OECD Rural Studies

Enhancing Innovation in Rural Regions of Switzerland

This document, as well as any data and map included herein, are without prejudice to the status of or sovereignty over any territory, to the delimitation of international frontiers and boundaries and to the name of any territory, city or area.

Please cite this publication as:
OECD (2022), *Enhancing Innovation in Rural Regions of Switzerland*, OECD Rural Studies, OECD Publishing, Paris, https://doi.org/10.1787/307886ff-en.

ISBN 978-92-64-97739-6 (print)
ISBN 978-92-64-80764-8 (pdf)
ISBN 978-92-64-70489-3 (HTML)
ISBN 978-92-64-97626-9 (epub)

OECD Rural Studies
ISSN 2707-3416 (print)
ISSN 2707-3424 (online)

Foreword

Innovation is a fundamental driver of growth and key to tackling the many megatrends our economies and societies face, including digitalisation, climate and demographic change. Each of these trends, and indeed more generally, economic shocks, affect regions in different ways. While many urban regions, for example, are able to quickly adapt, and leverage their agglomeration effects, rural regions often struggle to adapt. They also typically lag in innovation creation and up-take, measured by patent-intensity and R&D technological innovation. However, that narrow view may not fully reflect the notion of innovation for rural areas. As such, policies that focus on this narrow view may not take advantage of the full potential of rural places areas. This report adopts a broader perspective and provides analysis and guidance on how innovation can support regional and rural development in Switzerland.

Across Switzerland, peri-urban regions close to urban cities record the highest growth rates in labour productivity, outperforming urban and other types of regions. In contrast, productivity and innovation activity have been lagging in rural and remote regions. Given the differences in productivity and innovation performances across different types of rural regions in Switzerland, a one-size fits all approach can fall short in tapping the main drivers of innovation and reducing bottlenecks. This publication, *Enhancing Innovation in Rural Regions: Switzerland*, calls for a place-based approach and focuses on a broad perspective of innovation that also includes regional innovation systems and entrepreneurship.

The OECD, through the Regional Development Policy Committee and its Working Party for Rural Policy, has created a programme focusing on enhancing innovation in rural regions, building on over 2 decades of policy and economic analytical experience.

The first chapter describes the economic structure of rural economies, explores statistics on the geography of research and development and finally identifies how innovation can help manage demographic decline and ageing in rural regions. The second chapter describes the framework conditions that govern policies for innovation, notably those through the programmes in the State Secretariat for Economic Affair's programme on Regional Innovation Systems. The last chapter describes the agricultural innovation system in Switzerland and how it can build on the experiences of the Regional Innovation System.

Acknowledgements

This publication was produced in the OECD Centre for Entrepreneurship, SMEs, Regions and Cities (CFE), led by Lamia Kamal-Chaoui, Director, as part of the programme of work of the Regional Development Policy Committee (RDPC). This report was prepared by the Regional Development and Multi-level Governance Division of the OECD, headed by Dorothée Allain-Duprè. The process that led to the final version of this publication was directed by Nadim Ahmad, Deputy Director of CFE. It was co-ordinated by Michelle Marshalian and was approved by the Regional Development Policy Committee.

The report was drafted and co-ordinated by Michelle Marshalian (Chapters 1 and 2), and co-authored by Lisanne Raderschall (Chapter 3) and Dalila Cervantes-Godoy from the Directorate for Trade and Agriculture (Chapter 4). It benefited significantly from the guidance of Dorothée Allain-Duprè, Head of RDG, and Jose Enrique Garcilazo, Deputy Head of RDG. Contributions from other OECD Secretariat members included Urban Sila (ECO), Michael Keenan and Andres Barreneche (STI), Paolo Veneri, Franciso Martes Porto Macedo, Alexandre Lembcke, Maximilian Günnewig-Mönert and Philip Chan (CFE).

The report greatly benefited from the expertise of the State Secretariat for Economic Affairs (SECO) and the Federal Office for Agriculture (FOAG), notably Valerie Donzel, Sylvianne Gostelli, Lukas Gunti, Sabine Kollbrunner, Marc Plancherel, Fabienne VanDamme, Alexander Wuerzer (SECO), Jean-Marc Chappuis, Daniel Baumgartner and Vinzenz Jung (FOAG). We received critical feedback from colleagues managing data on national statistics in Switzerland, notably Sam Banatte, Pierre Sollberger and David Tesar (OFS). Substantial reflection for this work came from the consultations with Heike Mayer, University of Bern, who is part of the academic advisory committee for this report and project.

Consultations for this report included valuable insights given by Eric Jakob (SECO); Emile Dupont, Angelina Keller, Marc Pauchard, Inès Rosetti (Innosuisse); Jon Erni (Graubünden Digital); Gianluca Giuliani (Flury&Giuliani GmbH); Roland Scherer (University St. Gallen); Patrick Albert , Margaret Collaud, Paul-Albert Nobs (ARI-SO); Regula Egli (SERI); Nicole Bachmann Raschle (Canton of Lucerne); Christoph Lang (Zentralschweiz Innovativ); Bruno Imhof (Zentralschweiz Innovativ); Miriam Shergold (Swiss Conference of Cantonal Directors of Public Education); Georg Bregy, Claude Pottier (Canton of Wallis); Markus Hodel (Lucerne University of Applied Sciences); Matthieu Delaloye (University of Applied Sciences of Western Switzerland); Pierre-Alain Berret, Cédric Koller, Claude-Henri Schaller (Canton of Jura); Samuel Hess (Canton of Basel-Stadt); Thomas Kübler (Canton of Basel-Landschaft); Christof Klöpper, Frank Kumli, Sébastien Meunier, Frédéric Nicolet (Basel Area); Prof. Dr. Hans-Florian Zeilhofer (University of Basel); Georges Humard (HUMARD Automation SA); Mireille Gasser (Arc jurassien); Guillaume Lachat, Emilie Moreau (TalentisLAB); Raphaël Conz, Raymond Cron, Raphaël Tschanz (Switzerland Innovation); Magali Estève, Astrid Gerz (AGRIDEA); Nathanaël Dériaz, Jean-Baptiste Leimgruber, Philippe Leuba, Véronique Martrou, Samuel Monachon (Canton of Vaud); Urs Zaugg (Canton of Fribourg); Caroline Choulat, Jean-Kley Tullii (Canton of Neuchâtel); Julien Bugnon, Philippe Michiels (DICIFOOD); Dr. Jean-Marc Brunner (Microcity); Nathalie Lesselin (Kokoro Lingua); Jean-Michel Stauffer (Innovaud).

Special thanks are due to Jeanette Duboys (CFE) who prepared the report for publication, and to Nikki Trutter, François Iglesias and Pilar Philip (CFE) for editorial support.

Table of contents

FIGURES

TABLES

BOXES

Follow OECD Publications on:

http://twitter.com/OECD_Pubs

http://www.facebook.com/OECDPublications

http://www.linkedin.com/groups/OECD-Publications-4645871

http://www.youtube.com/oecdilibrary

http://www.oecd.org/oecddirect/

Abbreviations and acronyms

Agroscope	Swiss Federal Research Institute for the Agri-food Sector
AIS	Agricultural innovation system
ARE	Federal Office for Spatial Development
CEAT	Urban and Regional Planning Community
DEGURBA	Degree of urbanisation
DETEC	Federal Department of the Environment, Transport, Energy and Communications
EAER	Federal Department of Economic Affairs, Education and Research
EMPA	Swiss Institute for Materials Science and Technology
EPFL	Swiss Federal Institute of Technology Lausanne
ERI	Education, research and innovation
ETH	Swiss Federal Institute of Technology
ETH Zurich	Swiss Federal Institute of Technology Zurich
EU-LFS	European Labour Force Survey
FiBL	Research Institute of Organic Agriculture
FOAG	Federal Office for Agriculture
FOEN	Federal Office for the Environment
FSVO	Federal Food Safety and Veterinary Office
GSSE	General Service Support Estimate
HAFL	School of Agricultural, Forest and Food Science
HHI	Herfindahl-Hirschman Index
ICT	Information and communication technology
IPRs	Intellectual property rights
ISDC	Interdepartmental Sustainable Development Committee
NRP	New Regional Policy
OECD	Organisation for Economic Co-operation and Development
PSE	Producer support estimate
PSI	Paul Scherrer Institute
R&D	Research and development
R&I	Research and innovation
RIPA	Federal Act on the Promotion of Research and Innovation
RIS	Regional innovation system
SECO	State Secretariat for Economic Affairs
SERI	State Secretariat for Education, Research and Innovation
SNSF	Swiss National Science Foundation
SSC	Swiss Science Council
TL2	OECD Territorial Level 2
TL3	OECD Territorial Level 3
TOPO	Geodetic Engineering Laboratory
TRQ	Tariff rate quota
ZHAW	Zurich University of Applied Sciences

Executive summary

A new vision for innovation in rural regions of Switzerland

With strong entrepreneurship rates, leading universities and research institutions, a competitive market and policies that enable the free flow of individuals and encourage firm linkages between territories, Switzerland is a leader of innovation among OECD countries, with an exemplary and advanced regional innovation strategy consisting of six regional innovation systems (RIS).

However, this strong innovation performance can be improved by addressing disparities across territories. The unequal diffusion of innovation across territories is in part due to the nature of innovation in rural places that focuses more on incremental innovation in processes, including in business models and less on product innovation in science and technology fields. In line with the publication on the OECD *report Rural Well-being: Geography of Opportunities* (2020[1]), a new vision of innovation in rural areas calls for a place-based framework that offers analysis of innovation policies through a rural lens.

Switzerland has a competitive environment and is a leader in innovation, yet disparities between regions still exist

The economic structure of Switzerland lends itself to innovation through highly a competitive market structure and high levels of innovation, by many of the standard innovation indicators. In Switzerland, the Herfindahl-Hirschman Index (HHI) of market competition demonstrates high levels of competition, with an index of less than 0.25, in all major sector and territorial categories. Compared to other OECD regions, Swiss regions perform strongly in most indicators for innovation. Five out of the seven large (TL2) regions of Switzerland perform above the OECD in shares of co-publications while all regions have higher than OECD regional average shares of tertiary educated workforce.

Yet there are still disparities within Switzerland between rural and urban regions that impact innovation, such as unequal shares of older workers and women in the active workforce. These disparities reflect many factors including the structure of regional economies, skills gaps and, indeed, at least in part, place-blind innovation policies. Rural areas, for example, typically have a larger share of small-sized firms with relatively less propensity to engage in the types of innovation activities that are traditionally supported by government subsidies, such as those in high-technology research and development (R&D).

Simultaneously, productivity, as a measure of innovation adoption, is diverging across territories in Switzerland. From 2012 to 2019, labour productivity grew by only 1% per year on average, yet high-density peri-urban areas saw double that rate and rural remote areas and peri-urban low density saw productivity fall by 14% and 5% respectively over the period. Relatively low productivity growth has also been experienced in most OECD economies, giving rise to a new productivity paradox and a number of possible theories to explain the slowdown, including more marginal technological shifts (Gordon, 2016[2]), less substantial impacts of technologies (Akcigit and Ates, 2019[3]) and longer lags before the benefits of innovation can be realised (Brynjolfsson, Rock and Syverson, 2021[4]). Rural areas are exposed to these risks but they are also compounded by those of an ageing workforce (especially in manual occupations in sectors going through transition) and associated skills gaps, exacerbated by the movement of younger workers out of rural regions.

Policies for innovation in rural regions need to reflect their size and structure

On average, rural firms in Switzerland are small, accounting for a larger share of employment than those in metropolitan areas. Similar to other European OECD countries, a third of firms and a quarter of jobs are in rural and peri-urban areas of Switzerland, according to the national definitions of rural. Smaller firms typically have lower productivity than larger firms, in large part reflecting economies of scale. At the same time, young firms and firms with young founders and managers are often highly innovative and, in turn, productive (Acemoglu, Akcigit and Celik, 2020[5]; Breschi, Lassébie and Menon, 2018[6]). Policies for innovation in rural regions (including more broadly entrepreneurship policies) should therefore leverage the potential of new firms, whilst also looking to boost innovation in older small- and medium-sized enterprises (SMEs). Those policies also need to better target and nurture the types and modes of innovations that can be adopted by rural firms, which typically have less of a focus on standard product innovations and a comparative advantage in the development of original or incremental innovations (OECD, 2020[7]; Freshwater et al., 2019[8]; Lee and Rodriguez-Pose, 2012[9]). Initiatives to support innovation and entrepreneurship beyond the technological realm and traditional manufacturing sectors are underexploited.

Policies for innovation also need to take into account the sectoral structure of the economy. While agriculture, professional services and manufacturing remain the most dominant sectors of activity in rural areas, the growth of the broader service sector, with typically higher salaries, also provides opportunities to boost innovation and productivity as well as increased female participation and scope for less labour-intensive older worker participation in rural economies.

Innovation has a larger potential for promoting productivity and well-being in rural regions of Switzerland…

Firms in rural places innovate differently than those in urban areas. In addition, R&D activities in rural regions are still positively associated with increases in productivity in non-metropolitan regions of Switzerland. However, this link is not so clear in metropolitan regions of Switzerland. Rural firms tend to spend R&D investment differently than those in other areas. In 2019, close to 35 cents per Swiss franc spent on R&D was outsourced; in rural regions, only 4 cents per Swiss franc left the firm for R&D expenses. While R&D activities are stronger in metropolitan areas and, in general, in the manufacturing sector, there are increasing R&D investments in the trade and services sector in rural areas, which is also associated with increasing R&D jobs. This correlation suggests that there is also an opportunity to simultaneously support R&D innovation and employment-enhancing policies through place-based approaches to innovation policies.

Supporting policies for innovation should also include addressing challenges for non-metropolitan regions, such as accessing markets and boosting skills. Although the New Regional Policy (NRP), the Swiss multi-annual regional programme focusing on reducing regional inequality, tries to address territorial inequalities in many ways, more needs to be done to integrate rural and urban areas and align other federal policies to support rural innovation. This includes stronger co-ordination and collaboration between the State Secretariat for Economic Affairs (SECO), the Swiss Innovation Agency, Innosuisse, and the Federal Office for Agriculture (FOAG), as well as joint approaches to supporting entrepreneurs with cantonal offices.

Switzerland follows a strongly federal, decentralised approach to innovation policies through several independent policy areas that are co-ordinated as needed. Because of its decentralised nature, the Swiss innovation system functions as a complex ecosystem. It includes federal actors (e.g. Innosuisse), public education and research organisations, cantonal actors and programmes (e.g. Living Labs, individual projects) and RIS as well as private programmes. Part of the NRP is RIS. Complementary to national research-driven innovation activities, their focus is on demand and need-driven services targeting SMEs. Yet, RIS impact is geographically uneven. Evidence shows, that SMEs and entrepreneurs in dense areas benefit more from RIS support than those in more remote regions and mountainous areas.

… with gains to be made through innovation, including in the agri-food sector

The Swiss agricultural innovation system (AIS) is highly sophisticated, efficient and advanced. Private sector and public-private initiatives have been crucial for the sector, building critical infrastructure and advisory boards for innovation. However, at the cantonal level, formal and systematic collaboration and interaction between the RIS and the cantonal agricultural offices is limited, in part because of the decentralised structure of Switzerland and cantonal independence. Building incentives to bring continued collaboration between the cantonal and regional agricultural advisory services, including at a multi-cantonal level such as the example of Star'Terre, an association of local agri-food enterprises, and the RIS and FOAG is important for ensuring that regional innovation initiatives in rural regions are able to take advantage of all resources including those that may be involved in industries and services that support the agri-food chain.

The FOAG has a well-developed knowledge and innovation system in the agricultural sector but is looking for ways to support entrepreneurial farmers to become more innovative. Co-ordinating and jointly generating programmes for agricultural and agri-food entrepreneurs in rural areas with SECO may help avoid administrative overlap and increase the efficiency of resources.

Many of the challenges for firms to innovate in rural regions are related to demographic change…

Demographic disparities, based on gender and ageing populations, are a sharper challenge for non-metropolitan areas (including rural and peri-urban) than metropolitan areas. There are two men employed for every employed woman in low-density peri-urban areas, according to an analysis of employed workers. As in other countries, there is also a higher rate of older workers as compared to metropolitan regions. The size and skills mix in the accessible labour market are issues that impact the ability of people and firms to innovate.

… to address these issues, regional innovation system partners must consider demographically targeted programmes for delivering entrepreneurship and innovation support services, including for women, youth and older workers

Rural regions have an ageing workforce and often suffer from youth flight to varying degrees across all OECD countries. Activating all of the skills force of the region is important if regions want to address the massive shortage of skills in rural regions. Regional governments need to work with national and local governments to activate the female workforce as well as older workers and engage early with youth. In addition to programmes targeted at getting these populations into quality training and vocational programmes, they can also mainstream gender and age diversity requirements into projects and programmes.

Last, though entrepreneurship rates are strong in Switzerland, female entrepreneurship rates lag behind those for men in rural areas. Targeted programmes to support women entrepreneurs in the initiation, development and scaling up of business could increase opportunities in rural regions.

References

Acemoglu, D., U. Akcigit and M. Celik (2020), "Radical and incremental innovation: The roles of firms, managers and innovators", *American Economic Journal: Macroeconomics*. [5]

Akcigit, U. and S. Ates (2019), "What happened to U.S. business dynamism?", National Bureau of Economic Research, Cambridge, MA, https://doi.org/10.3386/w25756. [3]

Breschi, S., J. Lassébie and C. Menon (2018), "A portrait of innovative start-ups across countries", *OECD Science, Technology and Industry Working Papers*, No. 2018/2, OECD Publishing, Paris, https://doi.org/10.1787/f9ff02f4-en. [6]

Brynjolfsson, E., D. Rock and C. Syverson (2021), "The Productivity J-Curve: How intangibles complement general purpose technologies", *American Economic Journal: Macroeconomics*, Vol. 13/1, pp. 333-372, https://doi.org/10.1257/mac.20180386. [4]

Freshwater, D. et al. (2019), "Business development and the growth of rural SMEs", *OECD Regional Development Working Papers*, No. 2019/07, OECD Publishing, Paris, https://doi.org/10.1787/74256611-en. [8]

Gordon, R. (2016), *The Rise and Fall of American Growth*, Princeton University Press, https://doi.org/10.1515/9781400873302. [2]

Lee, N. and A. Rodriguez-Pose (2012), "Innovation and spatial inequality in Europe and USA", *Journal of Economic Geography*, Vol. 13/1, pp. 1-22, https://doi.org/10.1093/jeg/lbs022. [9]

OECD (2020), *Rural Well-being: Geography of Opportunities*, OECD Rural Studies, OECD Publishing, Paris, https://doi.org/10.1787/d25cef80-en. [1]

OECD (2020), "Second meeting of the OECD Academic and Business Expert Advisory Group on Rural Innovation", OECD, Paris. [7]

1 Assessment and recommendations

This introductory chapter sets out the report's overall assessment and recommendations. Switzerland is one of the leading OECD countries, systematically performing highly on innovation, yet, some areas within Switzerland still face acute challenges. To support Switzerland in maintaining its high level of innovation and activate innovation in rural regions, innovation stakeholders in the federal system of Switzerland need to continue to reinforce collaboration and co-ordination mechanisms in delivering innovation and entrepreneurial support.

Rural innovation in Switzerland has many forms. It occurs through networks in places, involves new actors in the traditional sectors, such as the watchmaking and manufacturing sectors, is fostered by a dynamic environment with high competition and benefits from the strong support of place-based policies.

Switzerland enjoys a stable political environment and a thriving economy, ranking among the top OECD countries on a number of innovation-related indicators. It has strong entrepreneurship rates, leading universities and research institutions, a competitive market and policies that enable the free flow of individuals and encourage firm linkages between territories.

As a highly decentralised federal country, Switzerland has a long tradition of consensus building and collaboratively working across federal, cantonal and regional levels. At the regional scale, it has an exemplary and advanced regional innovation programme consisting of six regional innovation systems (RIS). The RIS build functional, generally inter-cantonal and, in some cases, cross-border, economic zones.

The Swiss RIS is an exemplary practice that has incorporated some of the best practices in the field of regional innovation. The following assessments and recommendations are meant to provide guidance on refining the practices regarding innovation and entrepreneurship, considering that the current system itself is already well-developed and at the top of the field. Due to the richness of data and information from various resources, the analysis in this report is conducted on the level of Swiss rural-urban areas, as defined by the Federal Statistical Office (FSO). These include large categories associated with rural areas, peri-urban areas and urban areas. When there are international comparisons, they are conducted using a classification of regions based on the OECD Territorial Classifications in large (TL2) or small (TL3) regions.

Assessment

Switzerland is one of the leading OECD countries, systematically performing highly on innovation; yet, some areas within Switzerland still face acute challenges

Switzerland is a country with a system that provides several good practices and is largely at the top of the OECD countries in terms of promoting regional innovation. However, the strong performance of Switzerland is still hampered by challenges that all OECD countries face today. While innovation is still occurring on an everyday basis, productivity growth has reached a temporal frontier and innovation diffusion has slowed down across the globe (Acemoglu, Akcigit and Celik, 2020[1]; Akcigit and Ates, 2019[2]; Jones, 2009[3]).

Productivity, often used as a measure of innovation adoption, is diverging across territories in Switzerland. From 2012 to 2019, labour productivity grew by only 1% per year on average. Yet, high-density peri-urban areas saw double that rate and rural remote areas and peri-urban low density saw productivity fall by 14% and 5% respectively over the period. Relatively low productivity growth has also been experienced in most OECD economies, giving rise to a new productivity paradox and a number of possible theories to explain the slowdown, including more marginal technological shifts (Gordon, 2016[4]), less substantial impacts of technologies (Akcigit and Ates, 2019[2]) and longer lags before the benefits of innovation can be realised (Brynjolfsson, Rock and Syverson, 2021[5]). Rural areas are exposed to these risks but they are also compounded by those of an ageing workforce (especially in manual occupations in sectors going through transition) and associated skills gaps, exacerbated by the movement of younger workers out of rural regions.

The size and structure of the economy matter for how firms innovate in rural regions

A third of firms and a quarter of jobs are in rural and peri-urban areas of Switzerland, according to the national definitions of rural, in 2017. In comparison, 40% of firms and 30% of jobs are in non-metropolitan regions in other OECD countries.[1] Over 92% of firms in rural areas have less than 10 employees, as compared to 88% in urban areas. Likewise, small firms account for a larger share of employment in rural areas, close to 40% of the workforce, as compared to 25% in urban areas. In European OECD countries, firms with 1-9 employees account for close to 30% of the labour force in non-metropolitan regions. In metropolitan regions, this share decreases to less than 20%. The share and size of firms in rural areas in Switzerland reinforce the particular importance of targeting small- and medium-sized enterprises (SMEs) for innovation and entrepreneurship policies in rural regions. It also helps explain the trends in productivity and performance in standard measures of high-technology innovation.

Peri-urban and rural areas are continuing the long-term diversification process from traditional primary sectors into trade and services. While agriculture, professional services and manufacturing[2] remain the most dominant sectors of activity, the other services, which include wholesale and retail trade, transportation and repair, hospitality, information and communication, and financial and real estate, are gaining importance in rural regions. The growth of the services sector, and in particular activities in information and communications, and the financial services industry, is often closely linked to higher wages and salaries and provides opportunities for increased female and older worker participation in the local economy.

There is a strong level of entrepreneurship and competition in Switzerland

Entrepreneurship rates are stronger in rural areas of Switzerland than in other European countries. There are 28 entrepreneurs per 1 000 individuals in Switzerland, as compared to 20 entrepreneurs per 1 000 individuals in European OECD countries. In rural areas of Switzerland, there are close to 40 entrepreneurs per 1 000 individuals, a healthy indicator of dynamism in the private sector.[3] Likewise, competition is high across all of Switzerland. Based on regional analysis (TL3), Switzerland has a Herfindahl-Hirschman Index (HHI) of less than 0.25 across all major sector and territorial categories. Nevertheless, there is some evidence of a small share of firms in non-metropolitan regions capturing a large share of the market in the trade and services sector. For example, in the trade and services sector in non-metropolitan regions class to small cities, the HHI indicator is relatively higher than in other sectors and regions (0.18), with the top 10% of firms capturing 70% of the market in terms of sales. While not particularly alarming as the whole of Switzerland is still strongly competitive, this finding reinforces the importance of place-based policy-making for increased competitiveness.

Research and development (R&D) activities gain importance in non-metropolitan areas

Formal R&D investment and jobs are traditionally stronger in metropolitan areas and, in particular, in the manufacturing sector. This type of activity can bring growth and well-being to rural regions if they also produce spill-overs and bring quality jobs. Yet, R&D activities in the trade and services sector are also increasing in rural areas. The trade and services sector in rural areas is experiencing a 36% increase in average jobs per firm and a threefold increase in average R&D expenditure per firm. This demonstrates a shift away from traditional sectors dominating rural regions such as watch manufacturing and food processing activities. The growing importance of the trade and services sector in rural areas, along with a higher proportion of jobs associated with R&D activities in this sector in rural areas, suggests that there is an opportunity to simultaneously support R&D and employment-enhancing policies in rural areas, particularly in the trade and services sector.

Rural firms tend to conduct R&D activities differently than those in other areas. In 2019, close to 35 cents per Swiss franc spent on R&D was outsourced; in rural regions, only 4 cents per Swiss franc left the firm for R&D expenses. According to the statistics, rural firms tend to invest in R&D inwards, whereas those in other areas increasingly invest outward toward other firms and internationally. As a result, in rural areas, the likelihood of direct innovation spill-overs on well-being, for example through local jobs, is higher because rural firms tend to invest in the skills of their employees and equipment used for innovation.

The analysis finds that R&D-based innovation is positively associated with increases in productivity across regions in Switzerland, but there remains room to improve. One additional job in R&D or investment in R&D is not associated with increased productivity in the following period in metropolitan areas, while it is in non-metropolitan regions. Even though this association is positive, it can be reinforced through further reallocation of resources, providing an avenue through which place-based policies can directly reduce inequalities while simultaneously addressing the national productivity slowdown.

Activating female, young and older workers can help mobilise untapped potential for innovation and entrepreneurship in rural labour markets

Demographic disparities in the workforce, based on gender and ageing populations, are a sharper challenge for non-metropolitan regions than metropolitan regions. For example, in low-density peri-urban areas, there are approximately two men per woman working in the active labour force. As is the trend in most OECD countries, there is a stronger share of older workers in non-metropolitan regions. For example, workers aged 55-59 make up close to 11% of the working-age population in metropolitan regions of Switzerland. In most non-metropolitan regions of Switzerland, this figure is higher. In non-metropolitan regions close to small towns and suburbs, close to one-fifth of the population is between 55-59 years of age. The size and skills mix in the local labour market are important factors that impact the ability of people and firms to innovate. While labour markets are small in Switzerland's rural areas and regions, rural areas are missing out on potential labour when there are lower rates of the active female labour force and not enough support for upskilling the older working-age population. Both of these factors contribute negatively to productivity in rural regions, by reducing the pool of skilled workers accessible to rural firms placing upward pressures on wages and downward pressures on outputs. In addition, demographic change in rural regions often results in a relatively high share of retirees and inactive older citizens.

Entrepreneurship rates are favourable for women in Switzerland compared to other countries. There are more female entrepreneurs as a share of total entrepreneurs in Switzerland than European counterparts. According to European Labour Force statistics, in 2019, the ratio of male-to-female entrepreneurs in Switzerland was close to 1 (0.95). In comparison, the ratio of male-to-female entrepreneurs in European OECD countries was 1.5.

However, in Switzerland, as in other OECD countries, there is a penalty for women entrepreneurs in rural regions. In European OECD countries, the ratio of male-to-female entrepreneurs is 2 in rural regions and 1.1 in Swiss rural areas. While compared to Europeans, Switzerland compares very favourably; compared to Swiss metropolitan areas rural women are at a disadvantage. Furthermore, once women become entrepreneurs, challenges remain abundant. Among female founders, reported challenges include attracting venture capital and scaling up that disproportionately impact female founders.

How is Switzerland supporting innovation in rural places?

Switzerland, a federal country, is one of the most decentralised countries in the OECD. Because of its highly decentralised nature, the Swiss innovation system functions as a complex ecosystem. It includes federal actors (e.g. Innosuisse, the national innovation agency; RIS, the regional innovation system), public education and research organisations, cantonal actors and programmes (e.g. Living Labs, individual projects) and RIS as well as private programmes. A study by the State Secretariat for Education, Research and Innovation in 2016 recorded 138 innovation promotion offerings at the national, cantonal and regional levels. This organisation grants individual agents a high degree of autonomy and scope for action. It also allows for tailormade answers to new emerging challenges. Binding elements of this decentralised approach are principles shared by the main agents in the system, which are subsidiarity, the autonomy of agents, co-operation, competitiveness and quality awareness.

The federal government's New Regional Policy (NRP) is important in financially supporting subnational innovation projects and has allowed regional and cross-cantonal innovation initiatives to be established in most of Switzerland. Part of the NRP is RIS. Complementary to national research-driven innovation activities, their focus is on demand and need-driven services targeting SMEs. The RIS offer co-ordinated support and services in the areas of information, consulting, networking, infrastructure and financing. Yet, RIS impacts are geographically uneven. Evidence shows, that the SMEs and entrepreneurs in regional centres benefit more from RIS support than the more remote regions and mountainous areas. Following this, there are some stakeholders that would like to see a re-definition and re-consideration of the scale of policy intervention. More targeted support for remote rural regions has been part of the political discussion.

The RIS have a relatively strong institutional focus on traditional sectors and technology-driven innovation – there is further opportunity to enlarge the concept of innovation to benefit rural places. The support programmes of the RIS largely reflect the economic structure of the cantons as well as their different business fabric. Yet, specific rural innovation needs are often only partially reflected, leaving scope for improvement. Gaps can be found in catering for small businesses that would like to innovate outside of the technological realm or in opportunities for services that go beyond traditional sectors. Currently, even if many programmes are open to non-technology firms, a lot of support is technology-focused. For instance, the pharmaceutical and precision manufacturing industries are often earmarked for innovation programmes and support is only slowly broadening to other rural sectors such as tourism.

Foresight in anticipating changes to rural regions can be a source of inspiration for calibrating policies to close territorial inequalities and promoting growth and well-being. In light of fast-paced change, a strategic mechanism that helps to foster and implement anticipatory or forward-looking innovation support is lacking in Switzerland. Many OECD countries struggle with this missed opportunity, as programmes that encourage innovation can help solve upcoming social, economic or environmental challenges while also providing positive effects on local well-being and prosperity in rural regions. Detecting change and responding to megatrends and structural change currently happens through the council of spatial planning. The council publishes a report on territorial megatrends every four years. Yet, findings are only incorporated in a piecemeal manner and are limited to the leadership of individual people or entities. For example, in the case of the RIS run by the State Secretariat for Economic Affairs (SECO), demographic and climate change only marginally feature in strategy and programming.

There is a culture of experimentation in Switzerland that can be continuously reinforced to address challenges in rural regions. Building a culture of experimentation provides great potential for rural innovation but is currently underutilised, taking place in selected cantons and RIS. Experimental mechanisms such as regulatory sandboxes and Living Labs are policy instruments, which allow testing of future innovations at the local level, mimicking real-life situations before they are ready to be scaled. Rural places are often particularly suited for these types of experimentation. This is because, in comparison to more urban counterparts, they have the benefit of available space, function as a rather independent system and have lower living expenses. Consequently, by creating a regulatory environment that eases other pressures on firms, individuals in rural regions may experiment more easily than in high-income, high-turnover regions. These types of mechanisms can be useful for testing solutions that need to function in complex systems, reducing barriers to innovation and adjusting existing services on the basis of new learnings that can support experimental mechanisms.

Continuous and consistent monitoring and evaluation of the impact of the RIS programmes on different geographies and population groups can support reform in the future. Understanding what kind of innovation is most relevant in rural regions is an important first step. Continuously monitoring and evaluating how programmes to support innovation and entrepreneurship impact geographies and populations is an important second step. Most RIS do not prioritise an integrated analysis of the impact of current measures for different geographies and population groups, in part due to data privacy regulations. Although data exist and RIS do follow-up with each SME on the degree of satisfaction and collect percentages achieved within the NRP perimeter, results are not shared systematically and reduced importance is given to geographical components. Especially, within the NRP perimeter, the goal of evaluation is not to specify different kinds of rural geographies or the level to be achieved at each scale. This also means that there is little analysis done to understand if programmes have a substantial impact that varies between rural and non–rural SMEs, or whether participating companies largely come from more regional centres or from remote rural places. As a result, it would be difficult to argue for the need for additional funding to develop specific tools to address specific needs of rurality. More systematic analysis is needed to tailor policy responses to the diversity of rural needs in Switzerland (both in terms of geography and population). More policy evaluation is needed to better understand the impact of current measures within the context of the COVID-19 pandemic.

Despite advancements, access to public innovation support services in Switzerland remains complex with a multitude of competing offers– especially in rural areas. Due to the presence of a multitude of federal, regional and cantonal innovation services, beneficiaries face a complex supply of services that are sometimes duplicated. For example, some cantonal services in mentoring and coaching are provided in parallel to those of the RIS. Challenges are more pronounced in rural areas where the physical presence of services is reduced and can reduce much-needed trust-building processes with local communities. A more co-ordinated system can bring efficiency gains and complementarities to the various programmes. Ensuring simplification and access to public services within the scope of the RIS can improve user experience and uptake.

Closing silos between regional policies and other policies can improve regional innovation integration. The NRP is defined by a geographical range in which specific development problems and opportunities for mountainous and rural areas are the biggest. Only projects that have a majority impact in this area can be supported by the NRP. For instance, funding coming from NRP for the RIS programme areas "Point-of-entry-function of RIS" and "Coaching" requires that 50% of all supported firms fall inside the NRP geographic range. This so-called "funding compromise" regarding eligibility criteria addresses some territorial inequalities between rural and urban regions. At the same time, it also limits the integration of rural and urban areas in terms of innovation support. More needs to be done to integrate rural and urban areas. Especially with regard to other federal policies, there is scope to better support rural innovation. Short geographic distances between Swiss rural and urban areas make policy linkages crucial. There are policy fragmentations across and within federal ministries that are not beneficial to entrepreneurial needs. The fact that Switzerland distinguished between two policies that deal with rural-urban links in the broader sense, namely, the agglomeration policy and the policy for rural and mountainous areas, does too little to reduce institutional and policy fragmentation, in order to better support existing inter-dependencies among territories.

Agricultural policies in Switzerland seek to balance a variety of commercial, social and environmental objectives, yet strong market protections and subsidies impact incentives to innovate. On the one hand, Switzerland is a hub for research and innovation in several industries, including the agri-food sector. The agri-food sector has prospered in the stable and thriving Swiss economy. For example, the food giant, Nestlé, is a testament to the country's prominent role as an exporter of food and beverages.

On the other hand, farmers are highly supported by agricultural policies such as market price support (through border measures) and direct payments. This support may allow maintaining land and agricultural activities in less-productive uses for providing public services such as landscape conservation or the promotion of biodiversity, but it also slows structural adjustment and may impact innovation at the farm level.

While the Swiss agricultural innovation system (AIS) is advanced, further work on aligning and collaborating between the AIS and RIS could improve outcomes in rural regions. The Swiss AIS is highly sophisticated, efficient and advanced, with national institutions that provide the general agricultural innovation framework and fund and/or carry out agricultural R&D, and with cantonal agricultural offices that implement agricultural policy and execute advisory services and other agricultural matters. The role of the private sector and the public-private initiatives has been crucial for the sector. However, at the cantonal level, formal and systematic collaboration and interaction between the RIS and the cantonal agricultural offices is limited due to the independent nature of their institutions.

The Federal Office for Agriculture (FOAG) has a well-developed knowledge and innovation system in the agricultural sector but is looking for ways to support farm entrepreneurs looking to become more innovative. Co-ordinating and jointly generating programmes for agricultural and agri-food entrepreneurs in rural areas may help avoid administrative overlap and increase the efficiency of resources.

Recommendations

To support Switzerland in maintaining its high level of innovation and activate innovation in rural regions, innovation stakeholders in the federal system of Switzerland need to continue to reinforce collaboration and co-ordination mechanisms in delivering innovation and entrepreneurial support. The State Secretariat for Economic Affairs (SECO), which is responsible for the regional aspects of innovation promotion, has the important task of considering how to adapt its vision for innovation and ensuring its support is well targeted across all Swiss territories.

This report suggests that SECO, through its RIS programme and in collaboration with other relevant stakeholders such as the Federal Office for Agriculture (FOAG) and Innosuisse, should consider engaging in the following activities:

Policy design

SECO should expand the scope and target groups of rural and regional innovation initiatives by:

- Further broadening the **scope** of innovation programmes beyond purely tech-based innovation.
- Reinforcing the development of **programmes** targeted at small firms, start-ups and nascent entrepreneurs in rural places. This includes outreach to regions not typically covered by the current RIS. Such development can include:
  - Adopting the *OECD Recommendation of the Council on SME and Entrepreneurship Policy* (2022[6]).
  - Supporting SMEs by facilitating the adoption of digital technologies, strengthening digital skills and encouraging and supporting under-represented or disadvantaged groups; and keeping in mind the accrued challenges for access to finance and resources for rural regions.
  - Encouraging the expansion and development of initiatives to encourage the *creation of new firms* that provide diversified services.
  - Encouraging *networking* events, *challenge-based initiatives* (such as the Innovation Boosters managed by Innosuisse) and interaction with schools to build the *entrepreneurial mindset* from an early age.
  - Considering creating programmes to provide *specific support* to firms run by women and youth.
- Broadening the selection of **coaches and mentors** and increasing the number and variety of potential coaches to foster interlinkages between sectors to reduce existing silos by:
  - Diversifying qualifications for mentors.
  - Exploring more opportunities for peer-to-peer mentoring and coaching.
  - Supplementing coaches with R&D experience or understanding of Innosuisse programmes, such as those in the Innosuisse network, with those having a background in business development or other areas, and encouraging the uptake of information classes for coaches without knowledge of Innosuisse resources.

- Increasing the awareness and demand for **university linkages** among entrepreneurs, such that research initiatives are not primarily led by university research. This can involve awareness-raising initiatives and information dissemination through mentoring, counselling and network events and services.

Building a culture of experimentation

- Engaging in **collaborative initiatives in physical spaces**, such as innovation sandboxes, challenge-based initiatives, Living Labs and experimentation-specific grants that allow innovators to test solutions for the future at the local level, mimicking real-life situations. This could greatly benefit from closer co-ordination with other government bodies such as Innosuisse's Innovation Booster programmes and cantonal and municipal level innovation or development offices. Such initiatives can include:
  - o Innovation sandboxes with a narrow, time-limited focus. Based on the outcomes of such experiments, governments can decide whether to adapt policies to encourage the upscaling of such experiments.
  - o Challenge-based initiatives that tie funding, mentoring and other opportunities to solving regional priorities (both physical and online).
  - o Living Labs with a physical space where individuals may experiment with the development of new products and services, often accompanied by material and in-kind services.
  - o Specific grants that allow companies to access physical and digital networks that help them to think outside the box or test prototypes or new services.
- Increasing **flexibility and bottom-up solutions**, by:
  - o Allowing for certain agility in the programme, giving entrepreneurs the opportunity to bring forward ideas and requests for funding, for example, through an experimentation fund.
  - o Adjusting pre-existing programmes to integrate greater lead times, accept incremental advances as programme outcomes or encourage learning from failures.
- Promoting **public sector innovation** or innovation inside the policy-making process. This can include:
  - o The adoption of new policy tools (i.e. open government, foresight and planning tools).
  - o New methods of re-enforcing the consultation process with non-government actors.
  - o Funds for experimentation pools that can be accessed for testing out new ways of delivering public services before scaling up.

Monitoring and evaluation

SECO, in collaboration with other federal agencies and cantonal ministries, should contribute to monitoring and evaluating innovation programmes in rural regions by:

- Reinforcing how **monitoring and evaluation** practices, such as the existing regional development monitoring, feed into innovation strategies, as is the case in science and technology foresight monitoring in Japan and the monitoring for demographic trends analysis in Korea. This could include:
  - o A central strategic unit of RIS in SECO that works in collaboration with the Federal Statistical Office (FSO) and cantonal offices based on:
    - – Access to shared data on RIS and non-RIS catchment areas.
    - – The sharing of results on good practices as part of the regular co-ordination meetings.

- The improvement of data-sharing and open data practices, between RIS, cantons and the FSO. Include precautionary measures such as aggregation and confidentiality controls that can help provide information while still respecting privacy regulation.
- The implementation of the *OECD Recommendation of the Council on Enhancing Access to and Sharing of Data* (OECD, 2021[7]) that, for example, recommends adopting and regularly reviewing coherent, flexible and scalable data governance frameworks; and adopting a technology-neutral and agile legal and regulatory environment.

- Piloting a **unified customer relationship management (CRM) system**, which would track individuals' access to different services across and between cantons and RIS, and other agencies such as the FOAG. This can be incentivised through financial mechanisms or through the role of a data champion that pilots the benefits of data-sharing and uses data-sharing best practices (OECD, 2021[7]) to demonstrate how practical, legal and financial barriers could be overcome. It could provide the following information and measures:
  - Account for the location (municipality/canton/RIS) of the companies, or persons who participate in coaching, information and networking events.
  - Account for the number of companies and location of companies referred by the RIS to other innovation promotion agencies (Innosuisse, etc.).
  - Account for the number and location of companies that are referred to coaches/funding agencies in other cantons of the RIS, as well as the number and location of companies referred to coaches/promotion in other RIS.
  - Account for the number and location of companies that used the individual cantonal antennas (points of entry) and the number of these that have then used: i) a service at the corresponding RIS; and ii) a service at another RIS or another innovation promotion agency and the location of these services.
  - Implementing impact evaluation and monitoring using rigorous measurement procedures that include counterfactuals or randomised control trials.

Co-ordination

SECO, Innosuisse and other cantonal providers of innovation services should increase co-ordination and coherence between and within agencies to improve outcomes in rural areas by:

- Developing strategic **consultations** with local partners and academics to provide input into the inter-agency and cantonal working group on rural and regional development. For example, this can be done at the phase of joint elaboration of Innosuisse and RIS strategies, or through a centre-of-government initiative such as was done in the United States in the White House Rural Council.
  - Reinforce consultation mechanisms with departments in the federal and canton offices in charge of continuous education and upskilling for older workers.
- Increasing horizontal **co-ordination** efforts with relevant federal, cantonal and RIS agencies.
  - This includes, for example, efforts to increase rural-proofing and co-ordination with those in the employment, education and spatial development networks, to create a strategy for addressing demographic disparities in age-based and gender-based participation rates in the rural economy.
  - Consider facilitating co-ordination mechanisms through institutionalising the role of regional brokers that act as a co-ordination mechanism between cantonal and public employment partners on cross-cutting issues such as regional skills development and digital skills strategies.

- Jointly build strategic programmes for rural areas or regions, in particular, programmes between the RIS and FOAG. For example, agricultural policy instruments or programmes such as *Projekte zur regionalen Entwicklung* (PRE), *Förderung von Qualität und Nachhaltigkeit* (QuNaV) or resource projects can be complemented by the RIS, Innosuisse and cantonal programmes.

- Fostering **policy coherence** through rural-urban linkages for innovation across territories, federal agencies, SECO and cantonal offices by:
  - Strengthening the consultation and convening power of the Federal Network on Coherent Urban-Rural Spatial Development to be aware of and assess ongoing co-ordination needs between the Agglomeration Policy, the Policy for Rural and Mountainous Areas, and synergies for sectoral policies.
  - Giving RIS a more prominent role in the promotion of urban-rural partnerships for innovation.
  - Providing incentives to accelerate the adoption of supra-cantonal development strategies.

Enabling conditions: Access to services

SECO, with its relevant federal and cantonal partners, should focus on how to reduce administrative complexity and simplify access to services for innovation, especially in rural areas, by:

- Complementing physical entry points with an *online one-stop-shop* that contains access and details about public innovation support, from RIS, Innosuisse and cantonal offices, making support accessible from anywhere and allowing for the integration of programmes and measures across sectors. This, for example, can be similar to Scotland's Business Gateway programme.

- Designating an *outreach person* that contacts rural SMEs directly and speaks to them to inform them about offers, such as those in the Rural Partners Network in the United States, or the Community Futures programme in Canada.

- Developing *targeted communication and branding strategies* and making sure information is shared in rural areas and through channels in the region, such as entrepreneurs who already live in remote places. This can also include developing specific entry events that inform about the offers of RIS.

- Considering further integrating Innosuisse and RIS services by creating shared support roles where more mentors and coaches jointly take on RIS mentoring and Innosuisse counselling.

SECO and the RIS can better accommodate regional innovation support to address change from megatrends by:

- Considering establishing an **inter-agency monitoring observatory** to monitor trends that signal structural change and projected trends within rural regions that feed into innovation strategies. This entity should:
  - Participate in co-ordination and provide guidance for national and regional innovation strategies and agendas.
  - Be composed of partners from regional and local authorities, academic institutes, the FSO, the private sector and social partners.
  - Anticipate change and develop strategies for supporting the transition of current firms in rural areas into new business models.
  - Encourage adaptability to new market conditions or other global factors such as climate and demographic change, while avoiding over-dependence on traditional industries.
  - Monitor challenges for women, youth, migrants and older workers.

Demographic change

- Improving **knowledge and data** gathering on women- and youth led-innovation and entrepreneurship in rural areas, including by measuring the impact of policies on harder-to-reach populations such as women, older workers and younger workers in the strategy for monitoring and evaluation.
- **Mainstreaming** gender and age diversity requirements into projects and programmes and improving the outreach to these groups.
- Setting **targets** for encouraging entrepreneurship and opportunities for women and other harder-to-reach communities in the NRP through business support measures targeted to different population groups.
- Establishing a **gender and youth strategy** within the RIS structure to evaluate how programme policies can better accommodate female and young entrepreneurs and workers in science, technology, engineering, and mathematics (STEM) learning and adult education.
- Considering adding corporate succession planning and innovation for succession to the RIS coaching to better cater to rural needs.

Climate change

- Adapting RIS coaching to feature **business support on innovation for climate change and net-zero-emission targets**, including by:
  - Considering requiring all businesses that receive support for innovations to demonstrate their compatibility with net-zero-emission targets and contributions to climate change.
  - Helping firms assess possible climate risks (physical, price, product, regulation) and improve energy and waste efficiency in their businesses and across value chains.
  - Supporting firm know-how on building data and monitoring practices for firms focused on emissions and net-zero progress.
  - Encouraging good practices on power sourcing from new renewable resources, minimising waste, saving energy, water and materials, and recycling and reusing materials or waste, while offering green products and services.
- Encouraging RIS staff to facilitate **networks and dialogue** around innovation for climate change, including by:
  - Fostering system thinking and collaboration amongst public, not-for-profit actors and businesses.
  - Exploring assessment tools and competitions for climate-friendly innovations.
  - Strategically connecting to other circular economy initiatives and measures being developed in Switzerland. In this context, the RIS could also further leverage learning from the circular economy toolbox, currently under development, though the NRP.
  - Establishing a strong connection to the Innosuisse Innovation Booster "Applied Circular Sustainability".

Special focus: Agri-food innovation

To support agricultural innovation, the FOAG, in collaboration with SECO, should work on:

- Considering the implementation of R&D and innovation and technology adoption **data collection and survey** to the agricultural sector, in collaboration with the Swiss FSO and university partners such as the KOF Swiss Economic Institute that conducts innovation surveys on behalf of SECO. Currently, the national R&D survey excludes the agricultural sector.

- **Re-orienting public expenditures** to support agriculture towards investments in innovation systems, covering both knowledge generation and its transfer to the sector, should be made central to agricultural support policies.
- **Co-ordinating and collaborating** with the RIS, for example by:
  - *Incorporating* offers to support entrepreneurs by the RIS in the agricultural supply chain and ecosystem, supplementing with programmes from the FOAG and the independent cantonal agricultural offices.
  - Improving *collaboration* between RIS, the FOAG and independent cantonal agricultural offices, when offering support and services in: information, consulting, networking, infrastructure and financing between RIS and cantonal agricultural advisory services, some of which offer similar but tailor-made support for farmers, for example, Innovativi Puure.
  - Promoting more systematic communication of successful innovation cases from RIS (such as Star'Terre) to improve scaling up and institutional learning.
  - Improving *systematic knowledge exchange* between research, advisory services, education and the needs of farmers, to speed-up innovation and technology adoption:
    - Consider creating *a digital platform for a systematic exchange* between research and advisory services, such as those offered by the RIS, that takes into account the needs of the farmer and/or agricultural processing firms, whether these needs are technical, process-related, funding, entrepreneurial or others. This digital platform or website can have two main tabs, one outlining institutional offers and services that farmers can access, the other geared towards knowledge sharing and peer learning for researchers, academics and the like. This online platform can be incorporated as a part of a new structure of supply chain known as "net chains" (a combination of networks and chains). Such a platform would also help outline the knowledge base and analytical tools that are made available and guide decision-making processes, as identified under the monitoring and evaluation recommendations.
  - *Building an FOAG-SECO co-ordination strategy* may include one of the following options:
    1. The FOAG creates a system that mirrors the structure of SECO's RIS, in consultation and co-ordination with pre-existing efforts.
    2. The FOAG and SECO co-create a national system that incorporates the agri-food subsector into the RIS initiatives. This can be considered an *extension of RIS services* jointly with the FOAG and the cantonal agricultural advisory services, in rural regions.
    3. Cantonal and regional agricultural advisory services, including on a multi-cantonal level, and RIS work closer together by jointly providing discretionary funds that individuals and associations may apply for to request support from the bottom up, through cantons and their choice of beneficiaries. For example, a centralised portal for support and funding available, as outlined previously, could be the platform for this co-ordination.

    Under Options 1 to 3, the role of SECO would be to collaborate, co-create and provide access to its network of institutions, mentors, counsellors and advisory services.
  - Under the current legal framework, creating *systematic networking* between all AIS actors that engages both the federal and regional levels including universities, research institutes, agricultural colleges and agricultural offices that provide extension services at the canton level. The FOAG can continue to co-finance multi-actor research and extension projects and networking activities. This initiative can be managed at both federal and cantonal levels, as it proposes a collaboration and knowledge sharing of innovations pertaining to agriculture amongst different relevant stakeholders.

    ○   Developing initiatives by other institutions such as Agroscope or AGRIDEA to *expand efforts to better connect to farmers* through already-created publicly available platforms and by integrating the work of their decentralised research stations and insights from their pilot and demonstration projects on different themes.

References

Acemoglu, D., U. Akcigit and M. Celik (2020), "Radical and incremental innovation: The roles of firms, managers and innovators", *American Economic Journal: Macroeconomics*. [1]

Akcigit, U. and S. Ates (2019), "What happened to U.S. business dynamism?", National Bureau of Economic Research, Cambridge, MA, https://doi.org/10.3386/w25756. [2]

Brynjolfsson, E., D. Rock and C. Syverson (2021), "The Productivity J-Curve: How intangibles complement general purpose technologies", *American Economic Journal: Macroeconomics*, Vol. 13/1, pp. 333-372, https://doi.org/10.1257/mac.20180386. [5]

Gordon, R. (2016), *The Rise and Fall of American Growth*, Princeton University Press, https://doi.org/10.1515/9781400873302. [4]

Jones, B. (2009), "The burden of knowledge and the "death of the Renaissance man": Is innovation getting harder?", *Review of Economic Studies*, Vol. 76/1, pp. 283-317, https://doi.org/10.1111/j.1467-937x.2008.00531.x. [3]

OECD (2022), *Recommendation of the Council on SME and Entrepreneurship Policy - OECD/LEGAL/0473*, OECD, Paris, https://legalinstruments.oecd.org/en/instruments/OECD-LEGAL-0473 (accessed on 22 June 2022). [6]

OECD (2021), *Recommendation of the Council on Enhancing Access to and Sharing of Data - OECD/LEGAL/0463*, OECD, Paris, https://legalinstruments.oecd.org/en/instruments/OECD-LEGAL-0463 (accessed on 23 June 2022). [7]

Notes

[1] The countries with available data included in this statistic are Austria, the Czech Republic, Estonia, France, Hungary, Italy, Lithuania, Poland, the Slovak Republic and Spain.

[2] The services categories are based on the national industrial classification harmonised to International Standard Industrial Classification of All Economic Activities (ISIC) rev 4 classifications. The agricultural sector refers to agriculture, fishing and forestry; manufacturing sectors used in this report refer to all forms of manufacturing, including textiles and chemicals; and the professional services sectors refer to all professional scientific and technical activities, and administrative and support service activities.

[3] Author's own calculations using European Labour Force Statistics from 2019.

2 Understanding innovation in rural Switzerland

Switzerland is an innovation leader, with a long history of federalism, regional collaboration and bottom-up consensus-building. While several regions in Switzerland are top international performers in innovation, rural regions are on average lagging behind. This underlines the importance of understanding innovation through a rural lens and providing support to entrepreneurs, firms and innovators across rural regions. This chapter sets the scene for the report. It outlines the structure of rural regions, discusses trends in innovation across all types of regions, and identifies challenges in promoting well-being and adapting to changing societies.

Creation, destruction and the proliferation of advances in innovation shape how our societies respond to the challenges today and in the future. Regional governments across OECD countries count on innovation and the diffusion of innovation advances to spread prosperity and opportunities to all places. Rural regions, in particular, are experiencing fundamental changes to the way people, places and firms work and interact with each other. This is in part, due to megatrends in digitalisation, innovation, demographics and environment. When crises, such as the COVID-19 pandemic, require heavy support in public service delivery and tailored approaches for recovery, rural regions often do not have the same opportunities as more densely populated regions closer to metropolitan areas (OECD, 2020[1]; 2021[2]).

The governance structure of Switzerland is federal. Critically, in the context of Switzerland, this means that Swiss cantons[1] have a strong mandate to propose and shape policies, levy taxes[2] and distribute government resources, including those directly or indirectly related to promoting innovation. Unlike countries with centralised systems of governance, the Swiss system works on the basis of subsidiarity, i.e. cantonal and regional competition and self-determination within the federal framework. More specifically, the innovation ecosystem in Switzerland is characterised by a structure of cantons that associate themselves and then apply for funding of their respective regional innovation systems (RIS).[3] To overcome challenges of scale, and build synergies and cohesion within and between functional urban areas, cantons are incentivised to associate with each other before developing an RIS. As of 2022, there are currently six inter-cantonal RIS. These entities have a mandate to provide support, in particular to small- and medium-sized enterprises (SMEs), to promote innovation and competitiveness. They are co-ordinated at the federal level within the State Secretariat for Economic Affairs (SECO).[4]

While entrepreneurs and innovators all share certain entrepreneurial, risk-taking or problem-solving characteristics across cantons, differences in sectoral, occupational and territorial resources affect how innovation occurs and, more importantly, the societal or business purpose they serve. As elaborated by the OECD (forthcoming[3]), focusing on improving the conditions that encourage innovation adoption and entrepreneurial activities is more relevant for well-being in rural regions than an innovation that focuses on high-technology (high-tech) sectors alone.

Structure of rural areas in Switzerland

The socio-economic, territorial and multilingual structure of Switzerland is an important characteristic of its economy today. Territories in Switzerland are composed of a historical confederation of different communities with various linguistic and cultural attributes, with some territories specialising in specific sectors including agri-foods and manufacturing. Today it is thriving as one of the capitals of luxury manufacturing (notably precision watchmaking) and as an international hub of financial markets and the pharmaceutical industry. As one of the few OECD countries in continental Europe that is not a member of the European Union, it affords a certain autonomy in determining national policies while also incurring additional complications in trade and foreign affairs.

Within Switzerland, the development of industries and activities are dispersed across regions with different territorial attributes. Likewise, differences in demographics and labour supply within Switzerland are important aspects of understanding opportunities in Switzerland. The rest of this section defines rural areas in Switzerland while exploring economic activities and demographic trends across Switzerland and within the large RIS regions of Northwestern Switzerland, Central Switzerland and Western Switzerland, with examples from the cantons of Jura, Lucerne and Vaud in each of those respective regions (see Figure 2.1 for a graphical description of typology of municipalities and areas visited for the case study).

Defining rural Switzerland

Rural regions in Switzerland are defined centrally, with most ministries aligning with definitions provided by the Federal Statistical Office (FSO). In the case of Switzerland, the national classification is based on density, size and accessibility of places, with the base unit for the classification at the level of the *commune*. Communes, a relatively small local area unit akin to *municipalities*, are first split into three categories that determine characteristics as urban, peri-urban or rural, then categorised into a typology with nine categories based on density, size and accessibility (Figure 2.1 and Box 2.1). One further typology with 25 categories differentiates each of the 9 categories with criteria based on socio-economic factors. For the purpose of readability, the report refers to the typologies based on either the 3 or 9 categories of communes. According to this definition, the case study areas for the report are primarily peri-urban and rural areas. The report also uses the more aggregate OECD definition of administrative regions based on travel time and distance to functional urban areas (FUAs), to address privacy concerns flagged by the Swiss FSO, as described in Box 2.1.

Figure 2.1. Administrative typologies for classification of territories

Municipalities (communes) of Switzerland

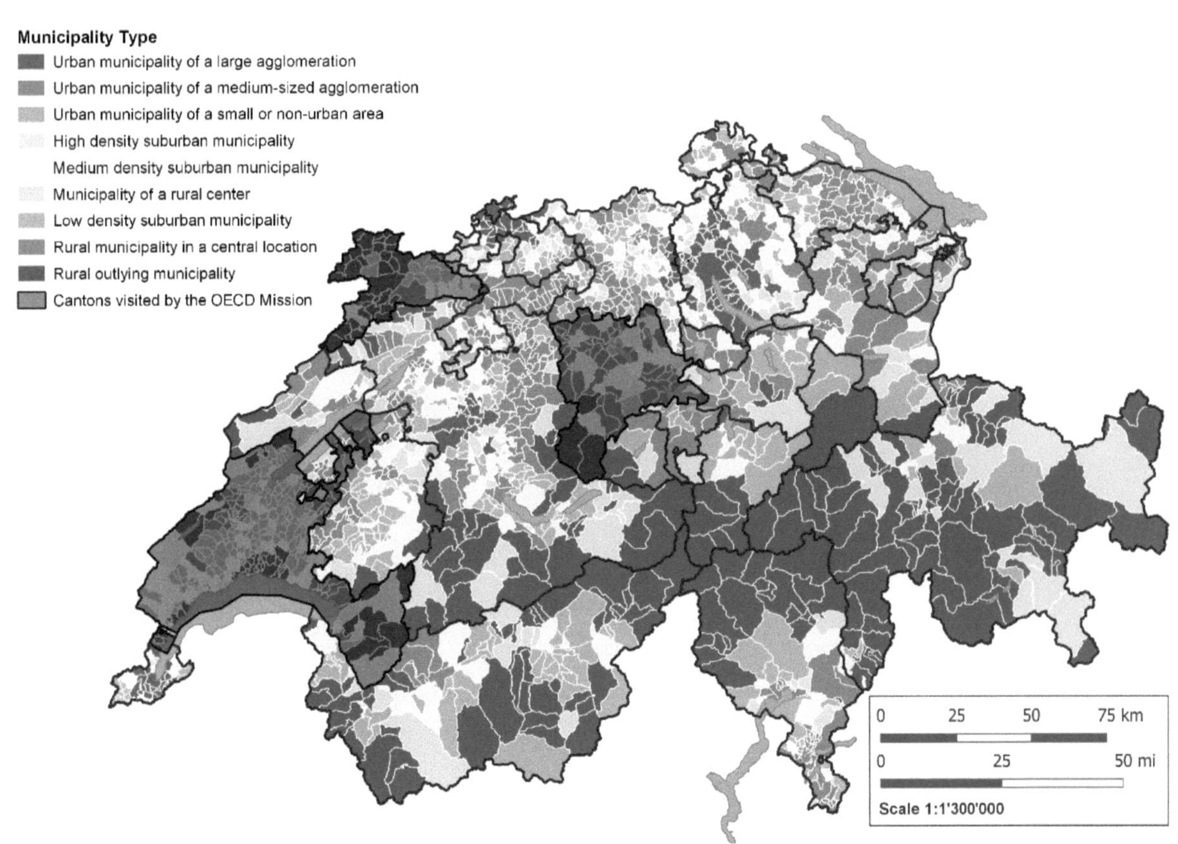

Note: The shaded areas in the map above reflect the cantons that were selected as the "entry point" into a study of the larger regions, exploring implications on rural and peri-urban areas. These include Vaud, Jura and Lucerne (from left to right).
Source: Federal Statistical Office, elaborated by SECO staff.

Box 2.1. Territorial and sectoral classifications

Using consistent classifications of territories and sectors enables harmonisation and comparability between different sources of information. When possible, the report will prioritise using national classifications of territorial characteristics but may have to adjust when it may be necessary, either because of privacy concerns or comparability purposes, to use alternative classifications. Unless otherwise stated, sectoral classifications are aligned with international definitions and are only adapted if the data resource in question only contains a limited sample of the sectors.

Swiss territorial classifications

The standard for territorial analysis in this report will be the Swiss National Territorial Classifications (FSO, 2017[4]). For the purposes of this report, we use the nine-tiered classification system that aggregates small administrative zones (communes) into nine key categories and three sub-categories. The Swiss national classification of territories is based on the criteria of density, size and accessibility. The nine categories are based on characteristics of communes, including: urban municipalities of a large agglomeration; urban municipalities of a medium-sized agglomeration; urban municipalities of a small or non-urban area; high-density suburban municipality; medium density suburban municipality; municipality of a rural centre; low-density suburban municipality; rural municipality in a central location; and rural outlying municipality.

For the purposes of readability, the nine communal categories are grouped into metropolitan, peri-urban and rural areas. In Figure 2.1, metropolitan regions refer to the three categories in red hues, peri-urban regions refer to the three categories in yellow hues, while rural areas refer to the categories in green hues. When comparative data is available or if, for data privacy regions, analysis needs to be grouped at a larger level, the report uses the most recently adopted definitions of territorial disaggregation elaborated recently by Fadic et al. (2019[5]). OECD territorial classifications are elaborated in more detail below.

Figure 2.2. National typology of Swiss communes

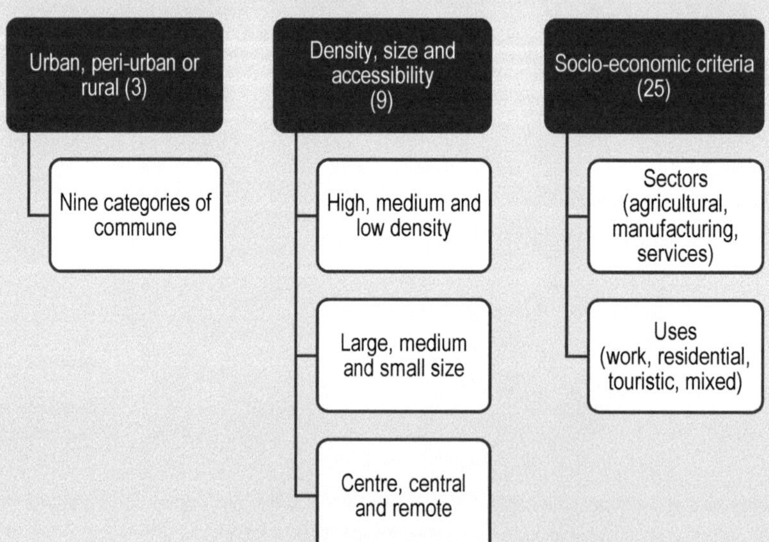

Source: FSO (2017[4]), *Typologie des communes et typologie urbain-rural 2012*, https://www.bfs.admin.ch/bfs/fr/home/bases-statistiques/niveaux-geographiques.assetdetail.2543324.html; Fadic, M. et al. (2019[5]), "Classifying small (TL3) regions based on metropolitan population, low density and remoteness", https://doi.org/10.1787/b902cc00-en.

> ### OECD classification of rural regions: Defining rural using physical and driving distances within administrative boundaries
>
> Rural is everywhere and exists as a continuum. What we commonly understand as rural is implicitly spatial and relative. In practice, governments delineate typologies of territories but there is no clear cut-off between regions or areas. Rural characteristics can exist within more urbanised regions and rural attributes are apparent across the spectrum of territorial characteristics. This continuum of rurality is delineated in the recent OECD publication on rural well-being (2020[1]).
>
> The term rural is often used to describe territories that have relatively low-density human settlement patterns, with relatively large distances to more densely populated areas. Often, rural regions are characterised as regions with activities closely related to natural resource industries such as mining and agriculture. However, this sectoral definition overlooks many of the different varieties of rural territories, and what this means for political agenda-setting in rural regions. Indeed, a region identified as "rural" has implications on government finance and wider regional policy making.
>
> In consultation with OECD member national governments, the OECD harmonised a set of guidelines for classifying territorial characteristics across countries that avoid the traditional, and sometimes harmful, rural-urban dichotomy. This unified definition of rural provides the basis for analysis across countries within rural economies (OECD, 2020[1]). The most recent definitions of rural regions have benefitted from a reflection on the combination of physical ("first-nature") and human ("second-nature") geographies. Rural regions are defined by economic remoteness, with three distinct features related to the physical distance to major markets, economic connectedness and sector specialisation. Considering these features, rural regions are physically distant to major markets, with specialisation in niche markets and those linked with natural resources such as agriculture and tourism. The degree of economic connectedness with surrounding areas may vary by relative density, infrastructure availability and complementarities between and within rural regions.
>
> In 2019, the OECD published a new classification based on FUAs, which incorporates density and the driving estimations in terms of the time it takes to access dense metropolitan areas. To the furthest extent possible, rural will be defined as 1 of 3 types of regions with less than 50% of the regional population living in metropolitan areas. This includes rural regions inside FUAs (where at least 50% of the population is within a 1-hour driving distance away from a dense urban area with a population larger than 250 000 inhabitants), rural regions close to small or medium cities of populations smaller or equivalent to 250 000 inhabitants, and rural remote areas. When this is not possible, the second-best definition will include EUROSTAT's degree of urbanisation classification which consists of cities, towns and suburbs and rural areas. Finally, when no other method of measurement is available, we will use a measure of the degree of rurality within large regions (TL2) or within the country. This is based on a simple calculation of the population total within each of the five access-to-city typologies over the total TL2 or country population. The three non-metropolitan categories within the access-to-city typology in the entire population are then used as a proxy for the degree of rurality of the TL2 region, or country.
>
> The diverse types of rural regions all have different characteristics and policy needs. There are three types of non-metropolitan regions (NMRs) that are considered to share more rural characteristics than urban ones, to various degrees. NMRs are defined as having less than 50% of the population living in an FUA with a population larger than 250 000 inhabitants. The three types of NMRs include regions with access to a metropolitan region, non-metropolitan areas with access to a small- or medium-sized city, and NMRs in remote areas.
>
> - NMRs with access to a metropolitan region: These regions have 50% or more of the regional population living within a 60-minute drive to a metropolitan area. This is similar in part to towns and suburbs surrounding the distant periphery of major metropolitan centres. An example of such regions includes Tyrolean Oberland in Austria (AT334), Montmagny in Quebec, Canada

(CA2418), Jura in France (FRC22), and Nagasaki in Japan (JPJ42). The challenges of such regions are often tied to economies of metropolitan areas, while focusing on industries such as tourism, without some of the infrastructure barriers of less densely populated areas.

- NMRs with access to small- or medium-sized cities: These regions are regions with 50% or more of the regional population living within a 60-minute drive from a small- or medium-sized city. Examples of these types of regions include the administrative district of Neufchâteau in Belgium (BE344), San Antonio in Chile (CL056), South Bohemia in the Czech Republic (CZ031), East Lancashire in the United Kingdom (UKD46) or Springfield in Illinois, United States (US158). These regions have a strong manufacturing base and linkages to neighbouring economies.

- NMRs without access to cities (remote): These regions are regions with 50% or more of the regional population without access to an FUA (metropolitan) within a 60-minute drive. Examples of such areas include West Estonia in Estonia (EE004), Lapland in Finland (FI1D7), Sonneberg in Germany (DEG0H) and Lesbos in Greece (EL411). Rural remote areas have economies with fewer interlinkages with major cities and often focus on tourism, while rural remote regions, such as those in Canada, Chile, Colombia, Finland and the US often also have an important share of the population with an indigenous heritage that face distinct challenges.

The schematic breakdown is available in the figure below.

Figure 2.3. OECD typology for access to cities

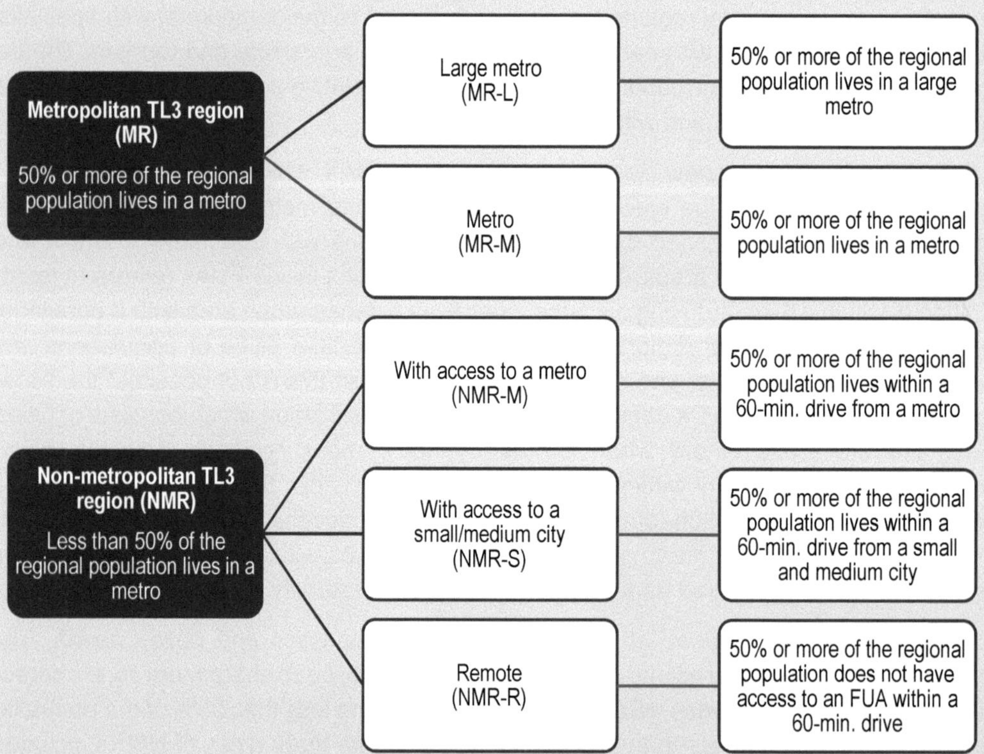

Note: Large metro: An FUA with a population larger than 1.5 million inhabitants; Metro: an FUA with a population larger than 250 000 inhabitants; Small or medium city: an FUA with a population smaller or equal to 250 000 inhabitants.
Source: Fadic, M. et al. (2019[5]), "Classifying small (TL3) regions based on metropolitan population, low density and remoteness", https://doi.org/10.1787/b902cc00-en.

Sectoral classifications

These statistics gathered from the Swiss National Enterprise Registry (STATENT), a Survey on Research and Development (R&D Survey) and a Survey on Value-Added (VA Survey) and base sectoral classifications on the national classification of sectoral activities (NOGA) harmonised to the International standard industrial classifications (United Nations ISIC 4th revision (UN, 2008[6])). For the purpose of readability, the sectoral classifications are grouped into the following ten major sectoral groups:

1. **Agriculture**: Agriculture, forestry and fishing (ISICr4 1-3).

2. **Mining**: Mining and quarrying (ISICr4 5-9)

3. **Manufacturing**: Manufacturing including Food, beverages and tobacco (ISICr4 10-12); Textiles and footwear (ISICr4 13-15); Wood and paper (ISICr4 16-18); Petroleum and chemicals (ISICr4 20-22); Metallics, computers, electrical and motor vehicles (ISICr4 23-30); and Other manufacturing (ISICr4 31-33).

4. **Utility and construction**: Electricity, gas, water and waste management (ISICr4 34-39); and Construction (ISICr4 41-43).

5. **Wholesale and retail trade, transportation and repair of motor vehicles**: Wholesale and retail trade (ISICr4 45-47); and Transportation and storage (ISICr4 48-53).

6. **Hospitality**: Accommodation and services (ISICr4 55-56).

7. **Information and communication**: Information and communication (ISICr4 58-63).

8. **Financial and real estate**: Financial and insurance activities (ISICr4 64-66); Real estate (ISICr4 68).

9. **Professional services**: Professional, scientific and technical activities (ISICr4 69-75); and Administrative and support service activities (ISICr4 76-82, 99).

10. **Public and community services**: Public administration and defence (ISICr4 88); Education (ISICr4 85); and Human health, residential care and social work (ISICr4 86-88); Arts and other service activities (ISICr4 90-98).

For illustrative purposes, some categories may be combined. In other cases, for privacy concerns, some sectoral categories had to be combined or excluded. In the report, the condensed categorical groupings include: 1) Agriculture; 2) Manufacturing; and 3) Trade and services (Groups 5-9 from the categories above). After discussions with the national statistical office, the public works and services (Groups 4 and 10 from the categories above) were excluded from some of the analyses. It was also suggested to group some of the categories further. The category of mining is often excluded because of a small number of observations.

Source: UN (2008[6]), *International Standard Industrial Classification of All Economic Activities (ISIC), Rev. 4*, https://unstats.un.org/unsd/publication/seriesm/seriesm_4rev4e.pdf.

Understanding economic activities and rural well-being in Switzerland

Most firms are located in metropolitan areas of Switzerland. Metropolitan areas, according to national territorial classification systems, account for two-thirds of the economy (Figure 2.4). Rural and peri-urban areas account for approximately equal shares of the rest of the economy. This share of jobs and firms in peri-urban and rural areas are similar to those in non-metropolitan areas in OECD countries. In most OECD countries, we observe close to 29% of individuals living in non-metropolitan areas based on OECD-wide harmonised definitions (Fadic et al., 2019[5]).[5] The relatively small territorial mass and driving distances on the scale of other OECD countries suggest that physical distances in Switzerland may be less of a constraint, although people in areas in the periphery and mountainous zones, such as those in the Jura region or the Alpine Arc for example, may nevertheless may find it relatively harder to access similar resources as those in dense metropolitan areas.

Compared to metropolitan regions, firms in non-metropolitan regions have fewer employees on average. While 36% of firms are located in non-metropolitan areas in Switzerland, only 25% of labour is located in non-metropolitan regions in 2019 (Figure 2.4). In comparison, 40% of firms and 30% of jobs are in non-metropolitan regions in other OECD countries.[6] In peri-urban regions, the share of firms and jobs vary less substantially. Among the six non-metropolitan territorial categories, the territories that demonstrate the largest gap in the shares of the economy are those in rural areas. The distribution of firms to jobs suggests that firms in non-metropolitan areas tend to employ fewer individuals per firm, with the majority of the difference due to a smaller share of labour of firms in rural areas. This observation is standard among other developed countries and underlines the importance of focusing on policies to support SMEs and entrepreneurship in rural areas.

Figure 2.4. Non-metropolitan areas contain 1/3 of firms and 1/4 of jobs in Switzerland

Share of firms and jobs, by Swiss National Classification of Territories, 2019

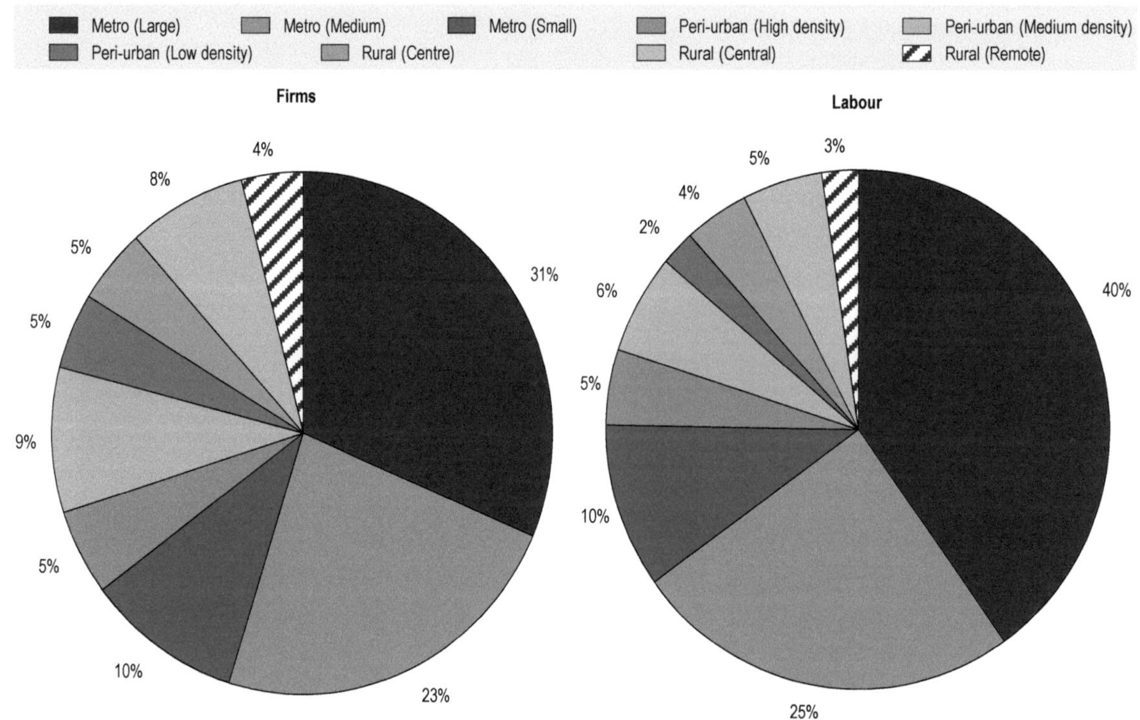

Note: Classifications are defined using the nine-tiered classification of rural areas as elaborated in Box 2.1.
Source: Swiss National Enterprise Registry (STATENT), Federal Statistical Office as elaborated by the OECD.

The agricultural, manufacturing and service sectors are the dominant sectors in non-metropolitan areas.[7] In rural and peri-urban areas, the economy is characterised by a sizeable agriculture and forestry sector, yet the firms in the sector do not employ an equal share of the economy (Figure 2.5). The strong share of firms in the trade, transport, finance and professional services in non-metropolitan areas is better reflected in the share of employment. As expected, there is also a sizeable share of hospitality services in rural and peri-urban areas. This is likely tied to the important role of tourism in rural mountainous regions.[8] Notably, there is a very small share of firms in the information and communication technology (ICT) services sector and a negligible share in rural areas, suggesting that policies only focused on innovation in the ICT services sector will not be relevant for development in rural areas.

The professional services sector is a small but increasingly important share of the economy in non-metropolitan areas. The sector is important for building amenable entrepreneurship ecosystems and support services. Firms in this sector include legal and accounting services, management consultancies, architectural and engineering activities, scientific research and development (R&D), advertising and market research and other professional and scientific-technical activities. We observe a sectoral shift in the period from 2012 to 2019 with a small relative fall in the share of the agricultural sector and a relative increase in the share of ICT activities and professional services sector activities in non-metropolitan regions (Figure 2.5). This change is small but simultaneously due to an absolute fall in the number of firms in the agricultural and forestry sector and growth in the absolute number of firms in ICT and professional services in rural areas.[9]

Figure 2.5. A fall in agricultural and manufacturing activities is accompanied by a rise in trade and services in rural and peri-urban areas

Total share of firms and jobs (full-time equivalent), by sector in 2012, 2015 and 2019

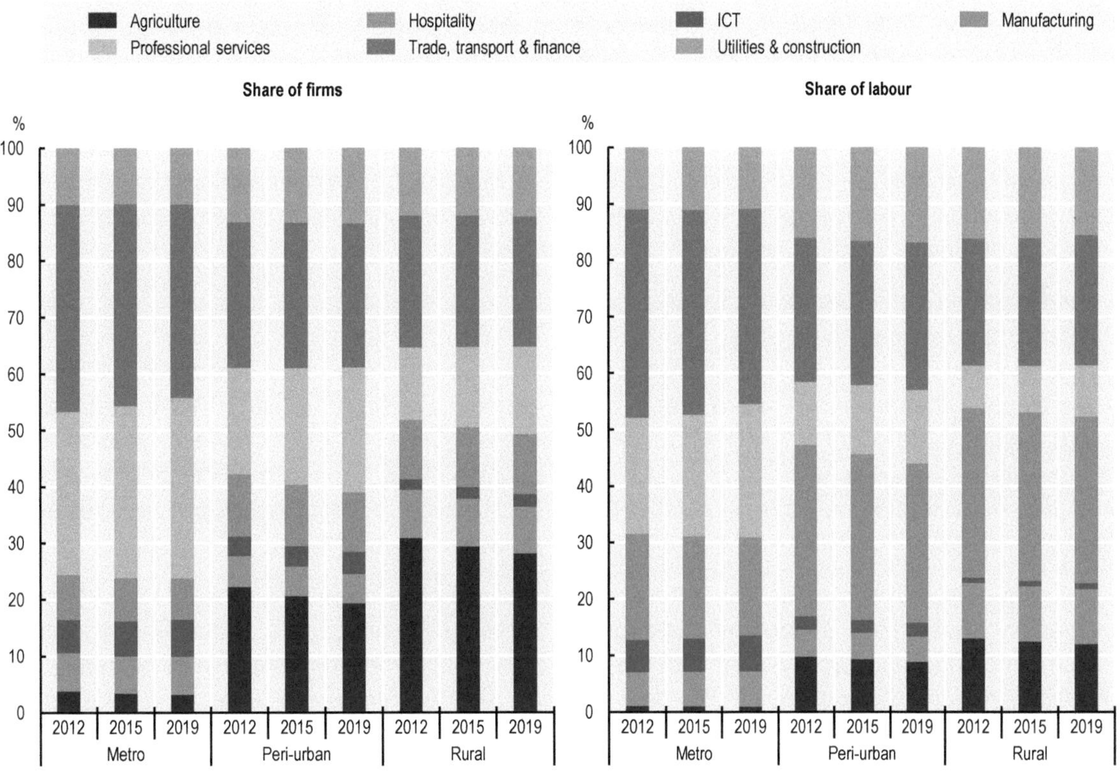

Note: To limit headquarter bias, data is presented at the plant level. Sectors were aggregated based on the NOGA08 codes. The "Utilities & construction" category includes electricity, water, waste and construction sectors; the "Trade, transport & finance" category includes the wholesale, retail, transportation, storage, financial, insurance and real estate activities; the "Professional services" sector includes professional, scientific, technical, and administrative and support service activities. All other categories are not aggregated across large sectoral categories. Mining is removed for visual purposes. Further information on sectoral categories is available in Box 2.1.
Source: Swiss National Enterprise Registry (STATENT), Federal Statistical Office as elaborated by the OECD.

The growing relevance of professional services sectors in non-metropolitan areas is an important observation and opportunity for policy makers in metropolitan and non-metropolitan regions. For rural development, focusing on innovation and entrepreneurship the traditional sectors of agriculture and natural resource-based activities, or the largest employment sector of manufacturing overlooks other opportunities and growing activities in rural regions. Taking into consideration the changing structure of rural regions, supporting the development of professional and ICT services is an important aspect of targeting policies for the future of equitable development in Switzerland.

Traditional manufacturing and agricultural sectors are likely to continue to hold a relatively stronger role in rural areas than in metropolitan areas. Policies that continue to support innovation through adoption are still important in these sectors. However, firms in these sectors are likely older and established. To encourage innovation, they would require either help in understanding how to change long-standing products and processes, or competitive pressures. On the other hand, supporting the development of professional services to such sectors can improve turnover, productivity and jobs in areas with traditional regional activities. For example, incentives in agricultural policy, as will be further discussed in Chapter 4, could increasingly focus on supporting innovation and development of professional services in the agri-food chain rather than primarily focusing on the traditional agricultural sectors where innovation could be supported through competition-increasing mechanisms. Such arrangements would be beneficial to the development of jobs and businesses in rural areas, helping to focus public services provided to support regional innovation, while simultaneously continuing to uphold agricultural output and exports.

Encouraging innovation and development in non-traditional, service sectors can support a welfare-improving approach to rural development. With higher levels of wages and benefits in services sectors, supporting firms and job growth in the professional services sector can provide jobs and productivity-driven improvement to the welfare of rural communities. The government of Switzerland's initiatives to focus on regional innovation as a driver for growth in SMEs and entrepreneurship should be reinforced to include a strong focus on quality jobs, in particular in the services sector.

The gender gap in peri-urban and rural areas of Switzerland is much larger than in metropolitan areas. Switzerland has reduced the gender gap in terms of full-time equivalent jobs since the early 2010s (Figure 2.6, Panel A); however, further progress is needed particularly in peri-urban and rural areas. In low-density peri-urban areas, there are over two men employed to every woman, while in metro areas the ratio was slightly more equal at 1.45 men to every woman.[10] While variations between types of territories were substantial, the areas with the highest disparities were those in peri-urban regions. A welfare-first approach to rural development can, at least partially, be achieved, by focusing on gender equality across territories.

The low gender gap in some service sectors, such as in ICT, is a promising avenue for well-being and innovation in rural areas. Encouraging the growth of the ICT sector can simultaneously target the development of innovation ecosystems and the creation of quality jobs for women in rural areas. Unlike in metropolitan regions, the gap in employment for men and women in ICT sectors is relatively small, suggesting that ICT jobs may be more amenable to employment for women in rural areas. It would be important for regional innovation initiatives to take into consideration what is driving the success in ICT-related employment and consider initiatives to encourage the development and upgrading of ICT-related firms and services in rural regions, including through STEM (science, technology, engineering and mathematics) education and programmes.

Without targeted programmes for women and gender mainstreaming, focusing on the growing services sector alone is likely to slow down the progress in closing the gender gap in Switzerland. The gender gap in the professional services sector is sizeable, even if it is not as substantial as in other sectors such as manufacturing, utilities and construction, and the transport sector (Figure 2.6, Panel B). With improvements in working conditions in this sector, alongside a focus on development, Switzerland can make a sizeable dent in the reduction of gender inequalities in peri-urban and rural areas by activating the female workforce and creating an environment for them to be productive. Recently, the autonomous Swiss Innovation Agency, Innosuisse, has taken a first step towards the inclusion of women in innovation-related projects in the services and ICT sector by establishing gender requirements in the new Innovation Booster programme (an instrument that encourages challenge-based innovation programmes, further described in Chapter 3. However, in other OECD countries, such as Canada, the United States and, forthcoming, Scotland (United Kingdom), regional development agencies and government departments directly create programmes to address the challenges of women in establishing and growing innovative businesses through specific women innovation and entrepreneurship strategies and programmes (ACOA, 2021[7]; ISED, 2021[8]; MBDA, 2022[9]). For example, in Canada, several regional development agencies including Atlantic Canada Opportunities Agency, Prairies Economic Development Canada (PrairiesCan), Pacific Economic Development Canada (PacifiCan), in collaboration with a federal agency, Innovation, Science and Economic Development Canada (ISED), deliver the Women's Entrepreneurship Strategy (Pacific Economic Development Canada, 2022[10]).

Figure 2.6. The gender gap in jobs is improving but still persistent across territories

Gender gaps in full-time equivalent (FTE) employment

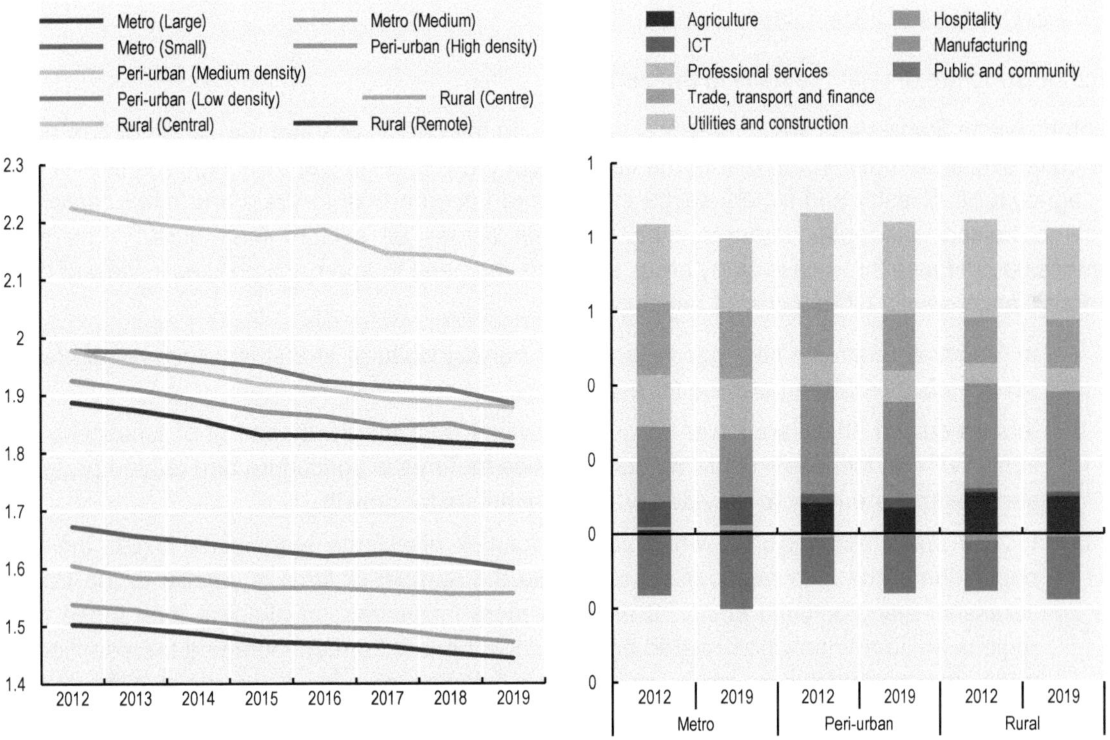

Note: Employment is estimated in full-time equivalents. The gender gap as measured in Panel A is the ratio of male-to-female employment within territories over time. The interpretation is the number of males to females in FTE employment. The gender gap as measured in Panel B is the yearly shares of the difference between FTE employment for males and females within territories. This is interpreted as a contribution to the total difference in the number of men to the number of women in each territory and in each year in FTE employment.
Source: STATENT, Swiss Federal Statistical Office.

With the normalisation of remote work in many OECD countries, supporting opportunities for women remote working in STEM occupations also requires reflection on work-life balance regulations. Work-life balance measures, such as remote work, are critical for women in the labour market (OECD/ILO, 2021[11]). Remote working could also be beneficial for women for several reasons (OECD, 2022[12]). In the post-COVID-19 transition, some governments are working towards generalising incentives to encourage remote work (OECD, 2021[13]). Country and regional governments that are taking active steps in promoting remote work tend to focus on strengthening enabling conditions, creating incentives for take-up of remote work for SMEs, awareness raising campaigns and other remote working attraction tools.[11] However, some studies are suggesting that it may hamper advancements, in particular for women in STEM, and lead to a heavier load of household labour and child care for women (Kossek, Allen and Dumas, 2020[14]). If work-life balance regulations and benefits, such as maternal, paternal, parental, sick-family leave regulations and child care benefits, are not able to adapt to the change in work arrangements, there is a likelihood that household burdens may increasingly fall on women. Countries like France, Italy, the Netherlands and Spain have increased care leave provisions to support women and families who are now remote working, while Japan, Korea and the United States have reformed parental leave schemes as a response to the COVID-19 crisis (OECD/ILO, 2021[11]).

Box 2.2. Cantons of Jura, Luzern and Vaud

Sectoral structure of select cantons in Switzerland

Cantons within Switzerland vary in sectoral intensity. In the canton of Vaud, the share of firm activities are quite similar to those in the rest of the country but there is a substantially higher share of firms in the agricultural, forestry and fishery sector in Jura and Lucerne than in Vaud and other cantons, with Lucerne having a sizeably larger number of firms across all sectors than Jura.[12] The sectoral composition of these three case study areas suggests the need to approach policies in view of both the territorial and sectoral differences. In particular:

- In Vaud, a relatively stronger reliance on non-agricultural industries such as professional services is a promising avenue for growth.

- In Jura canton, there are lower levels of activities, with the development of a nascent tourism industry[13] that focuses on building opportunities for firms in agriculture and related professional services that are likely to provide additional avenues for growth.

- In 2017, manufacturing firms, which account for 12% of all firms, employed a third of the working population in the Jura region. Critically, while the number of firms is smaller in the traditional Jurassian manufacturing sector, it employs more individuals on average than those in other regions. In Jura, innovation-related policies could benefit from encouraging the adaption of the traditional manufacturing sector to new technologies and focus on developing supporting services for encouraging the development of more diversity of industries.

- The region of Lucerne is a central tourist destination characterised by a relatively high level of activities in professional services and agricultural services. Addressing structural issues related to the clustering of innovation only around universities may help expand some of the benefits of innovation in this region. Overtourism is often a challenge in this region.

Size structure of cantons in Switzerland

Small firms are drivers of growth in the cantons of Jura, Lucerne and Vaud. The agricultural sector is a relatively strong sector in Jura and Lucerne, and the sector in these cantons is characterised primarily by small firms. However, as in the overall economy, the share of total employment attributed to small firms is lower than those in medium or large firms. Over time, we have observed an increasing share of larger firms but a fall in overall agricultural activities. Encouraging the growth of agricultural firms in the Jura and Luzern regions, while building the capacity of other professional support services in the agri-food chain can provide opportunities for employment-enhancing policies.

A small share of ICT firms in the Jura, Lucerne and Vaud regions account for a larger share of labour than those in other sectors. The ICT sector is an untapped potential for growth in rural regions but does not necessarily lead to more jobs. Jobs in these sectors tend to offer higher wages and, as previously discussed, can provide opportunities for reducing the employment gender gap in rural regions. In the Jura, Luzern and Vaud regions, 20-40% of firms in the ICT sector are small, but they account for close to 90% of employment in this sector in each of the areas. In contrast to other sectors, the share of small firms is much smaller, while its share of sectoral labour is equally as high. The interpretation is that each small ICT firm carries a more important share of cantonal labour than in other sectors.

Most professional services firms are small but there is a growing share of firms and employment in larger-sized firms in Lucerne and Vaud. Furthermore, there is a large and growing share of labour that is attributed to larger firms. Less than 10% of firms having more than 50 employees account for between 60% to 70% of labour. While there is a very small share of large-sized firms in Jura, Luzern and Vaud, they all account for a sizeable share of labour. Supporting the development and growth of such firms can improve jobs and the quality of jobs in the professional services sector. Focusing on scaling up firms in these cantons through more productive products and processes can support rural communities as they transition out of traditional manufacturing and agricultural sectors.

Source: OECD calculations using STATENT, Swiss Federal Statistical Offices.

Targeting programmes to SMEs in non-metropolitan regions

Small firms in rural and peri-urban areas account for a larger share of employment than in metropolitan regions.[14] The majority of firms in Switzerland are small (1-9 employees). In metropolitan areas in 2019, small firms accounted for 88% of the economy, while in non-metropolitan regions they accounted for 92% (Figure 2.7). As the share of small firms in non-metropolitan areas (rural and peri-urban) is slightly higher than in metropolitan areas, the share of labour employed in these firms is substantially higher. Small firms account for 40% of the labour force in non-metropolitan areas, while those in metropolitan regions only account for approximately 25% of total employment. In comparison, larger firms (with 50-249 employees and 250 or more employees) account for a very small share of firms (close to 0%) but a substantially larger share of employment in metropolitan areas (18% in metropolitan versus 9% in non-metropolitan areas).

While there are relatively more small firms in non-metropolitan regions, the territorial distribution of the size of firms in Switzerland is similar to those in other OECD countries (Figure 2.7, Panel C). In OECD countries the employment share in small firms (1-9) in non-metropolitan regions reaches between 35% to 40%,[15] while the same size of firms contributes to close to 20% of employment in large metropolitan regions. Based on the OECD categorisation of large Swiss regions (TL3), there are slightly fewer small firms in some of the most remote areas.

Encouraging national-level policies to focus on growth and innovation in SMEs will have a stronger impact in non-metropolitan areas. Federal innovation policies targeting SMEs are a key component of the Swiss regional innovation system (RIS), yet, as further explored in Chapter 3, most national policies have a harder time reaching SMEs and often are better targeted at firms with easier access to networks in metropolitan regions. As is already the case in Switzerland, encouraging innovation programmes and firm support directed towards SMEs is low-hanging fruit for uplifting productivity, growth and jobs through equitable development (EAER, 2021[15]).

Figure 2.7. Small firms account for a larger share of activities and labour in rural and peri-urban regions of Switzerland

Distribution of firms and labour (FTE), by size groups, 2012 and 2019

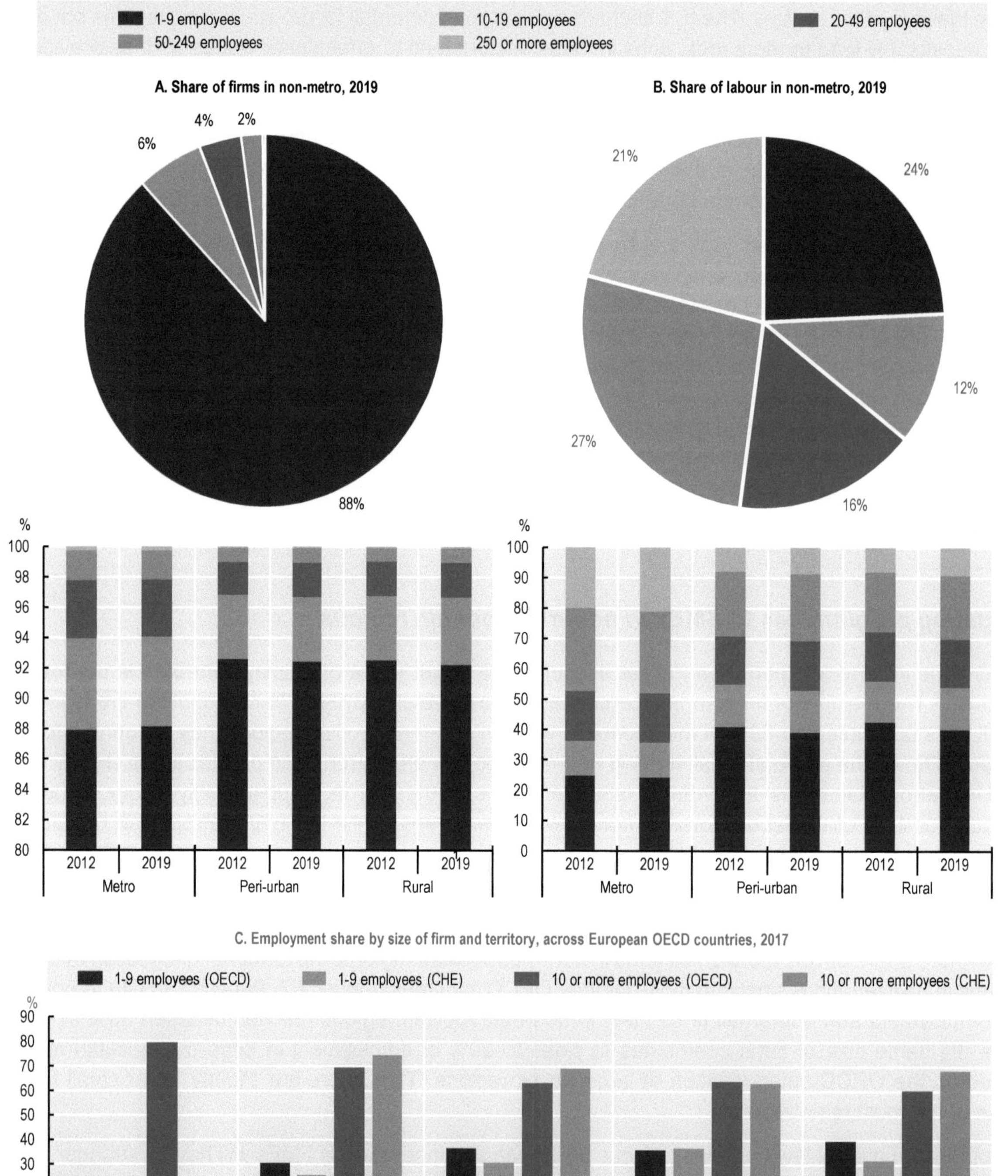

Note: Size groups refer to the number of full-time employees within each firm. They include firms with 1-9, 10-19, 20-49 , 50-249 and 250 employees and more. Countries included in Panel C for OECD comparison include Austria, the Czech Republic, Estonia, France, Hungary, Italy, Lithuania, Poland, Portugal, the Slovak Republic and Spain. In Switzerland, there is no large region (TL3) that has over 2.5 million inhabitants and is therefore not comparable to the OECD category "Large Metropolitan" region as described in Box 2.1.

Source: Swiss National Enterprise Registry (STATENT) and OECD Regional Business Demography statistics.

Key messages on the structure of rural areas in Switzerland

- Most firms are in metropolitan areas of Switzerland, as in other OECD countries.
- Yet small firms in rural and peri-urban regions account for a larger share of employment than in metropolitan regions.
- Compared to metropolitan areas, firms in non-metropolitan regions on average tend to employ fewer workers.
- The agricultural, services and manufacturing services are prominent sectors in non-metropolitan regions.
- The professional services sector is increasingly an important share of the economy in non-metropolitan regions, and the ICT sector may be an interesting sector to explore for further engagement with the less active female labour force.
- For reducing territorial inequalities and increasing well-being, focusing on encouraging innovation and development in sectors with higher levels of wages and benefits, and lowering gender gaps is critical.

Innovation in Switzerland

Innovation is a precursor of long-term growth, productivity and, in some cases, well-being (Aghion and Howitt, 1990[16]; OECD, 2016[17]; Romer, 1990[18]). Enhancing the creation, adoption and diffusion of innovative products and processes,[16] is often a target of policy makers and community leaders alike. While innovation can also be destructive and vary across industries and geographies (Autor, 2014[19]; McCann, 2019[20]), creative destruction in itself is a driver of innovation and resilient economies (Aghion, Antonin and Bunel, 2021[21]). This report considers that on average, innovation occurs and affects societies differently in rural regions than in urban regions, primarily due to the underlying sectoral, occupational and territorial attributes that characterise low-density areas with longer distances from metropolitan FUAs (OECD, 2020[1]).

Following the literature review, our current knowledge of drivers of innovation and rural development tells us that:

- Innovation is a predecessor of growth but not necessarily well-being for all territories (Aghion and Howitt, 1990[16]; OECD, 2016[17]; Romer, 1990[18]; McCann, 2019[20]).
- Framework conditions, such as access to labour, capital, markets and public services, encourage innovation and innovation adoption and diffusion but can be better targeted to satisfy the structure of rural regions (Aghion et al., 2001[22]; Andersson et al., 2009[23]; Bloom, Draca and Van Reenen, 2016[24]; Goos, Manning and Salomons, 2014[25]; Grossman and Helpman, 1990[26]; OECD, 2013[27]; 2020[1]).
- Innovation and its diffusion and adoption occur in networks and can be a source of growth for rural areas if barriers to physical and digital distances can be addressed (Akcigit, Grigsby and Nicholas, 2017[28]; Lengyel et al., 2020[29]; Sorenson, 2018[30]; Ahrend et al., 2017[31]).

In peripheral areas of Switzerland, the traditional view of innovation, one with a high and fast frequency of exchanges with innovation partners is not widely observed (Mayer, 2020[32]). This would suggest that innovation itself, in addition to innovation diffusion and adoption, may be limited. However, such an assumption precludes innovation as high-tech, based on quick interactions and firms that race to be first to the market. When studies have taken a territorial approach, this type of innovation is not as largely observed in rural areas as it is in dense cities. Economic geographers have started conceptualising alternatives such as what is considered "slow innovation" (Shearmur and Doloreux, 2016[33]), which is the occurrence of innovation based on isolated development and limited, but strategic interactions with partners. This leaves room for creativity based on the fringe and unconventional ideas, shielded from pressures to deliver fast to markets (Mayer, 2020[32]). "Slow innovation" has the advantage of not being time-dependent, meaning it does not lose value rapidly, with a lower frequency of interactions and a strategic search for knowledge. In the peripheral mountainous areas of the European Alps (Osttirol, Austria and Piedmont, Italy), Mayer (2020[32]) observes a selective in-migration of entrepreneurs and innovative actors that seek such assets of peripheral regions.

Most inventors live relatively close to FUAs and distances across regions are relatively small. Unlike other larger OECD countries, for much of the inhabited territory in Switzerland, individuals can physically reach territories across cantons with relatively shorter travel times. For example, while a relatively high percentage (over 45%) of individuals live outside of FUAs (Veneri, 2018[34]), the share of registered inventors with a travel time that is longer than 45 minutes away from an FUA is less than 5% (Figure 2.8).

Figure 2.8. Inventors in rural regions and travel times

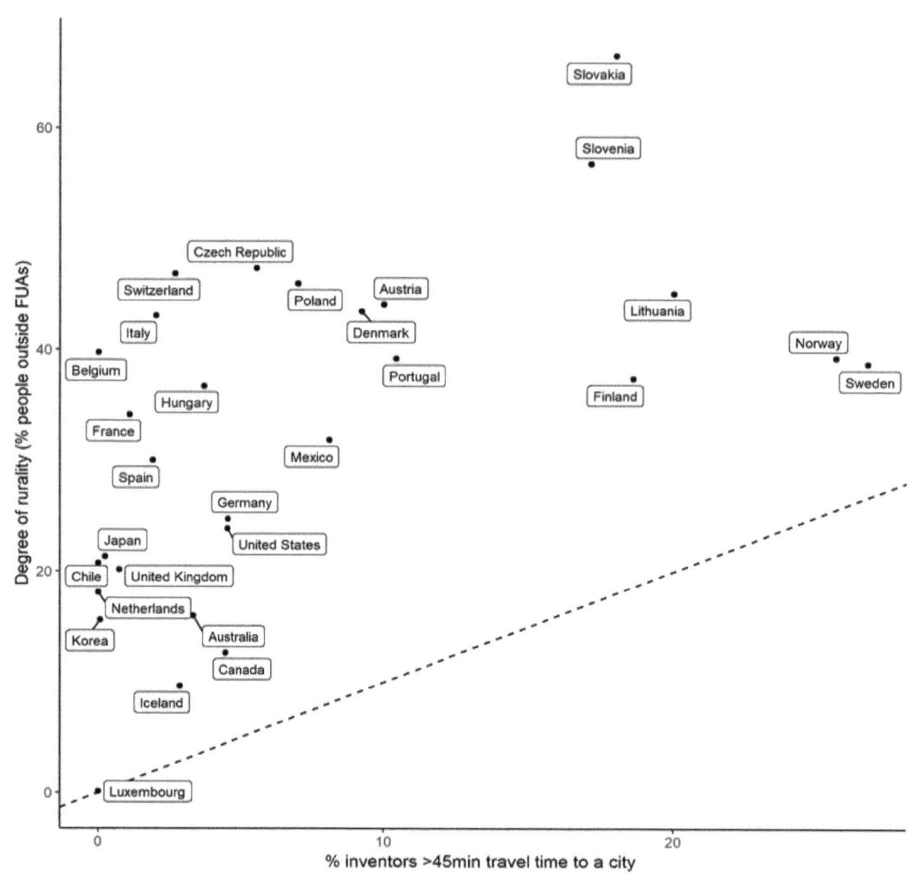

Note: Dotted line represents the 45-degree angle.
Source: OECD calculations based on PATSTAT and OECD (forthcoming[3]), *Enhancing Innovation in Rural Regions: Synthesis Report*, OECD Publishing, Paris.

Entrepreneurship rates are strong in Switzerland

There are 10 to 20 more entrepreneurs per 1 000 active workers in Switzerland, as compared to other European countries. According to European Commission (EC) Labour Force Statistics, there are more entrepreneurs as a share of the active labour force than in other European OECD countries (Figure 2.9).

For Swiss policy makers, focusing on encouraging start-up entrepreneurship (OECD, forthcoming[3]) and entrepreneurship in scalable activities is an important factor in generating employment growth and well-being in territories (McKenzie et al., 2021[35]). As actors of change, entrepreneurs, and in particular young entrepreneurs who start firms with high levels of education are better prepared for change (OECD, forthcoming[3]). While it is clear that entrepreneurs are playing a large role in regions across Switzerland, it would be important to explore what kind of entrepreneurs create scalable firms and what kinds of interventions can support entrepreneurship focused on more than mere subsistence.

Evidence from the European Union (EU) Labour Force Survey depicts that Switzerland has higher ratios of self-employed entrepreneurs across all territories than other European OECD countries. Furthermore, there is a higher share of entrepreneurs in rural regions than in cities or towns and suburbs (Figure 2.9). In most countries, rates of entrepreneurship in rural areas are high as a share of the active labour population, reflecting to some extent a different mix of opportunities for the labour force. The high level of entrepreneurship in Switzerland is a strong indicator of a dynamic economy and a promising avenue for encouraging change and innovation adoption in rural regions.[17]

Figure 2.9. Self-Employment in Switzerland and European countries, 2019

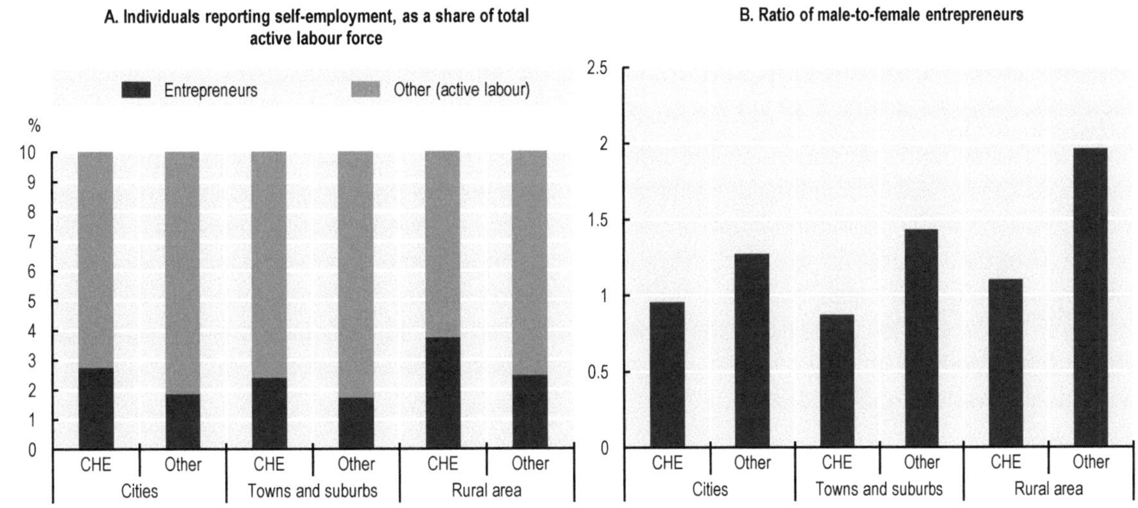

Note: The active labour force is defined as the part of the registered population between the ages of 15-64 who are either searching for work, in training, self-employed or in active employment. Areas are classified by Eurostat's degree of urbanisation.
Source: European Labour Force Survey (2019).

Entrepreneurship rates are promising for women in Switzerland. In European OECD statistics, one female entrepreneur is missing per three males in European OECD countries. While Switzerland has more gender parity in entrepreneurship than other European OECD countries, there is still a small rural penalty for female entrepreneurs in rural areas. While there is a smaller share of women entrepreneurs in rural areas, the rates themselves are a positive indicator of entrepreneurship in Switzerland. More recent findings from 2020 confirm the continued high trend of female entrepreneurship (Swiss Federal Statistical Office, 2021[36]).

Women still face acute challenges as entrepreneurs. Growing firms and gaining venture funding is still a challenge for women entrepreneurs and globally, the type of firms women tend to start are more often in wholesale retail (Global Entrepreneurship Monitor, 2021[37]). In traditional "start-up" sectors (new ICT firms), women only account for 20% of founders (Impact Hub Zürich, n.d.[38]). Notably, higher entrepreneurship rates for women come in stark contrast to the gender gaps in the active labour force across territories in Figure 2.6. It is well documented that female founders often have a more gender-balanced workplace, yet often firms with female founders hire fewer individuals (Global Entrepreneurship Monitor, 2021[37]). Supporting the well-being and growth of female-founded firms may help relieve at least some of the disparities in the territorial gender gaps.

Supporting fledgling female entrepreneurs is a promising opportunity for growth in rural regions. Accessing the hidden resource of female entrepreneurship in Switzerland may help diversify the labour force and economic activities across all regions, and in particular in rural and peri-urban regions that show lower levels of female participation in the labour force. In addition, some studies show that the kinds of firm women establish, tend to answer to otherwise unmet needs or have social purposes. While the opportunity is promising, women-led firms often face increasing challenges. Scaling up among female-owned firms is less common (Baldegger, Gaudart and Wild, 2020[39]). Unfortunately, there is little evidence of programmes to support female founders and very little is known about the challenges faced by female entrepreneurs specifically in rural regions of Switzerland.

Product and process innovation in Switzerland

Product and process innovation is driven by ingenious individuals and learning through networks. In some industries, this type of activity can be proxied by education levels and a number of co-publications for innovations in the high-tech sector that often occur in large firms, and involve patenting and sharing of findings with other experts. Swiss regions are often at the top of the charts in this type of innovation. For smaller firms, however, this type of innovation is often irrelevant.

Regions in Switzerland perform relatively strongly in standard indicators of high-tech innovation as compared to other OECD countries. In Figure 2.10, some of the standard indicators show that Swiss regions have repeatedly performed in the top quartiles of standard indicators of innovation. This includes the share of tertiary education workers, the number of co-publications as well as product and process innovations. Each one of these indicators suggests that the capacity for firms and workers to innovate is strong, even if some heterogeneities exist between large regions. In particular, this finding supports the argument that high-tech innovation, often characterised as an innovation that is more common in large firms, is quite advanced in Switzerland.

There is high innovation in both metropolitan and non-metropolitan regions. The large region of Ticino (CH07)[18] and Zurich (CH04) perform highly in indicators associated with high-tech innovation as well as those associated with innovation more widely in products and processes (Figure 2.10). However, programmes that support high-tech innovation are not necessarily the type of innovation that is most relevant to non-metropolitan areas. For example, in Central Switzerland, where the canton of Lucerne is located, indicators of high-tech innovation are relatively low, as compared to other Swiss regions, but are high for product and process innovation. With an economic structure in Luzern that has a relatively stronger share of professional services and wholesale and trade, firms in Luzern are more likely to benefit from innovation programmes that encourage the diffusion and adoption of already existing forms of innovation from other regions. In the large region of Lake Geneva (CH01), where the canton of Vaud is located, small and medium enterprises are lagging behind in basic product and process innovation adoption (Figure 2.10).

In the region of Espace Mittleland, process innovation is much more common than product innovation. Espace Mittleland (CH02), where the canton of Jura is located, has a relatively high level of co-publications for the share of tertiary educated workers (Figure 2.10), which may reflect the character of innovation in this large region. The region includes mountainous areas, as well as industrial parks and traditional manufacturing. It demonstrates a high level of process innovation and, while the level of product innovation is high, it is relatively less than expected given its industrial structure.

Figure 2.10. Innovation in large regions of Switzerland, 2020

Co-publications, tertiary education, process and process innovation as indicators of innovation and innovation diffusion

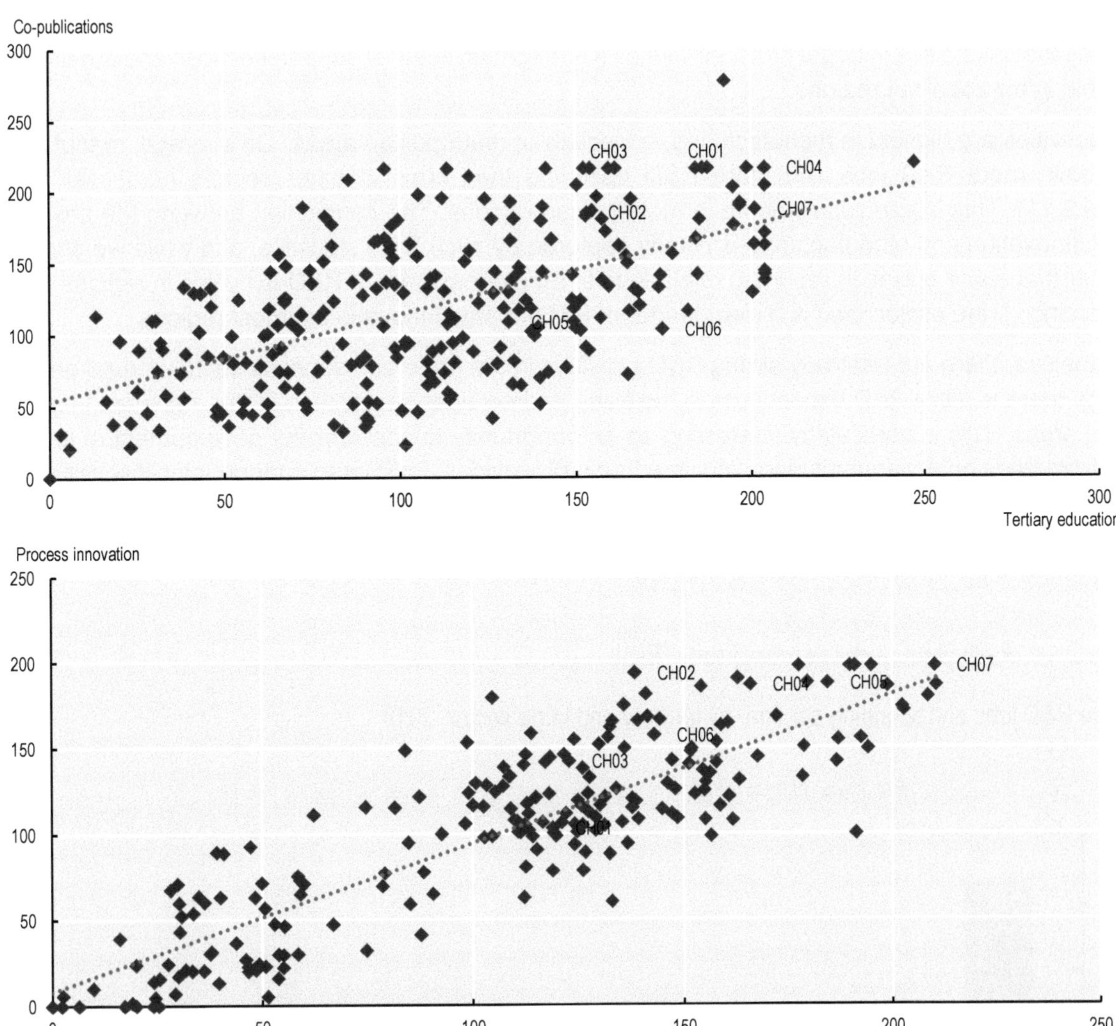

Note: Data includes TL2 regions with available data in all EU countries, Norway, Switzerland and Republic of Türkiye, as well as the EU average. Large regions of Switzerland refer to Lake Geneva Region (CH 01), Espace Mittelland (CH02), Northwestern Switzerland (CH03), Zurich (CH04), Eastern Switzerland (CH05), Central Switzerland (CH06) and Ticino (CH07). Co-publications refer to international scientific co-publications per million population, where at least one co-author is based abroad or outside the EU for the EU-27. Tertiary education refers to the share of persons aged 25-34 that have completed some form of post-secondary education over the population between and including 24 to 25 year-olds. Process innovation refers to the number of SMEs that introduced at least one business process innovation either new to the firm or new to the market, over the total number of SMEs. Product innovation refers to the number of SMEs that introduced at least one product innovation (new or significantly improved good or service) over the total number of SMEs.

Source: EC (2021[40]), *European Innovation Scoreboard (database)*, https://ec.europa.eu/growth/industry/policy/innovation/scoreboards_en.

Spending, jobs and firms in R&D

R&D activities to a large part, indicate whether firms participate in actively contributing to the production of new and improved products or processes. They are particularly relevant for innovation in high-tech industries but not necessarily the adoption and diffusion of such innovations. Nevertheless, in some regions, R&D jobs and expenditures indicate that firms are actively working on generating new-to-firm and new-to-market innovations and can still provide insights into some of the regional innovation puzzles.

R&D activities are higher in metropolitan areas. There are more R&D jobs and expenditures per firm in metropolitan regions than in peri-urban or rural regions (Figure 2.11). This trend is observed widely in the spatial literature on innovation. In part, this is reflected in the size of the market, the type of innovation activities that take place in larger firms, as well as a stronger diversity of support services and supply chains available in metropolitan regions.

R&D activities are highest in manufacturing, especially in metropolitan areas. On average, manufacturing firms have more R&D jobs and more R&D spending than firms in other sectors across all regions (Figure 2.11). This is particularly acute in metropolitan regions. The connection between the process for formal innovation and manufacturing is clearly captured by such R&D statistics, and while we should still consider that some biases in reporting might lead to an overestimate of R&D activities in regions (OECD, forthcoming[3]), the sector itself is a clear leader of R&D-related innovation in most regions.

Nevertheless, there are relatively strong R&D activities in the trade and services sector in rural areas. On average there is more R&D expenditure in the trade and services sector than in the manufacturing sector in rural areas. This is particularly interesting as an opportunity to consider the development of industries away from traditional manufacturing, into new forms of services. Policies to support inter-disciplinarily can help build the development of the growing ecosystem around firm activities. An example of an initiative that promotes interdisciplinary includes the Innovation Booster programme offered by Innosuisse and similar interdisciplinary programmes supported in innovation parks further described in Chapter 3.

Figure 2.11. R&D jobs and spending (per firm)

Average R&D jobs and spending per firm, by territory and large sector, 2019

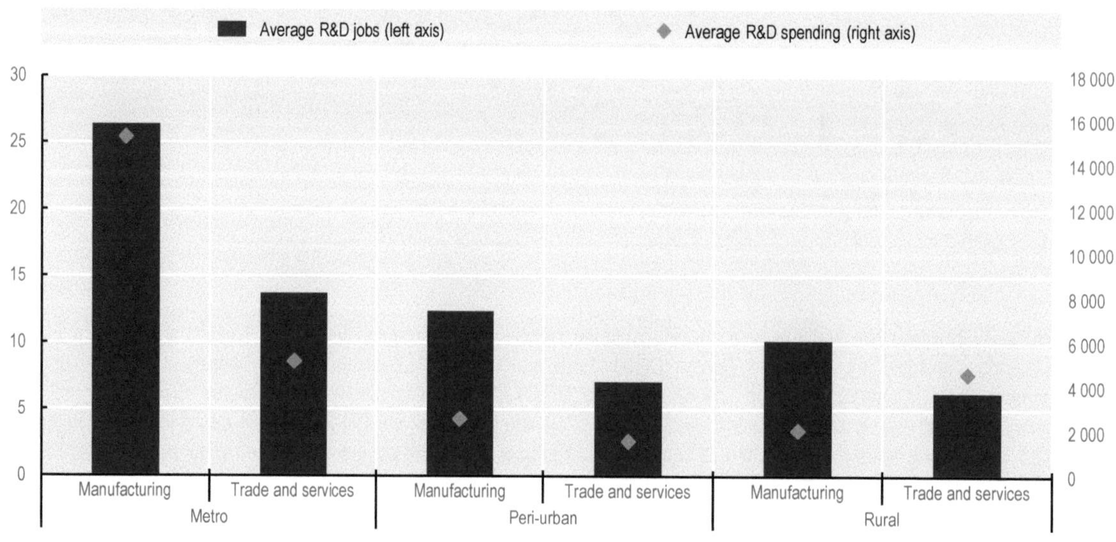

Note: Average R&D jobs refer to the average number of jobs involved in R&D in the sample of firms that reported any R&D activities. Average R&D spending is in Swiss Francs (2015). Groups of rural, peri-urban and metro areas are categorised in Box 2.1 and Veneri (2018[34]).
Source: Swiss R&D Survey, Swiss Federal Statistical Offices, as elaborated by the OECD.

The average number of R&D jobs grew from 2012 to 2019 in rural regions, while there is a strong decline in metropolitan regions (Figure 2.12). Likewise, there is a growth in R&D activities that peri-urban regions are observing in the trade and services sector. The increase in R&D activities per firm is a sign of the growth of traditional innovation activities. In line with an increasing transition to trade and services activities in rural regions, this trend indicates a promising opportunity for rural regions to contribute more fully to innovation in Switzerland, while also being able to benefit from the positive impacts of innovation in rural regions.

Figure 2.12. Changes in R&D jobs and spending, 2012-19

Average job (FTE) changes and spending changes, by large sector and territory

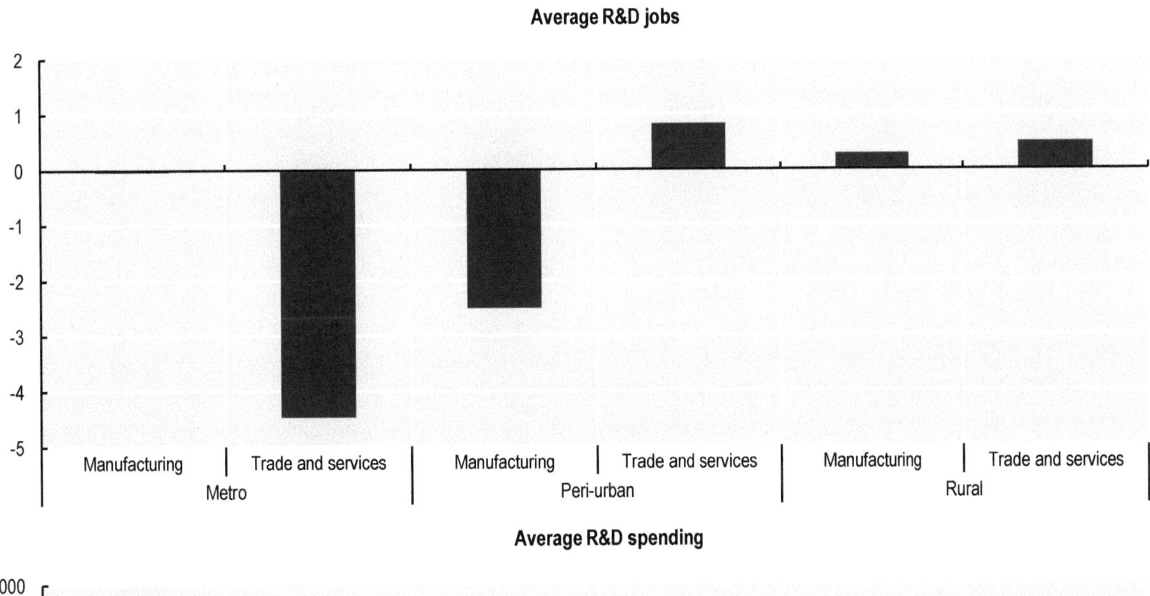

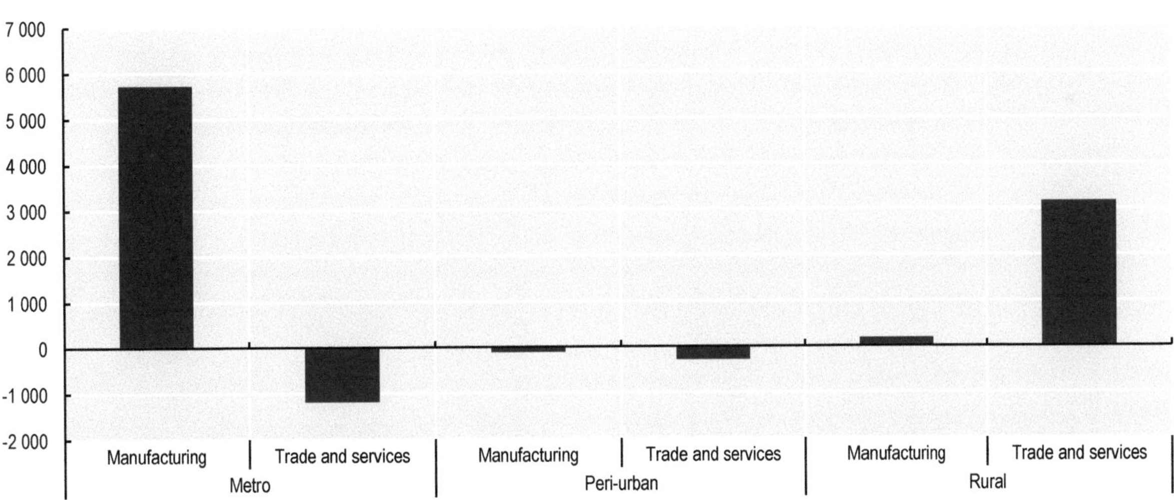

Note: Average R&D jobs refer to the average number of jobs involved in R&D in the sample of firms that reported any R&D activities. R&D in-house (intramural) expenditure refers to R&D expenditures within firms, per firm. Extramural expenditure refers to R&D expenditures in Switzerland and abroad. All currency is in Swiss Francs (2015).
Source: Swiss R&D Survey.

In metropolitan areas, a decline in R&D jobs per firm is accompanied by an increase in expenditure per firm, in particular in the manufacturing sector (Figure 2.12). In metropolitan regions, firm activities in R&D are shifting from those that require R&D staff to those that primarily involve R&D expenditures. It is not currently possible to understand whether this is due to higher input costs for R&D in some businesses, or because of changes in trends of outsourcing R&D activities. While we observe a fall in manufacturing R&D jobs on average across Switzerland from 2012 to 2017 and stagnant change in 2012-19, spending on R&D

in manufacturing is still increasing in metropolitan regions. Such a pattern could be explained if R&D activities are increasingly outsourced; other explanations for this pattern may be general equilibrium effects and competition from external sources of jobs during the Swiss Franc crisis in 2015.[19] Some evidence from the location of spending further explored below, suggests that in part, this is due to outsourcing of R&D in manufacturing in metropolitan regions (Figure 2.14). This is not observed in manufacturing sectors in rural regions, where there are small levels of growth in jobs and expenditure per firm.

R&D spending quadrupled in the rural trade and services sector from 2012 to 2019. According to Figures 2.12 and 2.13, the trade and services sector is particularly strong in leading to an increase in expenditure as compared to the manufacturing sector in rural regions. Expenditures on R&D in rural regions grew from CHF 90 000 (approximately EUR 83 000) to CHF 360 000 (approximately EUR 331 000) from 2012 to 2019.[20]

The trade and services sector in rural areas is experiencing a 36% increase in average jobs per firm and a threefold increase in average R&D expenditure per firm. The average number of jobs in R&D in the trade and services sector in rural regions grew close to one per two firms. Likewise, the growth in R&D expenditures per firm in the trade and services sector reflected a close to threefold increase in rural regions. A similar trend was not observed in metropolitan regions. This finding is promising for reducing gaps in R&D activities across regions. In the rural trade and services sectors, there are more R&D jobs, expenditure per firm and more firms operating (Figures 2.12 and 2.13). The relative increase of average R&D jobs per firm in the trade and services sector suggests that further activity is being picked up in the R&D sector, and R&D workers are still being hired to participate in innovative activities in rural regions, even if the same cannot be said in metropolitan regions.

Figure 2.13. R&D firms and jobs

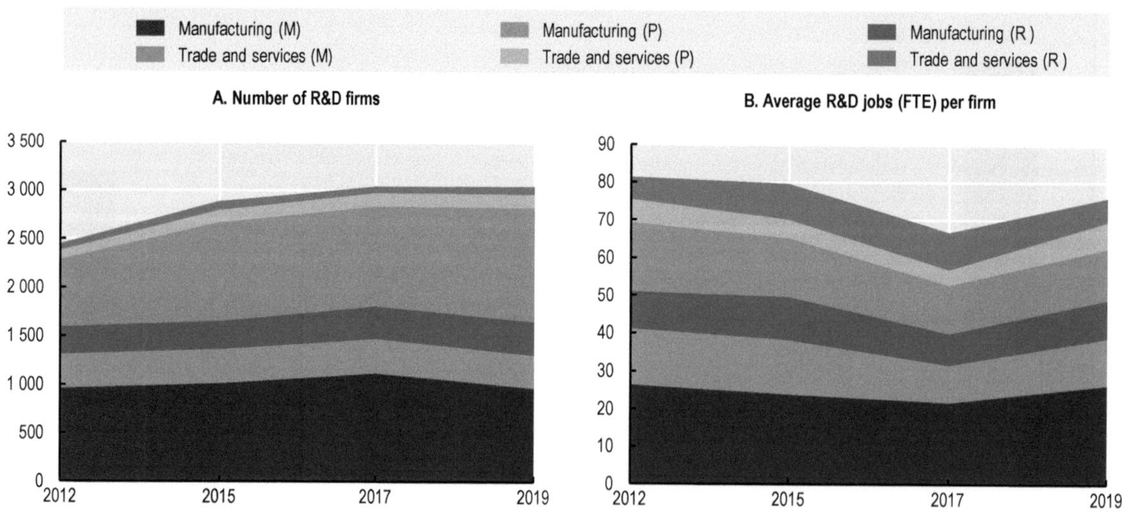

Note: R&D firms refer to the number of firms reporting any R&D activity. R&D jobs refer to the average number of full-time equivalent (FTE) jobs that participate in R&D in firms conducting any form of R&D.
Source: R&D Survey, Swiss Federal Statistical Office as elaborated by the OECD.

In 2019, close to 35 cents per Swiss Franc spent on R&D was outsourced; in rural regions, only 4 cents per Swiss Franc left the firm for R&D expenses. R&D spending in rural regions focuses more on internal R&D processes than on metropolitan regions. This trend has been increasing over time (see Annex A). In 2012, 18 cents per Swiss Franc were spent outside of the firm, while in rural regions this was only 2 cents. While spending within firms or investing in other Swiss or foreign firms may be preferable depending on the model of innovation the firm pursues, the lack of investment for in-house research may limit some of the immediate benefits of investments in innovation on the labour market and the diffusion of skills within regions.

Rural firms are increasingly spending a larger share of R&D investments in-house in the manufacturing sector and out of the firm in the trade and services sector. The change in R&D investments from 2012 to 2019 primarily went to R&D investments outside of firms (67% of the change) rather than within firms (33% of the change). However, in rural regions, we observe that 62% of the change in expenditures is due to increased external expenditure, with the majority of the increase in expenditure due to increases in the trade and services sectors outsourcing R&D expenditure (Figure 2.14 and Annex A).

Focus on bringing more support for R&D investments in rural regions could unlock the stagnant innovation and productivity rates. Firms in metropolitan and peri-urban regions may be choosing to invest in R&D outside of firms in metropolitan regions, either for cost-saving purposes (wages premiums may be lower in smaller firms, or firms not located in high-income regions) or because innovation in such firms is reaching saturation point. On the other hand, firms in rural regions are not yet fully saturated in terms of R&D expenditures and may be able to conduct more in-house research because of lower reservation wages, and fixed and variable costs. As will be discussed in the next section, because rural and non-metropolitan regions are not yet full saturated, focusing on R&D and innovation in rural regions may also help reverse the productivity slowdown.

Figure 2.14. The composition of R&D spending across territories and sectors

Spending by destination, territories, and sectors, 2019, in 2015 CHF

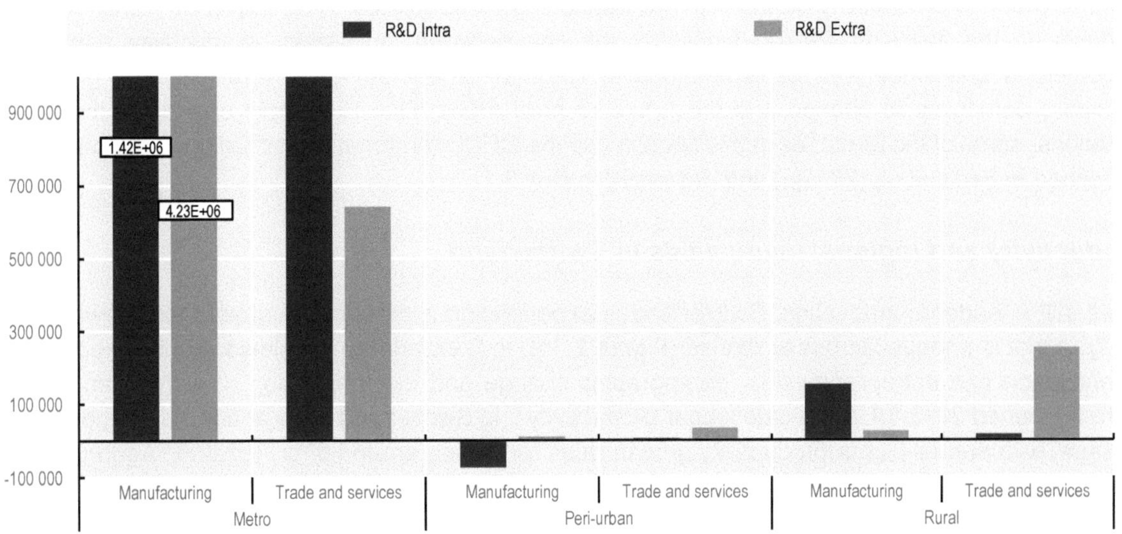

Note: Graph depicts the levels of R&D spending, by destination from in 2019 within aggregate sectors and territories. Due to sample size and interpretation, the public and community service sectors, the financial, insurance and real estate sector and utility and construction sectors are excluded.
Source: Swiss R&D Survey, Federal Statistical Office as elaborated by OECD.

Key messages on innovation in Switzerland

- Entrepreneurship rates are strong in rural regions of Switzerland but there is still a penalty for women in rural regions.
- Swiss regions perform relatively strongly in high-tech innovation but some regions are still lagging in basic product and process innovation.
- There are more R&D investments and jobs in metropolitan regions and, in general, in the manufacturing sector, however, increases in R&D spending are not contributing to the growth of R&D jobs in metropolitan regions.
- There is an increasing opportunity for R&D activities in the trade and services sector in rural regions, where increased R&D investment coincides with increased R&D jobs.
- Rural firms are increasingly outsourcing R&D spending in the services and trade sectors.
- Focusing on bringing more support for R&D investments and other innovation activities in rural regions could unlock the stagnant productivity rates in Switzerland.

Promoting equality and adapting to demographic change

Innovation is often used as a tool to bring prosperity to regions. While it often is linked to growth in jobs and wages, it can also accentuate territorial inequalities via trends in concentration and diversification. Productivity is often used as a proxy for innovation adoption; while it is not perfect, under the assumption that innovation is productivity-enhancing, the trends should be related. After exploring trends in territorial productivity, the following section highlights the link between innovation, productivity and firm-level outcomes. It concludes with considerations for promoting well-being as rural regional governments anticipate demographic change and the future of rural areas. Due to sample size and privacy-related limitations, some of the territories in this section use the OECD territorial classification of regions (cantons) as defined in Fadic et al. (2019[5]) and described in Box 2.1.

Productivity and regional inequalities in Switzerland

While still a leader in innovation, Switzerland is experiencing a productivity growth slowdown (Ollivaud, 2017[41]) that is unequal across territories (Figure 2.15). In Switzerland, the slowdown is linked to the role of innovation and entrepreneurship, demographic change and low integration of women and migrants. From the period 2012-19, aggregate labour productivity[21] in Switzerland grew at around 1% per annum on average, with annual labour productivity growth rates remaining around 0, or negative. Aggregate growth rates over the entire period reached their highest points in 2018 and 2019 at close to 4% as depicted in Figure 2.15. This came after positive growth in prior decades as reported in Ollivaud (2017[41]). The aggregate relative productivity slowdown masks territorial divergences. Whereas productivity in high-density peri-urban areas soared (at 2% in 2019 as compared to 2012), productivity in rural remote areas and peri-urban low-density areas fell behind, particularly after 2015.[22] In 2019, central rural regions and low-density peri-urban contracted by 14% and 5%. This reinforces the importance of strategies for innovation and entrepreneurship that consider spatial aspects to bring more inclusivity.

Innovation (R&D) is positively associated with increases in productivity but is contingent on territorial and sectoral attributes (Figure 2.16). A rise in jobs in R&D is associated with an increase in productivity in the next period for all of Switzerland. Likewise, a rise in R&D expenditure is associated with an 8% increase in productivity in the next period. Estimates are not significant when controlling for territorial and sectoral fixed effects but negative for non-metropolitan regions.[23]

Additional R&D expenditures are negatively associated with increases in labour productivity in metropolitan regions, yet positive in non-metropolitan regions. While the correlation is noisy, it describes a potential saturation of the R&D expenditure market in non-metropolitan regions, as suggested in the previous section.

Figure 2.15. The divergence of productivity across Swiss territories

Labour productivity growth, by nine-tier national territorial classifications

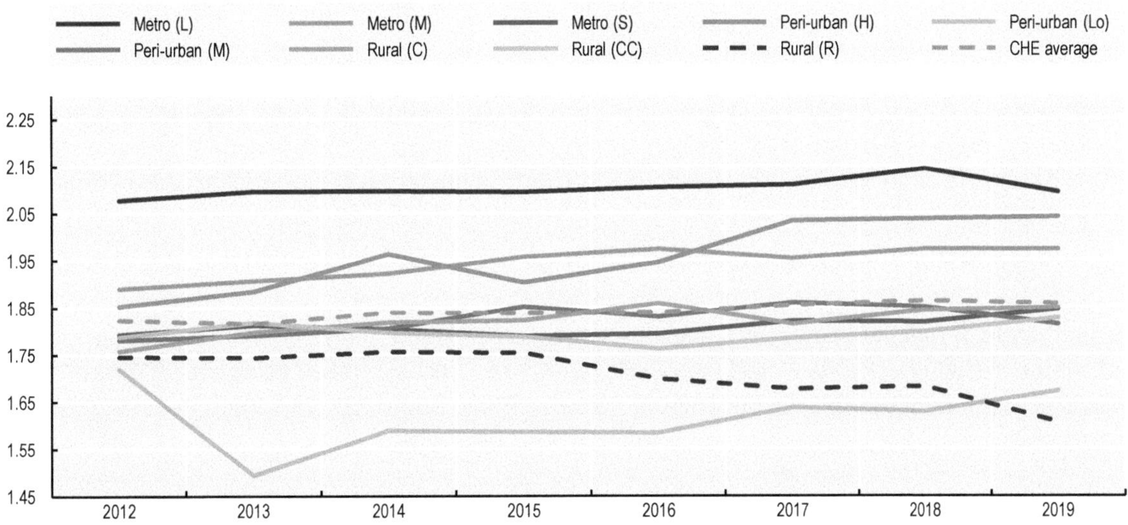

Note: Labour productivity is reported based on value-added over (FTE) employment. Areas are classified into the nine-tier classification of areas. All figures are deflated to 2015 CHF. The agriculture and fishery sectors are excluded because of the lack of data availability in the value-added survey. To facilitate interpretation and after consultation with the FSO financial, insurance and real estate sector, utilities and construction, as well as public and community services are excluded from this analysis.
Source: Swiss Value-Added Survey and STATENT, Federal Statistical Office.

Figure 2.16. Innovation activities and labour productivity

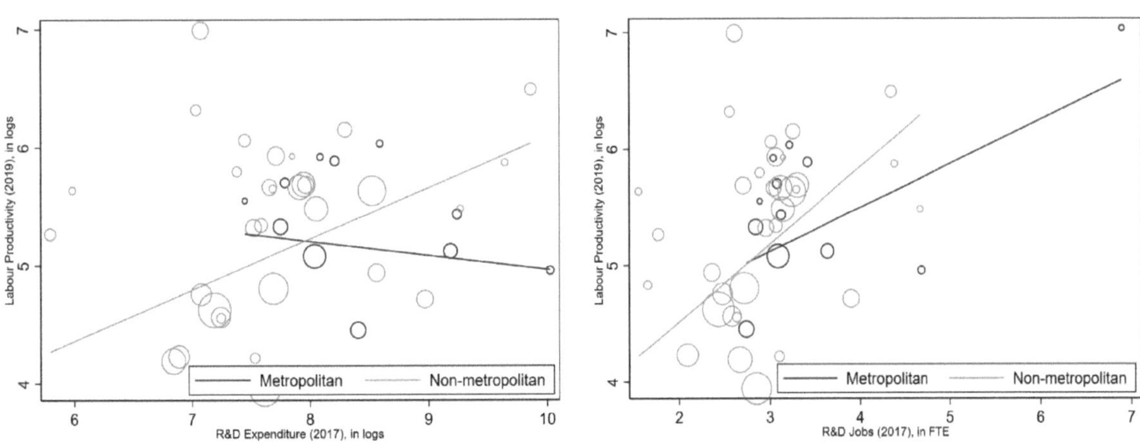

Note: Labour productivity is reported based on value-added over (FTE) employment. All expenditure and value-added figures are in millions of 2015 CHF. Observations are on a cantonal and aggregate sectoral level. To facilitate interpretation and analysis, the public sector and other community services sectors are excluded from the R&D statistics. Bubbles are weighted by labour (FTE). The figure includes only data from 2017 and 2019. To facilitate interpretation and after consultation with the FSO, activities in the agriculture and fisheries sector, financial, insurance and real estate sector, utilities and construction, as well as public and community services are excluded from this analysis. Classifications of territories are based on Fadic et al. (2019[5]).
Source: Swiss Value-Added Survey, STATENT and Swiss Research & Development Survey, Federal Statistical Office.

There is a higher return of R&D jobs on productivity in non-metropolitan regions. For each R&D job, there is a higher return to labour productivity in the following year for those in non-metropolitan regions. Non-metropolitan regions may have lower average levels of R&D jobs in sectors, as compared to metropolitan regions (Figure 2.16) but the return on R&D jobs on productivity is higher.

Nevertheless, there is a rural penalty on the return from R&D activities when controlling other factors such as the year, sector and region. The pure effect of belonging to a non-metropolitan region on labour productivity is negative. It is strongest and only statistically significant for non-metropolitan rural remote areas. In remote rural regions, belonging to a non-metropolitan region results in lower productivity in the following period as compared to metropolitan regions.[24]

Access to markets matters for innovation outcomes. Part of the productivity penalty in the previous figures is associated with access to higher sales volumes and prices. In Figure 2.17, for firms with the same level of productivity, there is a higher level of sales for metropolitan regions. This finding suggests that access to markets makes a larger contribution to innovation adoption and productivity in metropolitan regions than in non-metropolitan regions.

Access to larger labour markets is associated with higher productivity. Larger cantonal and sectoral labour markets (larger circles in Figure 2.17) tend to have higher sales, even for less productive activities in cantons. If firms in regions and sectors have access to larger labour markets, there is a larger possibility to find a large enough market for skilled labour. Rural regions may have fewer sales even if they are equally as productive, not necessarily only because of firm absorptive capacities, but also because of access to labour markets.

Figure 2.17. Sales and labour productivity

Annual labour productivity and sales by canton and sector, classified by access to cities, 2019

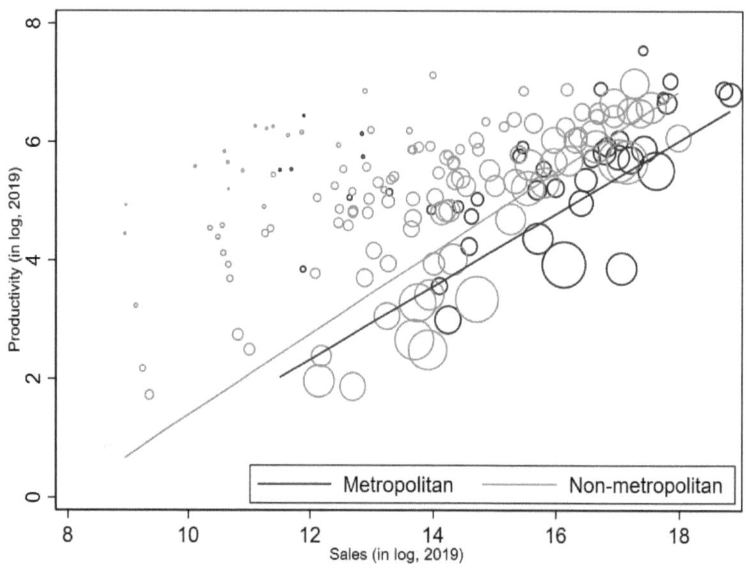

Note: Labour productivity is reported based on value-added over (FTE) employment. Value-added and sales are in millions of 2015 CHF. Observations are on a cantonal and aggregate sectoral level. Due to small sample size issues originating from the value-added survey, the canton of Graubünden is excluded from the analysis. Bubbles are weighted by labour (FTE). The figure includes only data from 2019. To facilitate interpretation and after consultation with the FSO, activities in the agriculture and fisheries sector, financial, insurance and real estate sector, utilities and construction, as well as public and community services are excluded from this analysis. Classifications of territories are based on the OECD classifications based on access to cities as explained in Veneri (2018[34]) and Fadic et al. (2019[5]).
Source: Swiss Value-Added Survey and STATENT Federal Statistical Office.

While sales volumes may be high in metropolitan regions, so is diversification; the opposite is true for non-metropolitan regions that are more concentrated (Figure 2.18). Using an indicator of territorial inequality (McCann, 2013[42]), we observe a stronger diversification between firms within metropolitan regions than those in non-metropolitan regions. Diversification of the shares of sales is highest in metropolitan regions and has been stable from 2012 to 2019.

Yet more concentration also coincides with less inequality between firms within non-metropolitan regions. Firms in the top 10th percentile of all firms have almost 40 times more sales than those in the bottom 10th percentile in metropolitan regions. In comparison, the top 10th percentile of firms have a little more than 20 times more than those in the bottom 10th percentile in non-metropolitan regions in rural remote areas (Figure 2.18). There are larger differences between outcomes for firms at the top and bottom of the distribution in metropolitan areas. Inequality at the top and bottom end of firm sales are stronger in more dense regions close to FUAs.

Figure 2.18. Territorial inequality and diversification

Territorial Gini on sales across territories and p90/p10 ratio of share, 2019

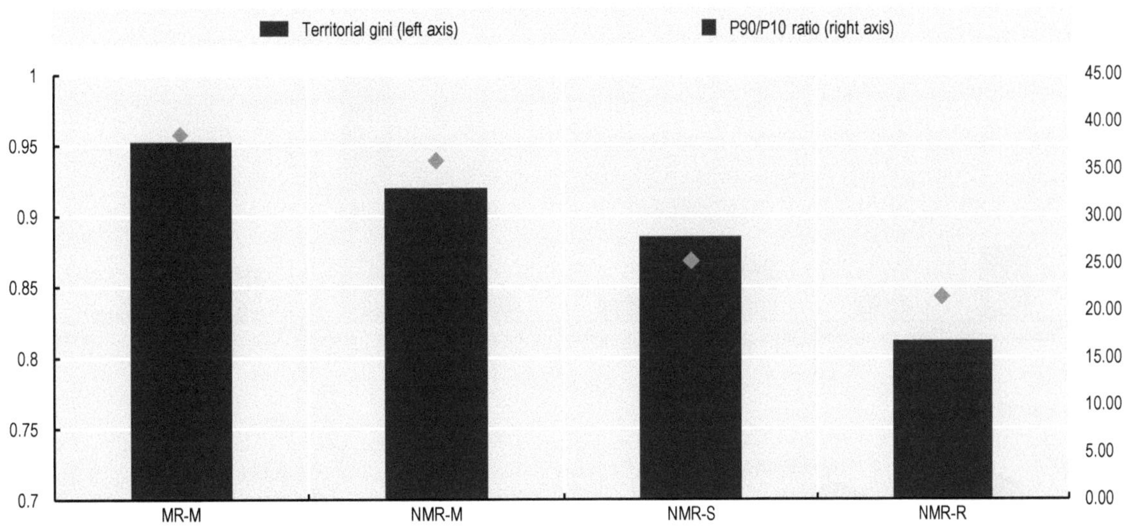

Note: Following McCann (2013[42]), territorial inequalities evaluate the parity between the share of individual firms within each of the territories. In this figure we use indicators based on firm sales. The Territorial Gini refers to the inequality of sales values between firms. The P90/P10 ratio is the ratio of total sales attributed to the top 10th percentile of firms, ranked by sales and the bottom 90th percentile of firms. Classifications of territories are based on Fadic et al. (2019[5]). Due to challenges with sample sizes, the report uses the OECD classification rather than the national classification for territories. The abbreviations refer to metropolitan regions (cantons) with a large city of more than 250 000 inhabitants (MR-M), non-metropolitan regions near a city of more than 250 000 inhabitants (NMR-M), non-metropolitan regions near a city with between 50 000 and 250 000 inhabitants (NMR-S), and non-metropolitan remote regions (NMR-R). Switzerland does not have any metropolitan regions classified as a region with a very large city of more than 1 million inhabitants (MR-L). To facilitate interpretation and after consultation with the FSO, activities in the financial, insurance and real estate sector, utilities and construction, as well as public and community services are excluded from this analysis.
Source: STATENT, Federal Statistical Office as elaborated by the OECD.

While diversification in metropolitan areas and concentration in non-metropolitan areas are not uncommon, it can be indicative of one of two main phenomena: i) that market failures are limiting competition and opportunities for some firms within the same sector; ii) that diversification of activities between sectors is high in the region, or a mixture of both. In the first scenario (market failures), governments should enact to ensure a fair playing field through competition policies and support for the development of diversified industries. In this second scenario (diversification), governments should not react unless outcomes are lagging.

In non-metropolitan regions, the low levels of inequality suggest that markets are working well despite less competition and more concentration. For regions in the phase of catching up to other regions, concentration can be a good strategy if firms are particularly productive. However, as observed from Figure 2.17, this is not necessarily the case in sectors in non-metropolitan regions. Non-metropolitan regions may need further diversification, before focusing on concentration.[25] This finding supports earlier recommendations that call for the need to diversify sectors in non-metropolitan regions of Switzerland. Furthermore, there may still be some sectors of activity, for example in the agri-food chain as discussed in Chapter 4, where more competition could be encouraged to counteract the productivity slowdown and encourage innovation.

On a sectoral level, markets are functioning competitively. While in some sectors and regions, the top 10% of firms capture over 70% of sales in metropolitan regions (Figure 2.19), the Herfindahl-Hirschman indicator of diversification is still within reasonable bounds.

Figure 2.19. Sales concentration and competition across territories

Share in sales of top 10% firms and Herfindahl-Hirschman Index (HHI) of concentration, 2019

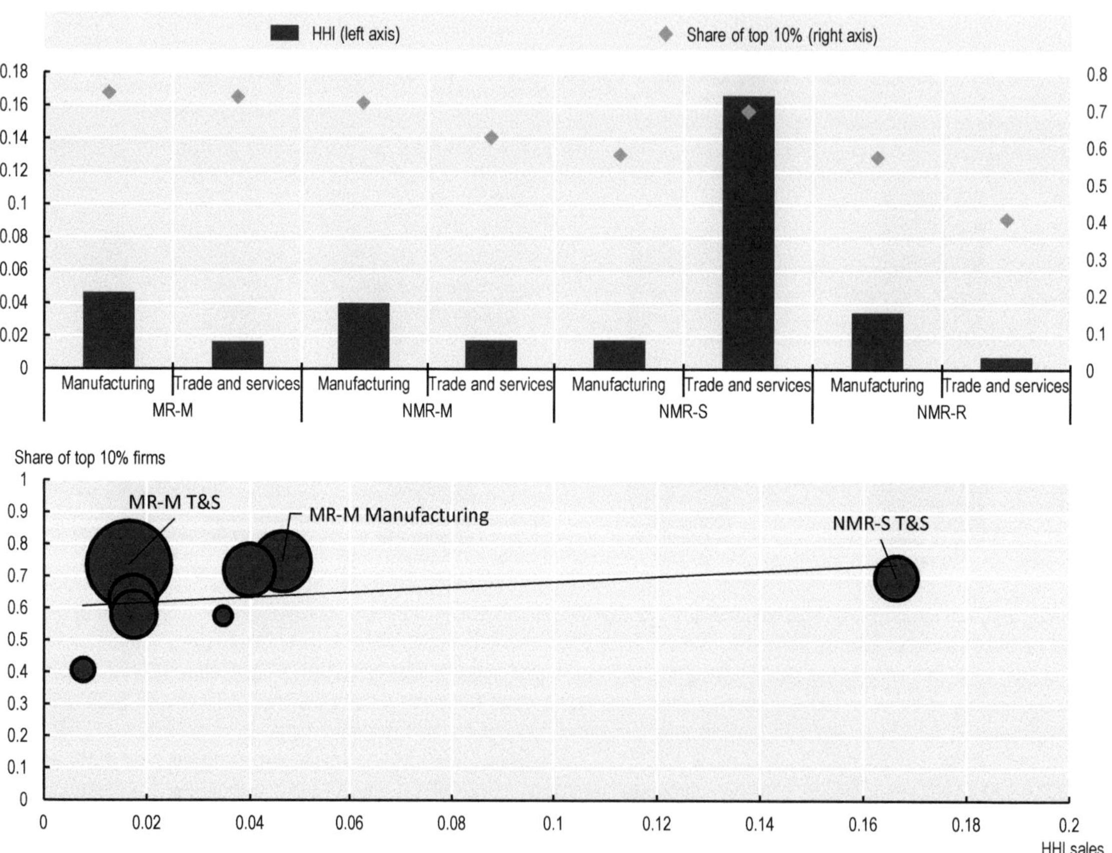

Note: The HHI measures the share of sales in each sector and region to determine market concentration and competitiveness. The formula consists of $HHI = \sum_{i=1}^{N} s_i^2$ normalised to 1. A low level of HHI indicates a highly competitive industry in the territory, while a high level of HHI indicates a highly concentrated industry in the specific territory. Because the indicators are split both by territory and sector, the numbers are slightly higher than anticipated. The share of the top 10% of firms refers to the share of sales that the top 10% of firms contain. Close to 1 refers suggests that the top 10% of high-sales firms have the quasi-totality of the market. Figures in the lower panel are weighted by the share of the labour force. Classifications of territories are based on Fadic et al. (2019[5]). Due to challenges with sample sizes, the report uses the OECD classification rather than the national classification for territories. The abbreviations refer to metropolitan regions (cantons) with a large city of more than 250 000 inhabitants (MR-M), non-metropolitan regions near a city of more than 250 000 inhabitants (NMR-M), non-metropolitan regions near a city with between 50 000 and 250 000 inhabitants (NMR-S), and non-metropolitan remote regions (NMR-R). Switzerland does not have any metropolitan regions classified as a region with a very large city of more than 1 million inhabitants (MR-L).
Source: STATENT, Federal Statistical Office as elaborated by the OECD.

Nevertheless, a relatively higher level of concentration is observed in trade and services[26] in non-metropolitan regions close to small cities. This could indicate opportunities for innovation through promoting competition and activity in this sector and type of region. A high Herfindahl-Hirschman Index (HHI) indicates high levels of concentration but not necessarily low competition if all firms are gaining equal shares of the economy. However, if we jointly observe an HHI with a high share of total sales activities in only the top 10% of firms, it can indicate market failures due to low competition.

In general, in Switzerland, competition is strong; however, relative to other regions, some sectors may be less competitive, with a high concentration of close to 70% of all sales going to the top 10% of high-sales firms in both the trade and services sector in non-metropolitan regions close to small cities. In line with previous recommendations and in lieu of specific intervention from competition authorities, working on encouraging entrepreneurship and innovation in this type of region and sector can provide some part of the solution to unlocking equity and growth in non-metropolitan regions close to small cities. As observed in Chapter 4, there are clear cases where export and sales markets are dominated by two to three firms in the agri-food chain that includes the wholesale and trade market for raw agricultural products and foods.[27] In this case, policies to encourage new firms in this sector may be needed to help entrepreneurs overcome anti-competitive practices.

Anticipating demographic change: Younger and older workers

A future-looking approach for rural regions and rural areas often starts by understanding how current trends are changing society and transforming policy implementation. It anticipates future trends with adaptive policies that can improve well-being and productivity regardless of the future scenario (OECD, 2021[43]). An integrated policy approach also includes a vision that is focused on the value-added of rural regions rather than just sectors (OECD, forthcoming[3]). While it is difficult to predict all future changes, governments with strategic foresight that includes a rural lens are prepared for adapting to change more quickly and have found the practice useful for building consensus and ownership. In some cases, to adapt to change, governments may also consider the use of experimental tools, such as regulatory sandboxes, or other experimentation processes that can provide new public services to a changing economy, as elaborated in Chapter 3.

There are two men employed for every employed woman in low-density peri-urban areas, as observed previously in this chapter (Figure 2.6). While the rate is still high in many metropolitan regions, it is lower than in most non-metropolitan regions. A forward-looking and inclusive strategy also addresses some of the barriers to participation in the labour market and entrepreneurship for the under-represented population, including women, youth and migrants. Rural and peri-urban regions suffer from a loss of opportunities for competitiveness, productivity and diverse labour market through a lower activation of the female workforce. Currently, no specific targets for encouraging entrepreneurship and opportunities for women and other harder-to-reach communities are included in the government's New Regional Policy (NRP), however, they are incorporated into some Innosuisse instruments. A more inclusive strategy might include specific support and targets that trace and make reforms to correct for market failures in access to government services for all parts of society, for all individuals in Switzerland. Furthermore, there are long argued gains in productivity through more inclusive policies.

Skills gaps and demographic change is a key challenge for innovation, as it often entails lower innovation activity rates and the need for continuous lifelong upskilling policies for younger and older workers. Cantonal authorities identified that their largest challenges had more to do with demographic change and migration patterns than those directly concerned with building more business opportunities. Demographic change has not spared Switzerland. In non-metropolitan regions of Switzerland, there is a higher rate of older workers as compared to metropolitan regions (Figure 2.20). In addition, some cantons are also suffering from a lack of young workers. This suggests that there is both a need for policies to ensure that older workers are productive and have access to lifelong learning opportunities in rural regions, including adult learning, lifelong learning and upskilling opportunities, reducing incentives for early retirement and considering health and other social services as part of a holistic approach (Lewis and Ollivaud, 2020[44]). Likewise, early engagement for entrepreneurship and leadership courses with youth in rural regions and increasing consideration for how to adapt economies to the change in the outflow of younger workers should be taken under consideration.

Migration is positively associated with innovation, entrepreneurship and firm performance across regions (OECD, 2022[45]; Kerr, 2018[46]; Guichard, Özgüzel and Kleine-Rueschkamp, forthcoming[47]). This is especially the case in Switzerland (Beerli et al., 2021[48]), even though, there is evidence of local labour market frictions (OECD, 2022[45]). In the case of Switzerland, daily cross-border migrants positively contribute to closing the skills gap, such as in the northern border Jura region. Recent work by Beerli et al. (2021[48]) found that the removal of barriers to European cross-border migrants in Switzerland impacted regions close to the border increasing wages for high-wage native workers, productivity, firm size and innovation in firms where there was a prior skills shortage. While the challenges may be outside of the direct programme of work of regional development agencies, co-ordinating with local cantons who make decisions on migration permits is an important step in shaping local policies to support closing the skills gap. Furthermore, encouraging a spatially conscious approach through co-ordination mechanisms with relevant skills, employment and migration authorities can help some of these issues.

Figure 2.20. Older workers across territories

Share of older working age population aged 55-59, 2018

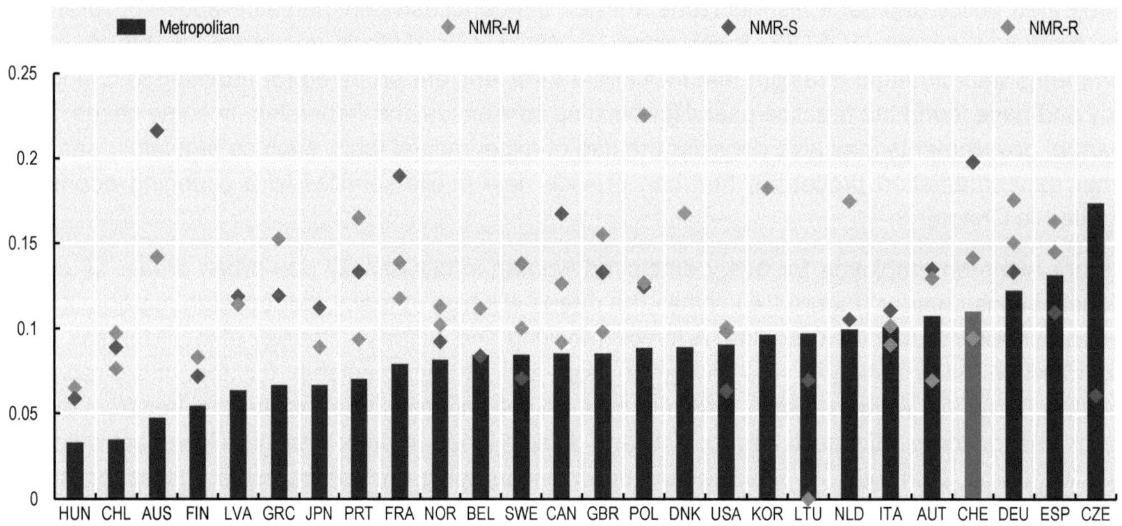

Note: Classifications of territories are based on Fadic et al. (2019[5]). The abbreviations refer to metropolitan regions (cantons) with a large city of more than 250 000 inhabitants (MR-M), non-metropolitan regions near a city of more than 250 000 inhabitants (NMR-M), non-metropolitan regions near a city with between 50 000 and 250 000 inhabitants (NMR-S), and non-metropolitan remote regions (NMR-R). Switzerland does not have any metropolitan regions classified as a region with a very large city of more than 1 million inhabitants (MR-L).
Source: OECD (2022[49]), *Regional Demography*, https://stats.oecd.org/Index.aspx?DataSetCode=REGION_DEMOGR (accessed on 15 June 2022).

Key messages on promoting well-being and adapting to change

- Productivity, as a measure of innovation adoption, is diverging across territories in Switzerland.
- R&D-based innovation is positively associated with increases in productivity particularly for non-metropolitan regions, even though the penalty for the rural remote region is persistent.
- Access to markets and the labour force matters for productivity and sales, but is a bigger challenge in non-metropolitan regions.
- While sales volumes may be lower in non-metropolitan regions, so are firm-level inequalities that may contribute to an easier environment for nascent entrepreneurs.
- In regions and sectors of Switzerland, markets still remain well functioning despite divergences between the top- and bottom-performing firms that are more pronounced in metropolitan regions.
- There is room for boosting competition in the trade and services sector in non-metropolitan regions close to small cities.
- Demographic disparities, based on gender and age, are an important challenge for rural regions that need to be addressed through co-ordination with other ministries.

References

ACOA (2021), "ACOA investments support resources and opportunities for women entrepreneurs across Atlantic Canada", Atlantic Canada Opportunities Agency, https://www.canada.ca/en/atlantic-canada-opportunities/news/2021/05/acoa-investments-support-resources-and-opportunities-for-women-entrepreneurs-across-atlantic-canada.html. [7]

Aghion, P., C. Antonin and S. Bunel (2021), *The Power of Creative Destruction*, Harvard University Press. [21]

Aghion, P. et al. (2001), "Competition, imitation and growth with step-by-step innovation", *Review of Economic Studies*, Vol. 68/3, pp. 467-492, https://doi.org/10.1111/1467-937x.00177. [22]

Aghion, P. and P. Howitt (1990), "A model of growth through creative destruction", *National Bureau of Economic Research*, Vol. w3223. [16]

Ahrend, R. et al. (2017), "What makes cities more productive? Evidence from five OECD countries on the role of urban governance", *Journal of Regional Science*, Vol. 57/3, pp. 385-410, https://doi.org/10.1111/jors.12334. [31]

Akcigit, U., J. Grigsby and T. Nicholas (2017), "The rise of American ingenuity: Innovation and inventors of the golden age", *National Bureau of Economic Research*, Vol. w23047. [28]

Andersson, F. et al. (2009), "Reaching for the stars: Who pays for talent in innovative industries?", *The Economic Journal*, Vol. 119/538, pp. F308-F332, https://doi.org/10.1111/j.1468-0297.2009.02277.x. [23]

Autor, D. (2014), *Polanyi's Paradox and the Shape of Employment Growth*, National Bureau of Economic Research, Cambridge, MA, https://doi.org/10.3386/w20485. [19]

Baldegger, R., R. Gaudart and P. Wild (2020), *Global Entrepreneurship Monitor 2019/2020: Report on Switzerland*, School of Management Fribourg (HEG-FR), HES-SO, University of Applied Sciences and Arts Western Switzerland, https://www.gemconsortium.org/economy-profiles/switzerland-2 (accessed on 22 November 2021). [39]

Beerli, A. et al. (2021), "The abolition of immigration restrictions and the performance of firms and workers: Evidence from Switzerland", *American Economic Review*, Vol. 111/3, pp. 976-1012, https://doi.org/10.1257/aer.20181779. [48]

Bloom, N., M. Draca and J. Van Reenen (2016), "Trade induced technical change? The impact of Chinese imports on innovation, IT and productivity", *The Review of Economic Studies*, Vol. 83/1, pp. 87-117. [24]

EAER (2021), *Switzerland's SME Support*, Federal Department of Economic Affairs, Education and Research, https://www.kmu.admin.ch/kmu/en/home/New/publikationen/politique-pme.html. [15]

EC (2021), *European Innovation Scoreboard (database)*, European Commission, https://ec.europa.eu/growth/industry/policy/innovation/scoreboards_en. [40]

Fadic, M. et al. (2019), "Classifying small (TL3) regions based on metropolitan population, low density and remoteness", *OECD Regional Development Working Papers*, No. 2019/06, OECD Publishing, Paris, https://doi.org/10.1787/b902cc00-en. [5]

FSO (2017), *Typologie des communes et typologie urbain-rural 2012*, Swiss Federal Statistical Office, https://www.bfs.admin.ch/bfs/fr/home/bases-statistiques/niveaux-geographiques.assetdetail.2543324.html. [4]

Global Entrepreneurship Monitor (2021), *Women's Entrepreneurship 2020/21: Thriving Through Crisis*. [37]

Goos, M., A. Manning and A. Salomons (2014), "Explaining job polarization: Routine-biased technological change and offshoring", *American Economic Review*, Vol. 104/8, pp. 2509-2526, https://doi.org/10.1257/aer.104.8.2509. [25]

Grossman, G. and E. Helpman (1990), "Trade, innovation, and growth", *The American Economic Review*, Vol. 80/2, pp. 86-91, http://www.jstor.org/stable/2006548 (accessed on 9 November 2020). [26]

Guichard, L., C. Özgüzel and L. Kleine-Rueschkamp (forthcoming), "Migrants and patenting across OECD counties", *OECD Regional Development Working Papers*. [47]

Impact Hub Zürich (n.d.), *Female Founders*, https://female-founders.ch/ (accessed on 17 May 2022). [38]

ISED (2021), *Women Entrepreneurship Strategy*, Innovation, Science and Economic Development Canada, https://ised-isde.canada.ca/site/women-entrepreneurship-strategy/en. [8]

Kerr, W. (2018), *The Gift of Global Talent*, Stanford University Press, https://doi.org/10.1515/9781503607361. [46]

Kossek, E., T. Allen and T. Dumas (2020), "Boundaryless work: The impact of COVID-19 on work-life boundary management, integration, and gendered divisions of labor for academic women in STEMM", https://nap.nationalacademies.org/resource/26061/Kossek%20et%20al%20-%20FINAL.pdf (accessed on 5 May 2022). [14]

Lengyel, B. et al. (2020), "The role of geography in the complex diffusion of innovations", *Scientific Reports*, Vol. 10/1, https://doi.org/10.1038/s41598-020-72137-w. [29]

Lewis, C. and P. Ollivaud (2020), "Policies for Switzerland's ageing society", *OECD Economics Department Working Papers*, No. 1600, OECD Publishing, Paris, https://doi.org/10.1787/3f8a12c6-en. [44]

Mayer, H. (2020), "Slow innovation in Europe's peripheral regions: Innovation beyond acceleration", in Döringer, S. and J. Eder (eds.), *Schlüsselakteure der Regionalentwicklung - welche Perspektiven bietet Entrepreneurship für ländliche Räume?*, Verlag der Österreichischen Akademie der Wissenschaften. [32]

MBDA (2022), "Women-owned and indigenous small businesses thrive with EDA and MBDA support", Minority Business Development Agency, United States Department of Commerce, https://www.commerce.gov/news/blog/2022/03/women-owned-and-indigenous-small-businesses-thrive-eda-and-mbda-support (accessed on 3 May 2022). [9]

McCann, P. (2019), "Perceptions of regional inequality and the geography of discontent: Insights from the UK", *Regional Studies*, Vol. 54/2, pp. 256-267, https://doi.org/10.1080/00343404.2019.1619928. [20]

McCann, P. (2013), *Modern Urban and Regional Economics*, Oxford University Press. [42]

McKenzie, D. et al. (2021), "Training entrepreneurs", *VoxDevLit*, Vol. 1/2, https://voxdev.org/sites/default/files/Training_Entrepreneurs_Issue_2.pdf. [35]

OECD (2022), "Mainstreaming teleworking and gender equality: A double-edged sword?", OECD, Paris, https://www.oecd-forum.org/posts/mainstreaming-teleworking-and-gender-equality-a-double-edged-sword (accessed on 5 May 2022). [12]

OECD (2022), *Regional Demography*, Regional Database, OECD, Paris, https://stats.oecd.org/Index.aspx?DataSetCode=REGION_DEMOGR (accessed on 15 June 2022). [49]

OECD (2022), *The Contribution of Migration to Regional Development*, OECD Regional Development Studies, OECD Publishing, Paris, https://doi.org/10.1787/57046df4-en. [45]

OECD (2021), *Forward-looking Public Service*, OECD, Paris, https://www.oecd.org/gov/pem/public-sector-leadership-implementation/pem-forward-looking/ (accessed on 15 October 2021). [43]

OECD (2021), *Implications of Remote Working Adoption on Place Based Policies: A Focus on G7 Countries*, OECD Regional Development Studies, OECD Publishing, Paris, https://doi.org/10.1787/b12f6b85-en. [13]

OECD (2021), *Policies for Present and Future Service Delivery Across Territories*, OECD, Paris. [2]

OECD (2020), *Rural Well-being: Geography of Opportunities*, OECD Rural Studies, OECD Publishing, Paris, https://doi.org/10.1787/d25cef80-en. [1]

OECD (2016), *OECD Regional Outlook 2016: Productive Regions for Inclusive Societies*, OECD Publishing, Paris, https://doi.org/10.1787/9789264260245-en. [17]

OECD (2013), *Regions and Innovation: Collaborating across Borders*, OECD Reviews of Regional Innovation, OECD Publishing, Paris, https://doi.org/10.1787/9789264205307-en. [27]

OECD (forthcoming), *Enhancing Innovation in Rural Regions: Synthesis Report*, OECD Publishing, Paris. [3]

OECD/ILO (2021), "Women at Work in G20 Countries: Policy Action Since 2020", OECD, Paris, https://www.oecd.org/gender/OECD-ILO-2021-Women-at-Work-P%C3%B6licy-Action-Since-2020-G20-Italy.pdf. [11]

Ollivaud, P. (2017), "Boosting productivity in Switzerland", *OECD Economics Department Working Papers*, No. 1443, OECD Publishing, Paris, https://doi.org/10.1787/a29cdbbe-en. [41]

Pacific Economic Development Canada (2022), "WeBC supports women entrepreneurs through the pandemic and beyond", Government of Canada, https://www.canada.ca/en/pacific-economic-development/campaigns/stories/stories-webc.html (accessed on 19 August 2022). [10]

Romer, P. (1990), "Endogenous technological change", *Journal of Political Economy*, Vol. 98/5 part 2, pp. S71-S102, https://www.jstor.org/stable/2937632. [18]

Shearmur, R. and D. Doloreux (2016), "How open innovation processes vary between urban and remote environments: Slow innovators, market-sourced information and frequency of interaction", *Entrepreneurship & Regional Development*, Vol. 28/5-6, pp. 337-357, https://doi.org/10.1080/08985626.2016.1154984. [33]

Sorenson, O. (2018), "Innovation policy in a networked world", *Innovation Policy and the Economy*, Vol. 18, pp. 53-77, https://doi.org/10.1086/694407. [30]

Swiss Federal Statistical Office (2021), *Swiss Labour Force Survey in Brief: 03 Work and Income*, https://www.bfs.admin.ch/bfs/en/home/statistics/work-income/surveys/slfs.assetdetail.18144207.html. [36]

UN (2008), *International Standard Industrial Classification of All Economic Activities (ISIC), Rev. 4*, United Nations, https://unstats.un.org/unsd/publication/seriesm/seriesm_4rev4e.pdf. [6]

Veneri, P. (2018), "Urban spatial structure in OECD cities: Is urban population decentralising or clustering?", *Regional Science*, Vol. 97/4, pp. 1355-1374, https://doi.org/10.1111/pirs.12300. [34]

Notes

[1] Cantons refer to the 26 small regions (TL3) in Switzerland.

[2] Not only do cantons propose policies and programmes, they also levy taxes. Through the New Regional Policy (NRP) that creates the framework for the regional innovation system (RIS), the Swiss Confederation provides matching funds for each Swiss franc invested by the cantons. Within the framework set by the confederation, the cantons set their strategies and objectives as well as invest their own money.

[3] For more information on the NRP and the RIS, see Chapter 3.

[4] For more information on multi-level governance and innovation policy in Switzerland, see Chapter 3.

[5] For Switzerland, the report by Fadic et al. (2019[5]) identified Switzerland as one of the countries with a very high level of non-metropolitan population, with 50% of the population living in non-metropolitan areas. However, this is due to the compatibility of territorial definitions across countries.

[6] The countries with available data included in this statistic are Austria, the Czech Republic, Estonia, France, Hungary, Italy, Lithuania, Poland, the Slovak Republic and Spain.

[7] For classification of territories and sectors, please refer to Box 2.1. Trade and professional services sectors include professional, scientific, technical and administrative and support services, as well as a grouping of other services that include wholesale and retail trade, transportation and motor vehicle repair, and financial and real estate services. The public services sector was excluded from this analysis

[8] The high shares of agriculture, public and professional services and manufacturing in metropolitan areas also holds when using alternatively classification of the OECD based on TL3 regions.

[9] The number of firms in the agriculture, forestry and fishery sector fell from close to 59 000 in 2012 to close to 53 000 in 2019. The number of firms in the professional services sector grew from 113 000 in 2012 to 132 500 in 2019. In the rural and peri-urban regions alone, the agriculture, forestry and fishery sector fell from close to 48 000 firms in 2012 to close to 34 000 firms in 2019. The number of firms in the professional services sector grew from close to 30 000 in 2012 to 35 000 in 2019.

[10] This is based on statistics of full-time equivalent (FTE) workers in Switzerland.

[11] This includes the Telearbeitsplats!Offensive (Austria), Live for the Moment (New Brunswick, Canada), the Our Rural Future strategy (Ireland), the Teleworking Strategy in Trentino (Italy), regional visas to attract remote workers (Estonia, Germany, Hungary, Spain, among others), and local grants (Portugal and United States). In other cases, countries like Sweden are focusing on building digital infrastructure and digital skills.

[12] According to OECD Territorial Classifications (TL3), Jura and Lucerne are considered non-metropolitan regions, close to small metropolitan regions, and Vaud is a medium-sized metropolitan region. In Switzerland, there are no large metropolitan areas as per the OECD definition of at least 2.5 million residents or more in the functional urban area of the city.

[13] See Chapter 3 for an example of innovation in tourism from the Jura region

[14] Metropolitan areas refer to the large category of "metro". Non-metropolitan areas refer to the large categories of "peri-urban" and "rural".

[15] Whether the share is closer to 30% or 40% depends on whether statistics include self-employed workers.

[16] This includes management and marketing practices.

[17] While this is promising, it is important to also consider that the structure of the economy in rural regions also lends itself to more self-employed entrepreneurs working in the agriculture and manufacturing sectors.

[18] See presentation by *regiosuisse* on high performance of the region of Ticino.

[19] This was due to an announcement by the government of Switzerland that they would no longer peg the Swiss franc to the euro on 15 January 2015.

[20] Currency is deflated to 2015 CHF levels. Exchange rate used for 31 December 2015: 1.0835 CHF to 1 EUR.

[21] Productivity estimates use value-added and full-time employment labour productivity estimates.

[22] This was also the year of the Swiss franc crisis.

[23] Estimates use a linear fixed effects model with year, sector, territorial and regional controls.

[24] This refers to estimates of R&D expenditures and jobs that are 0.53 and 0.56 points lower when in non-metropolitan regions as compared to metropolitan regions respectively.

[25] Diversification is normal in dynamic economies; however, high levels of market capture for a few firms, may nevertheless indicate barriers to opportunities for entry and growth of new firms. While Switzerland is not observing an increase in inequality between market shares of firms in 2019, inequality was still higher in metropolitan regions and lowest in non-metropolitan regions (Figure 2.18). In a sector specific analysis this tends to indicate potential for anti-competitive behaviour, which is associated with low productivity. In a territorial analysis, high levels of diversity may also enable spill overs from few firms fuelling smaller firms.

[26] Please see Box 2.1 for more information sectoral categories.

[27] Wholesale trade and services includes "activities of those involved in bringing sellers and buyers together or undertaking commercial transactions on behalf of a principal…such agents involved in the sale of: agricultural raw materials, live animals, textile raw materials and semi-finished goods; fuels, ores, metals and industrial chemicals, including fertilizers; food, beverages and tobacco; textiles, clothing, fur, footwear and leather goods; timber and building materials; machinery, including office machinery and computers, industrial equipment, ships and aircraft; and furniture, household goods and hardware" (UN, 2008[6]).

3 National, regional and local policy framework conditions for rural innovation in Switzerland

This chapter starts with an overview of the policy landscape for rural innovation and identifies drivers and barriers to innovation in rural Switzerland. Specifically, it investigates if local, regional and national framework conditions are conducive to and account for the specific characteristics of rural innovation using evidence from the case study areas around the regional innovation systems (RIS) in Basel-Jura, Central Switzerland and Western Switzerland. It also makes suggestions to address bottlenecks in the delivery of innovation support, broaden the concept of innovation, create a culture of experimentation, strengthen rural-urban linkages and improve skills shortages for rural innovation.

Innovation in rural areas is more incremental, making use of locally available knowledge and taking time to experiment (see Chapter 1). This is a result of both limited accessibility of knowledge, finance and other resources in the countryside and the size of firms and their focus on sectors that do not lose value as quickly, including natural resources. As such, rural innovation is less time-dependent and characterised by high levels of meaningfulness to the community while still competing successfully in the market economy. Rural entrepreneurs often bridge knowledge gaps strategically, building networks with partners such as suppliers and higher education institutions when looking to steadily improve their products. A key element of rural innovation is also passing down knowledge through inter-generational links. In times of demographical change and increasing numbers of younger people leaving for the cities, this can become an increasing challenge, not only in terms of succession but also because young people are more likely to be innovative and use newer products and processes.

This chapter makes recommendations to enhance rural innovation in Switzerland. It starts with an overview of the policy landscape and its stakeholders for rural innovation and identifies drivers and barriers to innovation in rural Switzerland. It draws on evidence provided by the federal administration on the Swiss decentralised innovation policy approach as well as three regional innovation systems, notably, RIS Basel-Jura, RIS Central Switzerland and RIS Western Switzerland (ARI-SO). Considering the vast innovation potential in rural Switzerland, it investigates if local framework conditions are conducive to and account for the specific characteristics of rural innovation. Specifically, it focuses on broadening the concept of innovation, future-proofing innovation agendas, building a culture of experimentation and simplifying access to services, and developing rural-urban linkages to increase the flow of knowledge and people. Overall, the chapter shows that for rural innovation, policy makers should focus on adjusting innovation support to focus on the comparative advantages of rural regions, while enhancing enabling conditions in currently lagging behind rural areas, adjusting for the variety of rural places in their programming.

Switzerland's decentralised innovation system

Switzerland has no overall innovation policy but follows a decentralised approach through several independent policy areas that are co-ordinated through mechanisms involving federal, cantonal and regional (cross-cantonal) actors. This organisation grants individual agents a high degree of autonomy and scope for action. It also allows for tailor-made answers to new emerging challenges. The binding element of this decentralised approach are principles shared by the main agents in the system. They include federal actors (e.g. Innosuisse), public education and research organisations, cantonal actors and programmes (e.g. Living Labs, projects), RIS and private programmes for start-ups. They form the basis of the structure of the Swiss innovation system and comprise subsidiarity, the autonomy of agents, co-operation, competitiveness and quality awareness. They are embodied in framework conditions, including democracy, federalism, liberal economy, social partnership and bottom-up institutions. This results in three other characteristics of the Swiss innovation system: diversity, stability and ability to adapt. The most important principles and framework conditions are presented graphically below (Figure 3.1).

Within the structure, both institutionalised and informal processes enable collaboration. Formal processes for instance include internal administrative procedures such as consultations and co-reporting procedures. This ensures that individual actors are informed about the activities of the others, insofar as they are affected by them. More informal or ad hoc processes also exist. They include steering groups, monitoring groups or other ad hoc bodies formed to contribute to individual projects. Co-ordination generally ensures that relationships between individual stakeholders are maintained and activities co-ordinates – especially if several actors are pursuing similar projects at the same time. Such co-ordination processes, which initially take place infrequently, can, if necessary, be institutionalised over time.

Figure 3.1. Swiss Principles, structures and processes of the decentralised Innovation System

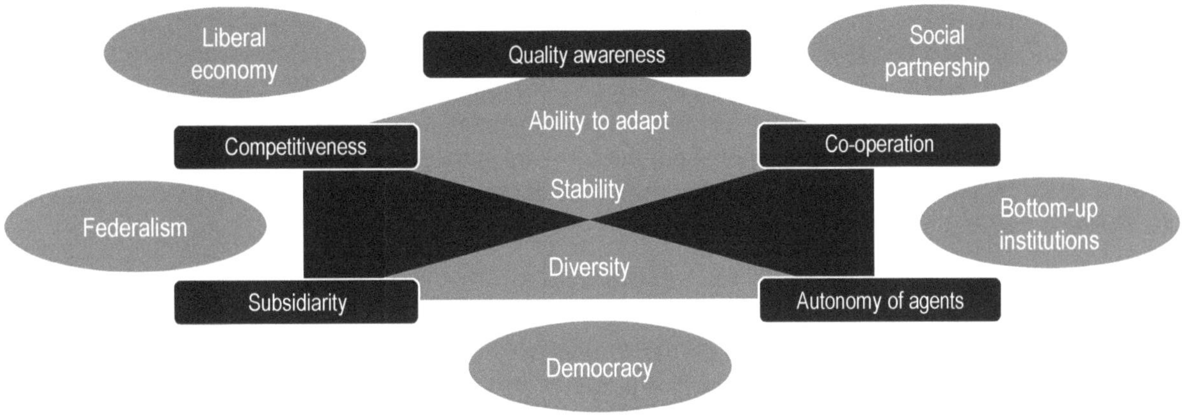

Note: Central principles of the Swiss Innovation system are depicted by the darker rectangular shapes, and the lighter oval shapes represent the framework conditions.

Source: Adapted from Swiss Federal Council (2018[1]), *Overview of Innovation Policy*, https://www.sbfi.admin.ch/sbfi/en/home/services/publications/data-base-publications/innovation-policy.html.

Institutional context

Because of its decentralised nature, the Swiss innovation system functions as a complex ecosystem. Figure 3.2 depicts the main elements of the decentralised regional innovation system in Switzerland, focusing on small- and medium-sized enterprises (SMEs) and entrepreneurs as the benefactors. A study by the State Secretariat for Education, Research and Innovation (SERI) in 2016 recorded 138 innovation promotion offerings at the national, cantonal and regional levels, which can sometimes be perceived as complex (SERI, 2016[2]).

Figure 3.2. Simplified representation of the Swiss decentralised innovation system

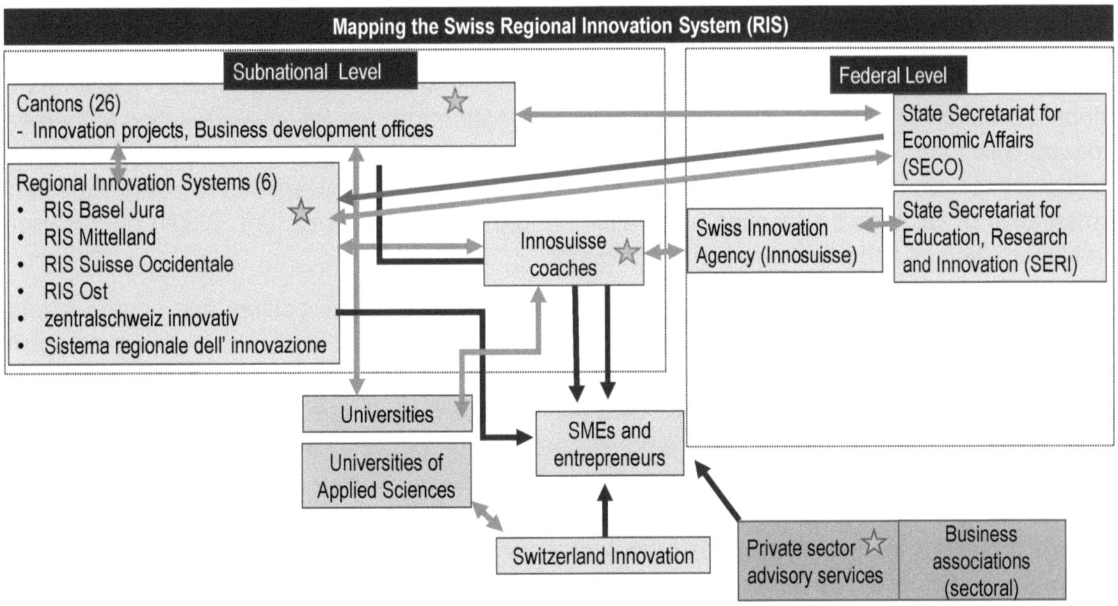

Note: Orange arrows show the flow of information, and blue errors show a service provided. Yellow fields describe the target groups (SMEs and entrepreneurs), blue fields show public actors and institutions, green fields depict public education and research organisations, stars signify advisory services or components, and red arrows describe framework settings and regulations.

Federal level

From a legal perspective, public research and innovation funding is the responsibility of the federal government. The promotion of innovation is regulated by Federal Act on the Promotion of Research and Innovation (RIPA). RIPA is a framework law that governs the objectives and funding of research and innovation by the federal government. It includes legally enshrined principles such as freedom of research, the scientific quality of research and innovation, the diversity of scientific opinions and methods as well as scientific integrity, and good scientific practice principles of research that define federal innovation funding (see RIPA, Article 6, Paragraph 1, Fedlex (2012[3])).

RIPA (see Article 6, Paragraph 3) also establishes overarching goals including the sustainable development of society, economy and environment and the (national and international) co-operation of the actors. The instruments of the innovation promotion policy according to RIPA primarily cover knowledge-based innovation. They support processes by which scientific knowledge can be developed into marketable products. As part of the business-oriented approach to innovation, instruments of economic policy are also added, specifically location promotion policy, growth policy, SME policy and intellectual property protection (Swiss Federal Council, 2018[1]).

The responsibilities in research and innovation (R&I) funding at the federal level are primarily shared among the Federal Department of Economic Affairs, Education and Research (EAER), SERI, the State Secretariat for Economic Affairs (SECO), the Swiss Innovation Agency Innosuisse, as well as the council of the Swiss Federal Institutes of Technology (ETH Board) on behalf of the institutions of the ETH Domain. Other departments such as the Federal Department of the Environment, Transport, Energy and Communications (DETEC) are also directly or indirectly involved in R&I funding. The Swiss Science Council (SSC) is the advisory body of the Federal Council for issues related to science, higher education and R&I policy.

Furthermore, there are additional innovation activities within various sectoral policy areas. These activities seek to achieve specific political goals, such as nationally and internationally set goals for environmental protection and reduction of energy consumption. The primary purpose of these programmes is therefore to reach the respective policy objectives, while innovations are the means to achieve these goals.

In terms of funding, the Federal Council submits a request to parliament on the promotion of education, research and innovation (ERI) every four years. As part of this, it formulates the guidelines and measures of its policy for ERI for which the Swiss Confederation has primary responsibility. These include the ETH, vocational education and training, R&I promotion and international co-operation in education and research. The request also formulates the confederation's commitment to those parts of the system that are primarily the responsibility of the regions (cantons), such as universities, universities of applied sciences, implementation of vocational education and training and the scholarship system. Based on this request, the parliament then decides on the funding framework.

Innovative entrepreneurship is largely executed by cantons, cities, municipalities and private actors, as well as the RIS. These will be discussed in more detail below. The federal level mostly tries to complement activities led by lower government levels and actors, for instance through its innovation agency Innosuisse. The role of the agency is to promote science-based innovation in the interest of the economy and society in Switzerland. To this end, Innosuisse promotes partnerships between academia and businesses and seeks to accelerate the transfer of knowledge from research to industry. It also helps innovators and start-ups to achieve a breakthrough in the market. The core of Innosuisse funding is the support of innovation projects. In these projects, innovative organisations such as companies, start-ups, administrative bodies and non-governmental organisations (NGOs) develop new services and products together with research institutions. Some projects also involve international partners. Further, the agency supports networking, training and coaching, with the goal of providing the foundation for successful Swiss start-ups as well as innovative products and services (Innosuisse, 2022[4]).

Box 3.1. Innosuisse Innovation Booster

The Innovation Booster programme powered by Innosuisse is designed to specifically support radical ideas in a culture of open innovation. Supporting the primary stage of an open innovation process, they provide the impulses for innovative ideas and help them to get off the ground into the market.

The main mission of the programme includes:

- Bringing together all interested players from research, business and society on various innovation topics.
- Promoting knowledge transfer and encouraging co-operation with partners along the entire value chain of a topic. Each booster has its own organisation and Leading House.
- Using design thinking methods and other user-centred methods. The Innovation Boosters support companies, start-ups and other organisations to identify and explore problems in interdisciplinary teams and develop new and radical solutions from scratch.
- Providing an apt funding amount to finance and support the testing and verification of promising ideas and assisting teams to get follow-up support to further develop or implement their idea.
- Fostering a culture of open innovation, to create sustainable competitive advantages for innovative Swiss organisations and SMEs.

Innosuisse selects Innovation Boosters with regular calls for proposals for a four-year period. The selection is based on a range of criteria which include:

- The current and future importance of the innovation topic.
- The likelihood that it will give rise to future innovation projects.
- The appropriateness of the methods and mechanisms used to promote the transfer of knowledge and technology.
- The competency to address the innovation topic and involve the relevant actors on a national scale.
- The plausibility of the budget and cost-benefit ratio, the degree of own-funding and the contribution of third-party funds.
- The contribution to the sustainable development of society, the economy and the environment.
- Measures to ensure appropriate gender representation in the organisation and at activities.

Key performance indicators (KPIs) on gender are supposed to motivate initiatives to proactively increase the percentage of women on their boards as well as among their speakers and participants. This is especially interesting in some fields which are historically unbalanced with respect to the participation of men and women.

Innovation Boosters are selected under a complementarity principle: Innosuisse supports initiatives that would not easily be supported by the private sector only, because of inherent risk, lack of resources or private investments or unclear economic return. They should all have the potential to involve actors from all over the national territory.

The above criteria should allow Innosuisse to select Innovation Boosters that will create an impact in Switzerland. This includes societal impacts such as an increase in quality of life, addressing major societal challenges, better population health or economic impacts such as job creation, increase in revenues, etc.

Source: Innosuisse (2022[5]), "Innovation boosters", Swiss Innovation Agency.

Subnational level

The vast majority of cantons engage in innovation and economic development activities. The range of services includes support for company start-ups or the promotion of regional networks or clusters in close contact with companies and sometimes specific coaching. Cantons generally have their own business development offices. They inform companies about location advantages, maintain contacts with investors, organise support for investors and handle customer care on site. Various cantons use tax breaks to promote businesses. Cantons also use their universities, universities of applied sciences and pedagogical universities to promote regional development and R&I. Cities and towns likewise are important in establishing technology or innovation parks (Swiss Federal Council, 2018[1]).

The federal government's New Regional Policy (NRP) (for an in-depth description, see the following section) is important in financially supporting these subnational innovation projects and has allowed regional and cross-cantonal innovation initiatives to be established in most of Switzerland. Overall, the NRP has the objective to "enhance the competitiveness and added-value creation of individual regions and thus contribute to the creation of jobs to preserve decentralized settlement and to reduce disparities between regions". The federal level is responsible for determining strategic objectives and spatial priorities as well as for ensuring legal conformity, while the cantons are in charge of policy implementation. They have maximum scope to define for their region how objectives are achieved, including project selection. The NRP is funded through the local promotion activities of the federal government (SECO, 2020[6]).

Part of the NRP is the regional innovation system (RIS). There are six RIS covering significant parts of the country (Figure 3.3). The RIS relate to functional (generally inter-cantonal and in some cases cross-border) economic zones. Complementary to the focus of the national research-driven innovation activities, their focus is on demand- and need-driven services, and a broader understanding of innovation that specifically targets SMEs. The RIS promote competitiveness and innovative capacity of SMEs by offering co-ordinated support and services in the areas of information, consulting, networking, infrastructure and financing. Following the principle of "no wrong door", the RIS are meant to consolidate innovation and support activities from different governance levels and actors and connect SMEs with other sources of funding and assistance if necessary. Overall, the central tasks of the RIS can be summarised as follows:

- Co-ordination of innovation promotion activities.
- Coaching on the topic of innovation for start-up companies and SMEs.
- Organisation of networking events.
- Point of entry, referring individual companies to the right innovation funding agency (including universities and federal funding agencies) (SECO, 2017[7]; B,S,S Volkswirtschaftliche Beratung AG, 2018[8]).

This study specifically focuses on the NRP and its RIS structures because they, within the overall innovation ecosystem, have a specific territorial and rural focus. Understanding and analysing how they deliver for rural SMEs is thus crucial to understanding what works and what does not with regard to rural innovation in Switzerland and how policies to foster rural innovation can be improved. At the same time, these geographically focused policies are only small and financially limited mechanisms that need to complement and work in synergy with the more general policy tools and mechanisms described in this section.

Figure 3.3. Map of Regional Innovation System in Switzerland

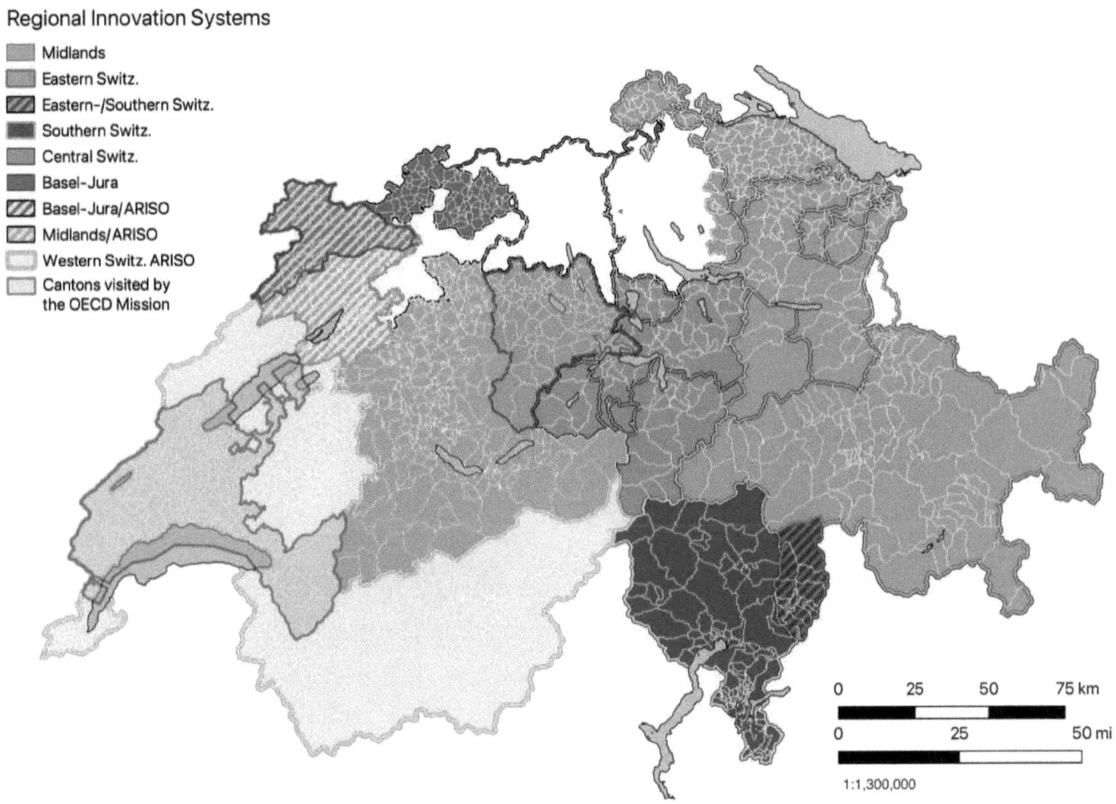

Source: OECD elaboration in consultation with local partners.

The NRP and its role in supporting rural innovation in Switzerland

Throughout the mid-1990s, the scope of Swiss regional policy shifted away from redistribution towards a new focus on impact orientation, competitiveness and the creation of value-added in rural areas. This shift was formalised with the introduction of the New Regional Policy (NRP) in 2008, which encourages an endogenous "growth-oriented" approach emphasising open markets, export capacity and competitiveness. The policy specifically targets rural and mountainous areas, which incorporate the vast majority of Swiss territory but excludes the large agglomerations of Basel, Bern, Geneva, Lausanne and Zurich and the urban cantons of Aargau, Basel-Landschaft, Basel City, Geneva, Solothurn, Zug and Zurich. Exceptionally, cantons may request that NRP funds be used for excluded areas (Figure 3.4). The seven urban cantons may also apply for NRP funds if they can demonstrate that the areas to be supported present the same structural challenges as the traditional target areas of NRP.

The NRP is a joint task of the federal government and the cantons. The Swiss Confederation is responsible for strategic management and orientation, while the operational responsibility for implementation and the decision as to whether a project can be supported with NRP funds lies with the cantons (OECD, 2011[9]). At the cantonal level, the NRP provides direct financial assistance (federal and cantonal) in order to enable the implementation of suitable projects and programmes. It also acts at a supra-cantonal level in order to enhance geographic coherence and economic functionality. This includes funding for Switzerland's participation in cross-border EU programmes, in particular Interreg, and funding for inter-cantonal RIS (OECD, 2019[10]).

Figure 3.4. Geographical range of the NRP, 2020-23

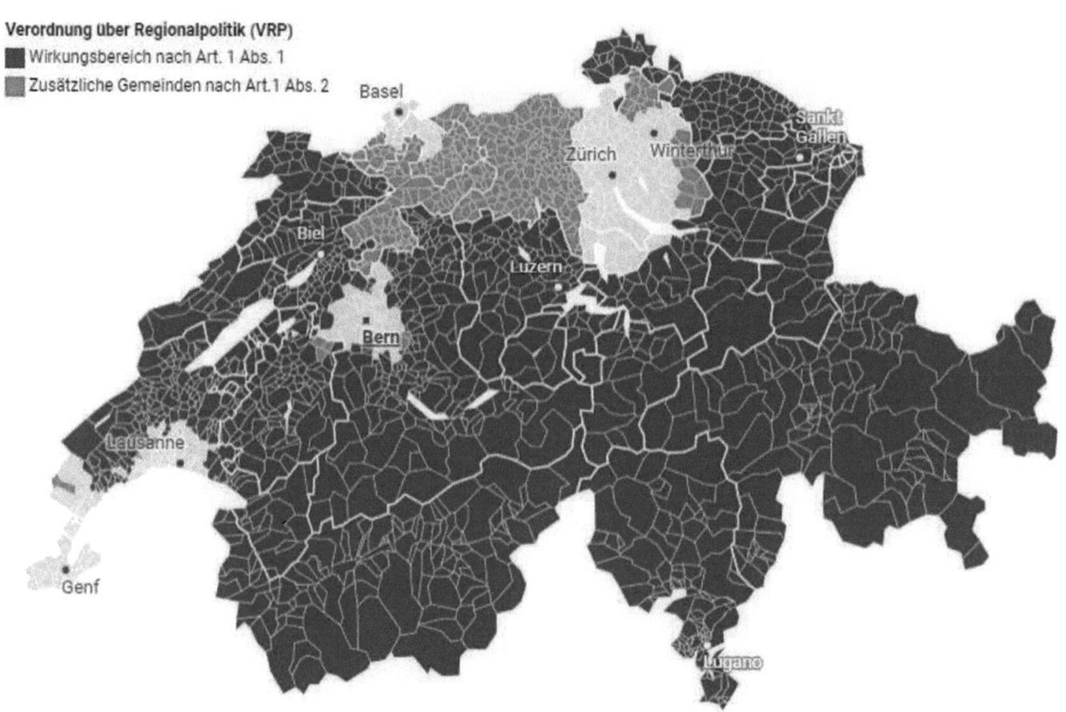

Note: The geographical range of the NRP defines the area in which the majority of specific development problems and development opportunities for mountainous and rural areas are the biggest. Only projects that have a majority impact in this area can be supported by the NRP. The geographical range of the NRP in dark blue (Regional Policy Ordinance, Article 1, Paragraph 1) and additional communities in light blue (Regional Policy Ordinance, Article 1, Paragraph 2).
Source: Regiosuisse (n.d.[11]), *Financial Instruments and Measures within the Framework of the NRP*, https://regiosuisse.ch/index.php/en/finan cial-instruments-and-measures-within-framework-nrp.

In 2016, the NRP multiyear programme started for a second eight-year period. The focus continues to be to "enhance the competitiveness and added-value creation of individual regions and thus to contribute to the creation and safeguarding of jobs in the regions, to the safeguarding of a decentralised settlement pattern, and to the reduction of regional disparities". Its three pillars address: i) an increase in the economic strengths and competitiveness of regions (85% of total funding); ii) co-operation and synergies between the NRP and other sectoral policies (5-10% of total funding); and iii) capacity building in the knowledge system of regional policy (5-10% of total funding). The NRP also offers tax breaks to industrial companies and service providers whose business is closely linked to industrial production. With this, the government hopes to support the creation of new types of jobs in innovative fields in structurally weak regional centres (OECD, 2019[10]).

The latest additions to the NRP 2020 include support for pilot programmes for mountainous regions to provide additional stimulus where it is needed. The pilot measurements offer more flexible eligibility criteria for support for example, small, less profitable infrastructure initiatives can be co-financed with à-fonds-perdu contributions. Another new feature is the support of project preparations and the development of Living Labs for the development and implementation of unconventional ideas (SECO, 2020[12]).

The implementation period 2016-23 has a stronger focus on innovation and tourism. The emphasis is on innovation in SMEs. One part of the promotion is the aforementioned RIS that provide coaching and networking for innovation. The federal government supports these networks provided they have a functional area orientation, i.e. if they extend beyond cantonal or even national borders and are adapted to the needs of the defined target groups. Second, the multiannual programme 2016-23 sets a specific focus on promoting tourism in the regions, a sector that was exposed to strong challenges in recent years due to foreign exchange rates and that is increasingly exposed to the effects of climate change. Digitalisation is considered an overarching goal for economic development activities and needs to be transversally addressed.

The emphasis on competitiveness mirrors the early shift observed in other member countries from a sectoral focus which was codified by the OECD New Rural Paradigm[1] in 2006. The OECD's most recent Rural Well-being Policy Framework published in 2020 (OECD, 2020[13]) builds on the paradigm and calls for an even more robust model for rural development, one that considers the economy, society and the environment (see Table 3.1). It also stresses the importance of innovation for rural places to be able to deal with structural change and identifies important policy measures to enhance innovation capacity (OECD, 2020[13]). Some of these include strengthening rural-urban links, addressing the rural-urban digital divide in connectivity, as well as enhancing education and skills. This comes at a time when recovery from COVID-19 is starting, while the impacts of the megatrends of globalisation, digitalisation, climate change and demographic change continue to shape the economic landscape of rural economies.

Table 3.1. Stages of Rural Well-being: Geography of Opportunities

	Old paradigm	New Rural Paradigm (2006)	Rural Well-being: Geography Of Opportunities
Objectives	Equalisation	Competitiveness	Well-being considering multiple dimensions of: i) the economy; ii) society; and iii) the environment
Policy focus	Support for a single dominant resource sector	Support for multiple sectors based on their competitiveness	Low-density economies differentiated by type of rural area
Tools	Subsidies for firms	Investments in qualified firms and communities	Integrated rural development approach – spectrum of support to the public sector, firms and third sector
Key actors and stakeholders	Farm organisations and national governments	All levels of government and all relevant departments plus local stakeholders	Involvement of: i) public sector – multi-level governance; ii) private sector – for-profit firms and social enterprise; and iii) third sector – non-governmental organisations and civil society
Policy approach	Uniformly applied top-down policy	Bottom-up policy, local strategies	Integrated approach with multiple policy domains
Rural definition	Not urban	Rural as a variety of distinct types of place	Three types of rural: i) within a functional urban area; ii) close to a functional urban area; and iii) far from a functional urban area

Source: OECD (2020[13]), *Rural Well-being: Geography of Opportunities*, https://doi.org/10.1787/d25cef80-en.

While the NRP is rural and peri-urban focused, the RIS can improve in delivering for all rural areas

In 2011, the OECD's territorial review (2011[9]) found that there were no explicit regional innovation policies in Switzerland. The report recommended that existing cantonal initiatives needed to be better co-ordinated and more effectively implemented, especially highlighting the potential of inter-cantonal initiatives (OECD, 2011[9]). Generally, RIS refer to functional economic spaces – usually cross-cantonal and sometimes cross-border – where networks of important actors for innovation processes, such as companies, research and education establishments, as well as public authorities work together in a network and contribute to the innovation processes of a region. In Switzerland specifically, the term is also used to describe the organisation that acts on the development and management of RIS. Overall, these RIS promote the competitiveness and innovative capacity of SMEs by offering co-ordinated support and services in the areas of information, consulting, networking, infrastructure and financing. In addition, they bundle other already existing support offers and refer SMEs to other funding bodies if required.

The concept of regional innovation systems (RIS) was introduced in its current form with the adoption of the federal government's multiyear programme for the implementation of the NRP 2016-23. It thus became the prerequisite for the further support of innovation promotion offers within the framework of the NRP. The cantons, in co-operation with the State Secretariat for Economic Affairs (SECO), have created RIS structures in six major regions of Switzerland (see also Figure 3.3).

The first RIS structures in the sense of an innovation promotion initiative motivated by regional policy date back to the activities in Central and Western Switzerland in the context of the 6th European Union (EU) Research Framework Programme. Building on already existing regional initiatives, the first RIS structure was created in Central and Western Switzerland until a federal regional innovation strategy was developed in a collaboration between SECO and the cantons in 2016. The introduction of RIS within the framework of the NRP established the RIS organisations as a central link between the federal government and the cantons in the operational implementation of an innovation-based regional policy (B,S,S Volkswirtschaftliche Beratung AG, 2018[8]). The system is also meant to provide complementary support to the national innovation promotion of Innosuisse, the Swiss Innovation Agency, focusing on knowledge absorption and more incremental innovation support.

The aim of the RIS created within the framework of the NRP is to simplify and harmonise innovation promotion for SMEs and start-ups. Thus, the innovation activity of companies in the NRP impact area is to be strengthened and the long-term economic development in these areas is to be supported. A central aspect of the funding activities to support innovation activity is the so-called "no wrong door" policy which is designed to ensure that a company's request is always forwarded to the right place, depending on its specific needs.

In order to assure that RIS support fits with diverse local needs, it is important to consider that innovation in more rural areas functions differently than in the regional centres or the larger agglomerations. It seems like the support currently provided does not sufficiently take all geographic specificities and the corresponding needs into account. While research is limited, evidence suggests that rural innovators take a different approach (Table 3.2). They are experimental and strategic in that they take the time to steadily improve products and processes without pressure and acquire information to fill knowledge gaps. In this process, the meaningfulness of the work to the community and passing down knowledge through generations is also important as it ensures holistically following projects through from beginning to end (Mayer, 2020[14]).

The current Concept RIS 2020+ recognises the specific challenges of rural SMEs in the innovation process. It also notes that rural SMEs are often smaller and have less access to other innovation actors. It includes a call for stronger efforts to facilitate access to innovation support for rural SMEs (SECO, 2018[15]). To ensure this, funding from the NRP for the RIS programme areas "Point of entry-Function of RIS" and "Coaching" requires that 50% of all supported firms fall within the NRP geographic range (see Figure 3.1). The strategy exempts the programme areas "Control and development of the RIS" and "Intercompany platforms (cluster, networking events)" from this rule.

Still, RIS impact within the NRP perimeter is uneven. Evidence shows that SMEs and entrepreneurs in regional centres benefit more from RIS support than those in more remote regions and mountainous areas (Egli, 2020[16]; SECO, 2020[17]). In view of this, some stakeholders would like to see a redefining and reconsideration of the scale of policy intervention of the NRP. While the success of the NRP is acknowledged in regional centres, more targeted support for very rural regions and a reduction of the NRP perimeter have been part of the political discussion. In opposition, other opinions consider it crucial to include larger agglomerations in the NRP to facilitate knowledge transfer and make use of synergies in spaces that work closer with each other for progressing digitalisation and increased mobility (SECO, 2020[17]).

Table 3.2. Characteristics and bottlenecks of rural innovation

Characteristics	Incremental and slower – less dynamic and short-lived, use of local knowledge for steady improvement
	Experimental – utilising space available to test until a solution is found
	Based on customer or client contacts
	Smaller firms requiring local leadership and dedication
	Natural resource focus (tourism, energy, agriculture, forestry)
	Strong use of social and human capital in innovation
	Community-driven – meaningfulness as an objective
	Targeting local markets
	Use rural-urban links to leverage knowledge outside their location for more radical innovations
Bottlenecks	Dependency on young generations – need for business succession and interest/ability to work on new products and processes
	Reduced accessibility of networks, knowledge and support readily available (missing links to universities or research institutions)
	Lack of digital connectivity and skills

Source: Mayer, H., A. Habersetzer and R. Meili (2016[18]), "Rural-urban linkages and sustainable regional development: The role of entrepreneurs in linking peripheries and centers", https://doi.org/10.3390/su8080745; (OECD, 2020[13]; Freshwater et al., 2019[19]; Lee and Rodriguez-Pose, 2012[20]; Jungsberg et al., 2020[21]; Mahroum et al., 2007[22]; Shearmur, Carrincazeaux and Doloreux, 2016[23]; Wojan and Parker, 2017[24])

Box 3.2. Outlook into the RIS 2024+ strategy

In preparation of the new RIS strategic framework for the 2024-31 multiyear programme period, the State Secretariat for Economic Affairs (SECO) prepared a consultation process to elaborate on this new strategy and identified a couple of key aspects specific to innovation and rural areas. The following points summarise the key elements mentioned by stakeholders taking part in the consultation. Many of them are very much in line with the wider findings of the Rural Well-being Policy Framework and suggest that there is significant potential for the NRP24+ to benefit from the learnings of other OECD countries.

- **Redefine and reconsider the scale of policy intervention of the NRP**. Different geographies have different needs, the biggest differentiations exist between the large agglomerations, regional centres and peripheral regions in Switzerland. Large agglomerations have their own policy and the current NRP policy, and thus its innovation support mechanisms focus on regional centres and peripheral regions. While the success of the NRP is acknowledged in regional centres, it seems to fail to take into consideration that innovation works differently in more rural areas. Some voices demand more targeted support for very rural regions and a reduction of the NRP perimeter. In opposition, other opinions consider it crucial to include larger agglomerations in the NRP to facilitate knowledge transfer and make use of synergies in economic and physical spaces that are growing closer to each other through progressing digitalisation and increased mobility.

- **Enlarge the concept of innovation present in the NRP**. Innovation support has a strong technical focus, while organisational and social innovation is a less prominent part of the NRP. Policies seeking to support innovation at the regional level need to recognise this and adjust their mechanisms accordingly. Suggestions are made to enlarge programmes to include non-technical sectors and work with a broader range of stakeholders on a variety of challenges and solutions, with proposals for a more agile, less risk averse innovation support and increased experimentation potential, for instance through Living Labs testing solutions for the future at the local level.

- **Complement economic policy objectives in the NRP with social and environmental ones**. Economic development can no longer be a single measure of success in times of climate change and demographic challenges. Rural economies are disproportionally affected by demographic decline and ageing and are highly sensitive to climate change effects. Regional policy needs to acknowledge its role in tackling these challenges and opportunities by including new objectives, such as the increased promotion of a circular economy, and better aligning with objectives of other sectoral policies such as climate policy, agricultural policy, social and labour policy.

- **Further promote digitalisation and digital skills in the NRP**. Digitalisation allows firms and entrepreneurs to innovate and bring products to the market no matter where they are. Remote working and flexible work hours further increase the potential for decentralised value creation. Digital ecosystems are suggested as a tool to foster and promote regional transformation processes and already exist in some cantons.

Source: SECO (2020[17]), *Weissbuch Regionalpolitik*, https://regiosuisse.ch/sites/default/files/2020-07/SECO%20%282020%29%20%C2%ABWeissbuch%20Regionalpolitik%C2%BB.pdf.

Shaping a future-proof vision for innovation that works for Swiss territories, including rural areas

Broadening the concept of innovation

Switzerland's federal system values cantonal independence, self-determination and local opportunities. In rural regions, there are smaller firms, higher shares of the agricultural, manufacturing and hospitality sectors and a growing services sector (see Chapter 1). While the current agenda for RIS includes a focus on SMEs, the relatively strong institutional focus is on research and development (R&D)-driven innovation. While there is already the possibility of coaching support in the tourism sector and further opportunity to widen the focus, support may be passing by some of the opportunities for innovation in other service sectors.

Despite a focus on bottom-up governance, innovation lacks diversity and is strongly focused on high-technology (high-tech) sectors, even if programmes are open to non-tech firms. The pharmaceutical and precision manufacturing industries are often the targets of innovation policies and programmes.

A large part of the offer of support that the RIS deliver is focused on coaching activities and providing space for SMEs and start-ups to work. RIS Basel-Jura provides different incubator and accelerator programmes that include support in: business plan development, funding, product development, communications, marketing, pricing and intellectual property. It also helps with business' needs for more than just RIS tasks. It supports and establishes contacts, for example specialists, research institutions or potential co-operation partners, and offer start-ups the opportunity to have their project or business idea reviewed by established industry experts, entrepreneurs and investors. These programmes are accompanied by three co-working spaces in Allschwil, Basel and Delémont (Jura). An overview of the innovation support provided can be found in Table 3.3 below. In addition to these services, digitalisation is seen as a key enabling condition for innovation in businesses (Regio Basiliensis, n.d.[25]).

Similarly, RIS Central Switzerland also offers individual coaching and business support as well as workspaces. Overall, the support is largely technology-focused and seeks to: support the generation of new ideas for products, and sometimes process innovations; provide feedback and insights from experts; help assess technological feasibility, regulatory barriers and market potential; help provide information on access to finance; provide special support and advice on patents and the patent landscape; and implement specific digitalisation programmes in mountainous regions. For example, a programme called Idea Check assesses projects from SMEs that have a maximum of 50 employees and are either based in mountainous regions or have a significant impact in those regions. The projects are assessed by a jury, the winners receive the support of CHF 15 000 (Zentralschweiz innovativ, 2020[26]).

Table 3.3. Basel Area Business & Innovation types of innovation support

Focus industries	Focus area	Initiatives
Biotechnology	Ecosystem activation and start-up support	Basel Launch Accelerator and Incubator - Participants have access to funding, expert coaching and infrastructure
Digital health	Ecosystem activation, start-up support and collaborative projects	Day One* - Participants have access to funding, expert coaching and infrastructure, fora on topics of value-based healthcare, health data, hospital innovation
Manufacturing and industry	Ecosystem activation, start-up support and collaborative projects	i4Challange* - Participants have access to funding, expert coaching and infrastructure, fora and projects on topics including artificial intelligence, robotics, digital transformation

Note: Further industries can be added in the future. Entrepreneurs, innovators and SMEs are supported in the best way possible according to existing possibilities and competencies. The programmes marked with * are available in Jura.
Source: Regio Basiliensis (n.d.[25]), *Interkantonales Umsetzungsprogramm zur Regionalpolitik 2020-2023 der Region Basel-Jura*, https://www.regbas.ch/de/assets/File/UP-Basel-Jura_NRP_2020-2023_24_6_2020.pdf.

In Western Switzerland, the RIS also support innovation in a broad sense focusing on business and technological innovation for SMEs and start-ups. The support is carried out by two agencies, Platinn and Alliance. Platinn seeks to develop companies' business innovation capacity by mobilising them and facilitating their access to innovation and providing coaching in different areas, while Alliance is a knowledge transfer programme whose mission is to develop synergies and set up technological projects between companies and universities or research centres in Western Switzerland, in order to enhance know-how and technology transfer. In addition, they also provide sectoral networking and knowledge exchange platforms in the life sciences (BioAlps), information and digital technologies (Alp ICT), micro-nanotechnologies (Micronarc) and clean technologies (CleantechAlps).

The support programmes of the RIS largely reflect the economic structure of the cantons as well as their different business fabric. Yet, in particular, rural innovation needs are often only partially reflected, leaving possibilities for improvement. Gaps can be found in catering for established but small businesses that are looking to innovate aside from the technological realm or in opportunities for services that go beyond traditional sectors.

Most RIS seem to conceptualise innovation mainly in technological and product innovation terms. For instance, many programmes are often specific to the high value-added industry within manufacturing industries such as precision watchmaking and pharmaceuticals. Continuously and sustainably growing the manufacturing industry may be a challenge. The Swiss manufacturing industry lost 30 000 jobs and 1 000 firms between 2012 and 2017, equivalent to 2% to 6% of manufacturing jobs in rural, peri-urban and metropolitan areas (see Chapter 1). Furthermore, even though an increasing amount of R&D funding is being spent in the manufacturing sector in metropolitan areas, it did not result in an increase in jobs associated with innovation in 2017, as observed in Chapter 1. In rural and peri-urban areas, there is both a drop in spending and jobs in the manufacturing sector.[2]

While local ties to precision manufacturing and expertise in the pharmaceutical industry may be an important determinant of current well-being and the logic of choosing high-value sectors is sound for attaining high levels of productivity, it underestimates the rate of change in the economy and overlooks opportunities for the future of industrial arrangements that include new sectors of activities and the importance of adapting traditional economies. For adaptions to pre-existing ways of working, traditional firms can benefit from the "fresh blood" of innovative SMEs through value chain links and strategic partnerships. For the development of diversified sectors, this can include supporting industries with services or encouraging the development of new industries. For example, in rural areas, we observe that increasing expenditures on R&D in the trade and services sector are also coinciding with increasing average jobs in research and expenditure. It is also notable that when R&D firms in rural areas spend funds on innovation, they are more likely to spend them within their own firms. Conversely, a higher share of average R&D spending in firms in metropolitan areas is spent outside the firm, either in other companies in Switzerland or outside Switzerland.

The wish to enlarge the concept of innovation present in the NRP and hence the RIS strategy also comes up in consultations for the new RIS strategy. Stakeholders perceive it as having a strong technical focus while organisational and social innovation are a less prominent part of the NRP. Public consultations have made suggestions to enlarge programmes to further include non-technical sectors and work with a broader range of stakeholders on a variety of challenges and solutions. A more agile, less risk averse innovation support and increased experimentation potential are recommended, for instance through Living Labs testing solutions for the future at the local level (SECO, 2020[17]).

Going forward, the RIS strategy and its implementation need to better recognise that, especially in rural regions, social, process and business model innovations can have positive effects and are needed to secure local well-being and prosperity. Therefore, to better reflect and enhance economic diversity, SECO, in collaboration with other national and regional actors, could lead to developing mechanisms that assure better reflection on needs in different geographies. One option would be to develop a high-level national innovation vision that incorporates experiences in the regional innovation system's trials, successes and errors, using consultation and agenda-setting with local partners to enlarge the concept of innovation beyond high-tech sectors, to include agriculture and tourism for example.

Future-proofing the innovation agendas

A future-looking approach for rural regions and areas often starts by understanding how current trends are changing society and transforming policy implementation. Future-proofing policy agendas anticipate how economies are changing, often before local entities have the time to react. While governments and individuals cannot anticipate all change, establishing observatories for change and benchmarking institutional performance and financial indicators to carry out projections across regions can help ensure that the government does not inadvertently block change by not reacting fast enough. Subsequently, once trends are identified, innovation support needs to accommodate them and help businesses and societies successfully manage these transformations.

Currently, detecting change and implementing the needs of different geographies happens through a report on territorial megatrends, which is published every four years by the council for spatial planning. The report makes 18 recommendations to the confederation, cantons and municipalities. Findings for 2019 specifically highlight:

- Automatising the agricultural industry.
- Safeguarding national capital, biodiversity and landscapes.
- Digitalisation as a basis for Industry 4.0, autonomous mobility and new modes of work and business.
- Service delivery for elderly people especially in rural areas.
- Reducing the use of resources and specifically enhancing renewable energy (Council for Spatial Planning, 2019[27]).

However, it is currently unclear how these findings are used to structure the RIS strategy and other innovation support given across territories. It seems that, within the RIS, identified megatrends are largely acted upon under the leadership of individual people or entities but not in a strategic way.

To address this gap, SECO could provide a regional lens for other national innovation outlooks and could, in collaboration with other government departments responsible for innovation at the federal and cantonal levels, reinforce existing monitoring practices, such as the existing regional development monitoring by *regiosuisse*. It could also contribute to establishing a cross-agency observatory to monitor trends that signal structural change and projected trends within rural regions. An example of a pan-government task force to monitor and anticipate change is available in Box 3.3. This entity should:

- Provide guidance for national and regional innovation strategies and agendas.
- Be composed of partners from regional and local authorities, academic institutes, the private sector and social partners.
- Anticipate change and develop strategies for supporting the transition of current firms in rural areas into new business models.
- Encourage adaptability to new market conditions or other global factors such as climate and demographic change, while avoiding over-dependence on traditional industries.
- Monitor challenges for women, youth and older workers.
- Consider extending and building a rural lens for the current Swiss Perspective 2030 described in Box 3.3.
- Promote innovation inside the policy-making process. This can include the adoption of new policy tools (e.g. open government) and re-enforcing the consultation process with non-government actors.

Box 3.3. Strategic foresight and initiatives to anticipate demographic change

Strategic foresight in policy making

Strategic foresight is a thought-driven, planning-oriented process for looking beyond the expected future to inform decision-making. It aims to redirect attention from knowing about the past to exercising prospective judgement about events that have not yet happened. For example, strategic foresight does not claim predictive power but maintains that the future is open to human influence and creativity, with an emphasis – during the thinking and preparation process – on the existence of different alternative possible futures (Wilkinson, 2017[28]). This generates an explicit, contestable and flexible sense of the future, where insight into different possible futures allows the identification of new policy challenges and opportunities and the development of strategies that are robust in the face of change. Some governments have conducted such exercises to define possible future scenarios and adapt public policies.

MetaScan 3, Canada

A possible-scenarios assessment (MetaScan 3: Emerging Technologies) was used by the Canadian government in 2013 to explore how emerging technologies will shape the economy and society, and the challenges and opportunities they will create. The study involved research, consultations and interviews with more than 90 experts. The key findings include some of the following policy challenges:

- The next decade could be a period of jobless growth, as new technologies increase productivity with fewer workers.
- All economic sectors will be under pressure to adapt or exploit new technologies, in which case having workers with the right skills will be essential.
- New technologies are likely to significantly alter infrastructures, forcing governments to decide whether to maintain old infrastructures or switch and invest in new, more efficient ones.

Megatrends analysis and scenario planning, United Kingdom (UK)

In 2013, the UK Government Office for Science launched a plausible scenarios-led foresight assessment (Futures of Cities). The goal of the project was to develop an evidence base for the future of UK cities (challenges and opportunities towards 2065) and to inform national- and city-level policy makers. The office commissioned working papers and essays and conducted interactive workshops, with over 25 UK cities participating. By combining megatrends analysis and scenarios planning, the study imagined a plausible future consisting of considerable climate shocks presenting key urban challenges by 2065 – e.g. drier summers and heatwaves affecting the UK's southern cities and higher levels of precipitation affecting western cities during the winter.

Perspective 2030, Switzerland

The first step of the *Perspective 2030* report by the Federal Chancellery used online questionnaires submitted to experts and think tanks to identify influencing factors, changing trends and megatrends that will impact Switzerland in the next 15 years. During the second step, the surveyed experts assessed the influencing factors and trends by assigning them a value between 1 (low impact/low degree of uncertainty) and 10 (high impact/high degree of uncertainty). Third, the report integrated influencing factors and trends into four different plausible world scenarios that analysed the interaction between the Swiss and international influencing factors as well as the resulting potential "winners" and "losers" for each scenario.

A long-term vision for rural areas, European Commission (EC)

The EC (2021[29]) elaborated its long-term vision for rural areas in the EU up to 2040 following a series of consultations with the public and experts. The long-term vision is accompanied by a Rural Pact and EU Rural Action Plan. The vision identifies: the importance of innovative solutions for service provision and social innovation; the importance of physical and digital infrastructure; resilience to climate change, natural hazards and economic crises; and bringing prosperity through attractivity to companies and digital skills. The EU Rural Action Plan focuses on rural proofing and building a rural observatory for monitoring and supporting the development of the rural action plan.

Science and Technology Foresight Centre, National Institute of Science and Technology Policy (NISTEP), MEXT, Japan

Looking beyond the next 20 years, the Japanese government is carrying out foresight activities through regional consultations looking into the impact of science and technology on regions in Japan. Involving policy makers across several government ministries, from universities and public research institutes, the business sector, civil society organisations, citizens and international participants, the initiative practices horizon scanning, trend analysis, scenario planning, the Delphi method, visioning and back-casting among other exercises.

The initiative started with a survey to identify trends in science, technology and society by horizon scanning and then created multiple future visions of society (desirable future visions to be realised by 2040) by visioning. Concurrently, 7 disciplinary committees identified 702 medium- to long-term R&D agendas (as "science and technology topics").

After consulting with more than 5 000 experts to evaluate each topic through the Delphi method, the initiative attempted to extract 8 cross-cutting areas and 8 areas based on 1 or 2 areas (as "close-up science and technology areas") using mechanical methods and experts' judgements. Finally, it created 4 conceptual scenarios based on the 50 social visions and 702 science and technology topics. From these, the initiative extracted 16 "close-up" science and technology areas from 702 topics, based on a mechanical process using artificial intelligence-related technology (analysing similarities and clustering topics through natural language processing) and experts' judgements. Eight areas are considered with high potential for multi/inter-disciplinary and the other eight areas are based on one or two specific fields. These areas are expected to have a possible high impact in solving social issues and/or also serve as common fundamental technologies and systems.

Before the next round, expected in 2024, the initiative plans to conduct several in-depth scenario analyses for several "close-up science and technology areas" defined in the 2019 exercise. It also plans to experiment with new methodologies and outreach by holding several regional workshops.

Anticipating demographic change through a pan-government approach, Population Policy Task Force, Korea

Demographic change has been a major consideration for the Korean government over the past decades, but anticipation and foresight on measures to address how change would impact society started to take a more central role in co-ordination of several related government institutions only towards the end of the 2010s. The initiative to address changes started with a cross-agency commission to measure, plan and take actions to ensure the well-being of individuals across territories.

The Korean Presidential Committee on Ageing Society and Population policy was launched in 2019 to address demographic challenges. As a pan-government initiative, the task force helped provide evidence to promote a co-ordinated approach to strengthen the entire society's adaptive capacity to the change.

The previous two task forces worked successively, addressing issues related to how projected demographic change would impact policies from April 2019 and July 2020 until January 2021. The first round prepared the government to discuss an extension of the legal retirement age in 2022 from 60 upwards in preparation for the projected 20% of the population that would be 65 and over in the near future. It also resulted in adjusting the supply/demand model for teachers and schools and reforming the military structure and personnel. The second round of consultations targeted initiatives to counteract the hollowing-out of small- and mid-sized regions and included plans for vacant housing and more elderly transport policies.

The issues in the current task force, starting in January 2021, address four major strategies around demographic change and sustainability. They include initiatives on: i) absorbing labour shortage shocks caused by demographic change; ii) responding to the shrinking society; iii) taking pre-emptive action against possible local extinction; and iv) improving the sustainability of the entire society. The strategies target improving opportunities for populations such as women, the elderly, as well as local citizens and the wider public, as defined in Table 3.4.

Table 3.4. Korean Population Task Force goals

How will Korean society change through population policy measures?

Women	Measures to provide more childcare services for families with children in elementary school.
	More hours of education for elementary school students; expanded one-stop services for all-day care; better management and supervision for private childcare services.
	Measures to promote the market for domestic services.
	Establishment of plans to boost the domestic service market.
	Measures to reduce the gender gap in the labour market.
	More aggressive action to improve employment conditions; better disclosure system for indication of gender equality; more incentives for women's entry to science, technology, engineering, and mathematics (STEM) areas.

Elderly	Measures to support more opportunities for older individuals to be economically active.
	Promotion of discussion on the reform of employment and wage system for the elderly.
	Measures to increase access to healthcare services to provide the elderly with a healthier life after retirement.
	Introduction of at-home medical centres; better medical services for patients in vulnerable areas using information and communication technology (ICT); development of non-face-to-face diagnosis/treatment services for the elderly.
	Measures to extend care services to all individuals for specific needs.
	Introduction of an integrated assessment system for healthcare, nursing and general care; more supply of care service workers and better service quality.
Local citizens	Measures to incentivise local talent to work in regions for regional development.
	Innovation of universities as a regional hub; lifelong vocational education in colleges linked to regional strategic industries; region-specific pilot visa projects to attract skilled foreign nationals.
	Measures to improve regional hub cities to increase competitiveness up to the level of the capital region.
	Review of reorganisation of local administrative systems, including the establishment of plans for supra-metropolitan areas and the integration of administrative functions at the regional level.
	Measures to increase the resilience of regions at risk of depopulation.
	Joint use of community infrastructure between regions; promotion of specialised regional projects.
General public	Measures to increase opportunities for adult skill upgrading.
	Interconnection between lifelong learning services and platforms; operation of various academic programmes and courses for adults at universities.
	Measures to secure a high degree of protection for platform workers.
	Promotion of the enactment of the Platform Workers Protection Act and the amendment of the Employment Security Act, the Framework Act on Employment Policy, and Framework Act on Labour Welfare; consideration of a comprehensive protection system.
	Measures to protect all families without discrimination.
	Expansion of concept for a family under the Framework Act on Healthy Families; greater support for single-person households; elimination of discrimination in laws and systems.
	Measures to support the development of skilled workers.
	Establishment of digital education centres; database setup and transfer of skills and expertise.
	Measures to support the evidence base for a broad range of other policies.
	Improvement of demographic statistics infrastructure; composition and operation of a research team for demographic policies.

Source: Author's elaboration based on information provided by the Korean Ministry of Land, Infrastructure and Transport and OECD Territorial Review of Korea; Strategic Foresight from OECD (2020[13]), *Rural Well-being: Geography of Opportunities*, https://doi.org/10.1787/d25cef80-en, adapted from OECD (2019[10]), *OECD Regional Outlook 2019: Leveraging Megatrends for Cities and Rural Areas*, https://doi.org/10.1787/9789264312838-en, using methodology from Wilkinson, A. (2017[28]), *Strategic Foresight Primer*, European Political Strategy Centre; EC (2021[29]), "Long-term vision for rural areas: For stronger, connected, resilient, prosperous EU rural areas", https://ec.europa.eu/regional_policy/en/newsroom/news/2021/06/30-06-2021-long-term-vision-for-rural-areas-for-stronger-connected-resilient-prosperous-eu-rural-areas.

Future-proofing the innovation agendas: Focus on demography

A forward-looking and inclusive innovation policy also needs to address barriers to participation in the labour market and entrepreneurship for under-represented populations, including women, youth and migrants. Increasing diversity, for example by activating female, young and migrant entrepreneurs increases positive outcomes for innovation and has the potential to solve challenges that may impact women and men unequally. For example, one Swiss start-up driven by a young female migrant, studying at the Swiss Federal Institute of Technology Lausanne (EPFL) has built a business based on a circular economy model that breaks down polyethylene terephthalate (PET) plastic (of which only 9% is recycled every year) at landfills and sells it back to industry. Another example is the start-up Kokoro Lingua, whose female migrant founder provides virtual English language classes for over 100 000 children taught by other children whose native tongue is English. Having started prior to COVID, this start-up was well-positioned to grow when education during lockdowns was transitioned on line.

As observed in Chapter 2, there is a lower rate of females participating in the workforce, where there are two men employed to every woman in low-density peri-urban areas. While the rate is still high in metropolitan regions, it is lower than in most non-metropolitan regions. Rural and peri-urban regions suffer from a loss of opportunities for a competitive and diverse labour market through a lower activation of the female workforce. Thus, there seems to be significant potential for supporting rural women in entrepreneurship by addressing the systemic barriers that many rural women face in growing their businesses. There is a growing understanding that gender-neutral business support measures do not assist women's enterprise development to the extent that they assist its male equivalent. Yet, no specific objectives for encouraging entrepreneurship and opportunities for women and other harder-to-reach communities are included in the government's NRP.

Young entrepreneurs have a high potential to innovate. However, given the relatively low share of youth in rural regions, in part due to the pursuit of higher education in denser areas, enjoying the benefits of innovation through young entrepreneurship is limited. According to recent work by the EC and OECD (2020[30]), young people between the ages of 18-30 consider entrepreneurship as a desirable outcome and have a higher potential to be innovative. In European OECD countries, in 23 out of 27 countries for which data is available, young entrepreneurs tend to offer products or services that their customers find to be new and unfamiliar. However, they also tend to report having the knowledge and skills to start a business and have difficulties accessing finance and entering networks, have few role models and low levels of awareness of programmes to support business ventures. The findings are similar to the analysis of characteristics of young start-up entrepreneurs from the upcoming report on *Understanding Innovation in Rural Regions* (forthcoming[31]).

More inclusive policies might include specific support, for instance through empowering initiatives, knowledge-building activities as well as reforms to correct for market failures in access to government services for all parts of society, including women and youth. Furthermore, there are long argued gains in productivity through more inclusive policies. Improved knowledge of the specifics of women-led or youth-led innovation, more supportive innovation ecosystems and smart solutions coming from women, youth and migrant-led innovations will empower rural people to act for change and get rural communities prepared to achieve positive long-term prospects, including jobs for all, in particular women, youth and migrants. Further guidelines on engaging with youth and women in rural areas are available in Box 3.4.

To achieve this, SECO and the RIS should:

- Improve knowledge on women, youth innovation in rural areas and create a better understanding of why the proportion of women in established start-ups is low.
- Set objectives for encouraging entrepreneurship and opportunities for women and other harder-to-reach communities in the NRP and develop business support measures targeted to different population groups.
- Consider analysing the impact of policies on harder-to-reach populations such as women, older workers and younger workers in the monitoring and evaluation strategy.
- Establish a gender strategy within the RIS structure to evaluate how programme policies can better accommodate female entrepreneurs and workers in STEM.

- Establish a youth strategy within the RIS structure to evaluate how programme policies can better accommodate young entrepreneurs.

Box 3.4. Support for women and youth in rural regions

Women's entrepreneurship, South of Scotland Enterprise, Scotland (UK)

Building a new strategy for Scotland's newest regional development agency, South of Scotland Enterprise (SOSE), presents opportunities for new thinking and approaches to regional, place-based development. With no previous record of delivering programmes, much of the leg work is still in the works. It was particularly disabled by the challenges of starting a new agency during COVID. SOSE are nevertheless looking to the future, beyond recovery efforts, and acting now to deliver transformational change. One of the key components of their regional innovation strategy under the head of the innovation and entrepreneurship unit is establishing new programmes specifically to address the needs of female entrepreneurs and barriers they encounter in accessing business support. The process is currently underway.

Women Entrepreneurship Strategy (WES), Canada

The Canadian Department for Innovation, Science and Economic Development (ISED) estimates that by ensuring the full and equal participation of women in the economy, Canada could add up to CAD 150 billion in gross domestic product (GDP). With only 17% of Canadian small- and medium-sized businesses owned by women, the government of Canada developed a WES with CAD 6 billion in investments and commitments to encourage access to finance, talent, networks and expertise. It includes an Inclusive Women Venture Capital Initiative, a Women Entrepreneurship Loan Fund, an Ecosystem Fund and the Women Entrepreneurship Knowledge Hub. Other similar programmes exist in the form of a Women Entrepreneur programme administered by Farm Credit Canada, a Women in Technology Venture Fund, a Women Entrepreneurs programme administered by the Business Development Bank of Canada and a Women in Trade programme administered by Export Development Canada.

Regional development agencies (RDAs) in Canada, such as ACOA, FedDev Ontario, PrairiesCan, PacifiCan and provinces across Canada provide specific support, consulting and advisory services to women. They deliver two aspects of the WES:

1. The Women Entrepreneur Fund (WEF) provides non-repayable contributions of up to CAD 100 000 to support women-owned and women-led businesses to scale/grow and reach new markets (programme completed).

2. The WES Ecosystem Fund, a National and Regional fund, is a four-year programme that runs until March 2023. Notably, the fund:

   o Provides non-repayable contributions to non-for-profit partners that deliver business services and support programming to women entrepreneurs.

   o Included an additional top-up to support women entrepreneurs to navigate the COVID-19 crisis.

Through WES, the RDAs seek to increase the number of women-owned and -led businesses and strengthen capacity within the entrepreneurship ecosystem and close gaps in service for women entrepreneurs.

The Women's Enterprise Initiative is an example of a distinct Canadian regional programme that addresses the challenges that women entrepreneurs face. The initiative, in partnership with PrairiesCan and PacifiCan, helps women entrepreneurs start, scale up and grow their businesses. There is a

Women's Enterprise Initiative organisation in each of the four Canadian western provinces (Alberta, British Columbia, Manitoba, Saskatchewan). These non-profit organisations provide a variety of unique products for women entrepreneurs, including business advisory services, training, networking opportunities, loans and referrals to complementary services (Government of Canada, 2021[32]; 2021[33]).

Funding diversity, United States (US)

The regional offices of the US Department of Commerce engage and activate programmes specifically to support female-run and minority entrepreneurs, including Indigenous and black entrepreneurs.

In the US, programmes are developed through the Minority Business Development Agency (MBDA) to help provide access to working capital and gap financing for women and minority communities. The MBDA is a federal agency solely dedicated to the growth and global competitiveness of minority businesses. In addition, the Department of Commerce's Economic Development Administration provides revolving loan funds (RLFs) to help bring access to capital and gap financing for minority-run firms, in addition to community development financial institutions (CDFIs) that help find and sponsor funding for rural communities.

Guidelines for attracting and retaining skilled young population in rural areas, US

According to the US Rural Policy Research Institute (RUPRI) and the associated programme Energizing Young Entrepreneurs (EYE), rural communities can promote a series of actions to benefit from the full potential of their young population:

- Invest time and resources in youth priorities and make communities more attractive for young people to live, work and develop activities.
- Improve the school-to-job transition by strengthening interactions between regional higher education institutions and firms.
- Map the community's assets in order to match educational and training programmes with career opportunities.
- Promote the development of a good business framework able to offer small business ownership and high-level job opportunities to young people.
- Provide entrepreneurial education within the school systems or as an extracurricular training programme, in which students can meet local entrepreneurs and gain hands-on knowledge.
- Offer access to technical assistance and business coaching for young entrepreneurs.
- Consult and involve young people in every phase of the economic activities in the region, to develop a sense of ownership and vested interest in their communities.

Source: OECD (2012[34]), *OECD Territorial Reviews: Småland-Blekinge, Sweden 2012*, https://doi.org/10.1787/9789264169517-en; OECD (2012[35]), *OECD Reviews of Regional Innovation: Central and Southern Denmark 2012*, https://doi.org/10.1787/9789264178748-en; RUPRI Centre for Rural Entrepreneurship; e2 Entrepreneurial Ecosystems (n.d.[36]), *Homepage*, www.energizingentrepreneurs.org (accessed on 19 Augest 2022); U.S. Department of Commerce (2022[37]), "Women-Owned and Indigenous Small Businesses Thrive with EDA and MBDA Support", https://www.commerce.gov/news/blog/2022/03/women-owned-and-indigenous-small-businesses-thrive-eda-and-mbda-support; Government of Canada (2022[38]), *Women Entrepreneurship Strategy*, https://ised-isde.canada.ca/site/women-entrepreneurship-strategy/en.

Future-proofing the innovation agendas: Focus on climate change

Transitioning to a zero-carbon economy and adjusting to climate change implications is the task of this century. Switzerland has set itself the goal to become climate neutral by 2050. Overall, rural regions are pivotal in the transition to a net-zero-emission economy and building resilience to climate change because of their natural endowments. Many rural economies (e.g. agriculture, forestry, tourism, energy, etc.) are already suffering from the increased frequency and intensity of extreme weather events such as storms, floods, torrents and landslides. In many rural regions across the world, increasing heat waves will contribute to water scarcity, with risks to food production. As nature loses its capacity to provide important services, rural economies will suffer significant losses as they rely on the direct extraction of resources from forests, agricultural land or the provision of ecosystem services such as healthy soils, clean water, pollination and a stable climate (OECD, 2021[39]).

Transitioning to net-zero will require a massive deployment of alternative energy technologies as well as new technologies that are not yet on the market or are currently in the demonstration or prototype phase. This means that significant innovation efforts must take place this decade in order to bring these new technologies to market (IEA, 2021[40]). Many of these innovations will need to occur in rural regions where their renewable energy can be generated from sun, wind and water and where there is massive potential to develop the circular economy and bioeconomy. Supporting innovation in these areas not only diversifies ongoing business activities, it can also create new businesses while contributing to environmental and climate protection.

The private sector, and particularly SMEs, are considered a potential driving force for the zero-emission transition – notably through innovation in their products and processes. Product innovations include design that replaces non-renewable materials and resources with renewable, recycled, permanent, biodegradable, non-hazardous and compostable materials and resources; and processes innovation involves the recreating processes, so that products are made to be more easily disassembled, recycled, modular (replacement of parts, recovery and reuse of systems and sub-systems) and repairable (OECD, 2020[41]).

In Switzerland, the circular economy has also gained in importance, especially through various parliamentary initiatives, interpellations and postulates that have been developed in recent years. Furthermore, at the federal level, a first National Research Programme (NRP 73) aims to combine research on all natural resources, all stages of the value chain and the integration of the environment, economy and society. A number of projects include a focus on the circular economy. Legal framework conditions for fostering a circular economy are still under discussion in the Swiss parliament[3] and the federal administration for the environment is in charge. More grassroots and private initiatives have also emerged. For example, in 2018, the initiative Circular Economy Switzerland was launched, supported by the MAVA Foundation and the Migros Group. The initiative aims to promote the circular economy in Switzerland with various projects and events such as a circular economy incubator, in which 27 Swiss start-ups are supported in building a more circular Switzerland (regiosuisse, n.d.[42]). At the regional scale, *regiosuisse* has developed a toolbox aiming to support regions, municipalities or cities in advancing on circular economy. The toolbox offers a methodological framework, inspiration, assistance and practical tips. The toolbox is set up in a modular structure or, depending on interests, consulted selectively (regiosuisse, n.d.[43]).

By providing the right support, RIS have the potential to become enablers of the net-zero transition and attaining climate objectives. Currently, climate change and the way businesses can move to more sustainable, less-emitting ways of doing business only marginally feature in the RIS programming (mostly events) and strategy.

There is great potential for the future NRP and RIS strategies to put greater emphasis on innovation that can advance climate change mitigation and adaptation. This can be done by:

- Adapting RIS coaching to feature business support on innovation for climate change: preparing businesses to assess possible climate risks (physical, price, product, regulation), improving energy and waste efficiency in their businesses and across value chains, and helping them to source power from renewable resources or minimising waste, saving energy, water and materials, recycling and reusing materials or waste, while offering green products and services.
- Facilitating connections and dialogue around innovation for climate change, fostering system thinking and collaboration amongst public, not-for-profit actors and businesses. In addition to workshops and events, RIS could also explore using tools and competitions for climate-friendly innovations similar to the ones organised by Glasgow, where businesses are asked to find a circular solution to local challenges.
- Ensuring the RIS strategically connects to other circular economy initiatives and measures being developed in Switzerland. In this context, the RIS could also further leverage learning from the circular economy toolbox under development through the NRP as well as establish a connection to the Innosuisse Innovation Booster "Applied Circular Sustainability", where appropriate, helping businesses to engage in this transition.
- Encouraging the development of any mechanisms related to innovation in line with net-zero-emission targets and contributions to climate change. Alternatively, requiring all businesses that receive support for innovations to demonstrate their compatibility with net-zero-emission targets and contributions to climate change. This way, the RIS and the businesses it supports function as a role model for other businesses and government agencies to climate-proof their work.

Box 3.5. Capacity building on the circular economy

The circular economy in Glasgow

Since 2015, the Glasgow Chamber of Commerce hosts Circular Glasgow and is responsible for delivering this initiative alongside Zero Waste Scotland, the Glasgow City Council (UK) and key stakeholders. Circular Glasgow aims to build best practices and capacity on the circular economy across Glasgow businesses, helping them identify opportunities to support and implement circular ideas. This is done through: workshops and events – a series of knowledge-sharing business-to-business networking events; Circle Assessment – a tool which helps businesses understand opportunities to become more circular; the Circle Lab – an online hackathon event to find a circular solution to local challenges. The Circle Lab sought solutions to make Glasgow's event industry more circular. From over 200 contributions, the 3 winning ideas include a deposit-based reuse system for food and drink containers, circular designs for event marketing and branding, and a scheme that will repurpose organic waste into energy and fertilisers. Ways to turn these ideas into pilot projects are now being explored. The city is currently developing a circular economy roadmap.

Source: OECD (2020[41]), *The Circular Economy in Cities and Regions: Synthesis Report*, https://doi.org/10.1787/10ac6ae4-en.

Building a culture for experimentation

Another way to prepare for and adapt to change is the use of experimental tools, such as regulatory sandboxes, Living Labs or other experimentation processes that can provide new public services to a changing economy. To develop and foster a culture of experimentation, Living Labs have provided good results across the globe (see Box 3.6). These mechanisms allow innovators to test solutions for the future at the local level, mimicking real-life situations. Germany for instance has developed a federal strategy to systematically establish Living Labs as an economic and innovation policy instrument in the area of digitisation. Since May 2017, a ministerial project group Reallabore has been conducting a needs analysis, contributing to a comprehensive research agenda on the requirements for Living Labs in digital transformation, has established a wide range of stakeholder contacts and developed an implementation agenda. The aim is to systematically establish Living Labs in Germany and to make a significant contribution to the development of Living Labs in contributing to a new digital regulatory framework. These temporally and spatially limited test spaces for predominantly digital innovation and regulation are an instrument for gaining concrete experience in the interplay of innovation and regulation, aiming to improve regulation in a digital age. To that end, temporary modifications to the legal framework, e.g. in the form of experimentation clauses, will create the flexibility for innovations, can be tested in practice and regulation can quickly be adapted to new developments (BMWi, 2018[44]).

Rural places are often particularly suited for these types of experimentation. This is because they, in comparison to more urban counterparts, have the benefit of available space, function as a rather independent system and have lower living expenses. Consequently, by creating a regulatory environment that eases other pressures on firms, individuals in rural regions may experiment more easily than in high-income, high-turnover regions. Likewise, government public innovation service delivery cannot only benefit from learnings and experiences but must also involve businesses that have found the practice useful for building consensus and ownership.

In Switzerland, Living Labs are largely being initiated at the cantonal level and in the forms of accelerator or co-working paces. For instance, in Jura, the programme Day One Accelerator supports innovative ventures that solve problems across a broad range of healthcare. Another example is the Innovation Park Biel/Bienne, which offers an innovative environment for around 500 people that work on and seeking an exchange in the areas of digitalisation/industry 4.0, and all kinds of interdisciplinary innovation projects in the fields of medical technology and health technology or the area of energy storage. It offers workstation rental as well as digitalisation and electronics laboratories workshops and clean rooms where innovations in the form of prototypes and small production series can be established (SIPBB, n.d.[45]).

Other programmes such as so-called "model projects" are also supported by the federal level, for instance, between 2020 and 2021, 31, innovative projects in villages, regions, agglomerations and cantons from the perspective of spatial development. These projects are supported with a total of CHF 3.9 million and are divided into five themes including digitalisation, development of local development strategies, the usability of public space, improving rural areas and demographic change. While not all of these model projects have the more "open innovation" laboratory characteristic of Living Labs, some do. For example, in the mountainous region of Albula und Prättigau/Davos, actors from the public sector, the housing industry and civil society join forces in lab structures and develop approaches and measures to investigate how to adjust housing stock to demographic change and increase liveability for elderly people (ARE, n.d.[46]).

In addition to fostering a culture of experimentation for SMEs and entrepreneurs, RIS can also consider doing this for themselves, creating more diversity, experimentation and flexibility and their own way of working. This can allow them to adjust to changes in client needs or to pick up specific trends.

Unlocking the potential of innovation in rural regions thus implies a need for the RIS to become more agile and increase the level of experimentation in the innovation support they provide. This would include broadening and changing the RIS support portfolio and adding more experimental measures and approaches to their work to improve outcomes.

They can do this by:

- Experimenting in delivering and adjusting already existing mentoring and coaching services. Such experiments should incorporate:
  - Varying offers based on the needs of different target groups, based on gender, age and territory, drawing on behavioural insights.
  - In the selection of coaches, an increase in the number and variety of potential coaches to foster interlinkages between sectors and reduce existing silos, paying attention to the different qualifications and backgrounds of coaches, supplementing R&D coaches with those with a background in business development or other areas.
  - Experiments with setting up peer-to-peer engagements, for instance through mentors who have already started a business and have solved similar problems. Matches with firms with well-performing peers have offered promising results in research (McKenzie and Woodruff, 2021[47]), although the impacts depend on the type of peer and only certain information will diffuse this way.
  - New methods of impact evaluation and monitoring, for instance using rigorous measurement procedures that include counterfactuals or randomised control trials.
- In addition to standard support provided, engaging in collaborative initiatives in physical spaces, such as innovation sandboxes and Living Labs that allow innovators to test solutions for the future at the local level, mimicking real-life situations. This would require close co-ordination with other government bodies on the cantonal and municipal levels.
  - Innovation sandboxes can be narrow in focus and time-limited. Based on the outcomes of such experiments, governments can decide whether to adapt policies to encourage the upscaling of such experiments.
  - Living Labs are physical spaces where individuals may experiment with the development of new products and services, often accompanied by material and in-kind services.
- Supporting a culture of experimentation by providing specific grants through cantons that allow companies to access networks that help them to think outside the box or test porotypes or new services. Furthermore, adjusting programmes to integrate greater lead times, accepting incremental advances as programme outcomes, or encouraging learning from failures as advances should be considered in RIS support.
- Allowing for certain agility in the programme, giving entrepreneurs the opportunity to bring forward ideas and requests for what they would like to see and provide bespoke support if a good case is made.

Box 3.6. Innovation sandboxes and Living Labs

Regulatory innovation sandboxes

In 2016, the first regulatory innovation sandbox allowed experimentation in the financial technology (fintech) industry. According to a recent study, since then, 73 fintech sandboxes have been established in 57 countries, with more than half between 2018 and 2019 (World Bank, 2020[48]). An innovation sandbox is a type of regulatory sandbox that encourages innovation, holding several regulatory requirements on pause while innovators experiment on whether outcomes of innovations may develop useful innovations that may solve greater issues or prove whether regulations may be needed. Regulators across the globe are using regulatory sandboxes to provide a safe environment for emerging technologies to test regulatory boundaries.

A recent report showed that they tended to serve as a base to test the necessity of regulations, facilitate firm start-up entrepreneurship and foster new partnerships. A few examples include a fintech sandbox in Australia and a digital sandbox in the UK. Additionally, initiatives in the agri-tourism sector of the Jura region of Switzerland fit a similar definition.

Fintech sandbox in Australia

The Australian government established an Australian Licensing Exemption Scheme through the Australian Securities and Investments Commission (ASIC) that allowed exceptions for eligible fintech companies on certain products and services for up to 12 months without a license. This allowed firms to begin operating quickly, with low barriers to starting a new fintech company through lower compliance costs. The firm is required to notify ASIC of its plans but remains momentarily free to experiment with the product and services offered.

Digital sandboxes in the UK

Starting with the beginning of the global COVID-19 pandemic in May 2020, the Financial Conduct Agency in the UK began piloting a "digital sandbox". The initiative is currently in its initial stages, attempting to provide guided support for firms looking for a digital testing environment with the aim of addressing some of the challenges of the pandemic. The initiative has a specific goal and is administered through a call for applicants who are given the right to participate based on whether their aim to accomplish one of the goals of the administration includes preventing fraud, improving the financial resilience of consumers and access to finance for SMEs.

Regulatory exemptions in tourism in the Jura region, Switzerland

While not directly marketed as such, two examples of regulatory sandboxes with the specific target of developing the tourism sector are found in the mountainous region of the Jura in Switzerland. Both initiatives were driven from the bottom-up and included the co-ordination efforts of the regional innovation system agencies.

A first example was built in collaboration with TalentisLab, which requested an exemption from environmental protection legislation that limited activities associated with ecotourism. After an application for exemption and a call for proposals, a new initiative to encourage eco-responsible tourism in the provision of campsite accommodation is being put into place.

A second example involves temporarily lowering prohibition from visiting publicly protected places while visiting local towns. The initiative provides access to a "secret route" (*circuit secret*) to groups of tourists that have acquired digital keys. The community of Porrentruy, in collaboration with the RIS agency services, worked on reducing regulations on access to public places that may be of interest to areas with an increase in tourism. This has allowed the town of Porrentruy, whose business was strongly impacted by the COVID-19 pandemic, to gain in visibility and attractiveness.

Innovation labs

Another increasingly popular way to encourage innovation are Living Labs, "fab labs" and similar initiatives to bring previously inaccessible tools to budding innovators. The Interreg Europe Policy Learning Platform (see note 1 below) is one of the agencies supporting the increased use of such tools that create a place to learn, experiment and enjoy the process of innovation. While the different labs vary, they generally provide a mix of services such as skills, materials and advanced tools to participants that can include university-industry collaborations and provide prototyping services for SMEs.

Living Labs, Portugal

The experience of implementing Living Labs in Portugal dates to the 1990s. Since then, they have been of crucial importance for the economic, social and business development of the country. To date, 18 projects have been developed, some of which are part of the European Network of Living Laboratories (ENoLL). There are diverse types – local, sectoral and thematic Living Labs – organised in regional, national and transnational networks. Sectoral and thematic Living Labs include labs for energy, well-being and health, e-government and digital participation, sustainable environment, mobility, rural and territorial development, and industry and logistics.

The Smart Rural Living Lab (SRLL) was founded at the end of 2007 and is located in Penela in central Portugal. It aims to develop new methods and technologies to identify the weaknesses and strengths of rural areas, find references for sustainable rural development, export the acquired knowledge to other rural areas and collaborate with citizens to promote rural areas. Key local issues are related to an ageing population and the weak development of the economic fabric. The goal of SRLL is to promote innovation and development in the exploration of innovative technologies, methods and applications to achieve better integration of rural areas into the global supply chain, create new services/systems/products and business opportunities, and promote citizen participation.

SRLL has established itself as a centre for innovation, best practices and sustainable development of rural areas where the agri-food and forestry sectors are strong. For example, for the problem of the lack of shepherds to take care of sheep needed for local Rabaçal cheese (protected designation of origin), a smart farm concept called FarmReal (see note 2 below) was tested. This involves investment in a community herd via crowdfunding and the adoption of individual animals by investors, who would then check their physical activity and milk production digitally via specific sensors. Users become "virtual shepherds" of real goats and can follow the day-to-day life of the adopted goats, monitoring their behaviour and socialisation through updated photos and videos, their GPS location, as well as the area and amount of vegetation used by the herd.

Living Lab e-Health and smart energy grids, Eindhoven, The Netherlands

As part of the Brainport Development Cluster, Eindhoven also houses an example of a Living Lab that focuses on the development of time-limited trial runs for new products and services. Brainport works with local stakeholders, higher education institutions, the government and a consortium of private sector parties, to focus on experimenting with new solutions to pre-existing issues. Through Living labs, individuals are given a license to test out a new initiative in a short time frame to get quick feedback and determine the feasibility, benefit and scalability of such a project. For example, Living Lab eHealth provides elderly people with the opportunity to try out new medical and healthcare services and a smart energy grids project provides new energy solutions for social housing.

The Center for Innovation and Entrepreneurship in California Polytechnic State University, US

As a service to students led by students, California Polytechnic State University has created a space for budding entrepreneurs to use materials involved in developing new products and services in a variety of sectors including but not limited to manufacturing, farming and services. This initiative provides some of the more advanced and often more expensive tools to experiment with innovative ideas. Some of the materials available for students to use include vinyl cutting, 3D printing, virtual reality, computer numerical control (CNC) routing and laser cutting resources.

The student-run organisation also offers workshops for learning engineering and artistic skills, as well as small grants that facilitate the development and starting of new student-run projects. Funds for grants are targeted toward bringing ideas from the innovation sandbox to entrepreneurial fruition.

> ### *Experimenting in the public sector*
>
> The use of "serious games" to support governments and make various options for courses of action visible through systems thinking and futurism has been increasing in the policy arena. This can be a good option to replace conventional brainstorming sessions with sticky notes and drawings on a board.
>
> The EC Joint Research Centre (JRC) has worked with experts in these types of games at the Hawaii Research Center for Futures Studies to create the Scenario Exploration System (SES). Participants explore their long-term objectives against scenarios and consider various stakeholders. By creating a realistic journey towards the future, SES generates a safe space to uncover perspectives and thinking, with a view to simulating possible responses linked to issues of interest to the participants.
>
> SES is available under a Creative Commons licence, which allows anyone to freely use and modify the game, as long as they share the results of their adaptation under the same conditions. The OECD has made freely downloadable details, instructions and templates available on https://oe.cd/ses.
>
> ### Augmented reality (AR) in policy making
>
> Governments are also realising the potential of AR and virtual reality (VR) for the public good. Similar to gamification, governments and their partners are using the technologies as tools to bring previously invisible insights.
>
> For example, in the US, the New York City suburb of New Rochelle was recently named city39 a 2018 Bloomberg Philanthropies' Mayors Challenge champion for its pioneering use of AR and VR to engage residents in plans for new buildings and public spaces in the city. Through this innovative project, residents can use AR applications on their smartphones to envision what a new park might look like, employ interactive software to design streets and use VR headsets to review different options for buildings and provide their opinions.
>
> Note 1: For more information, see https://www.interregeurope.eu/policylearning/news/11466/fablabs-and-makerspaces/.
> Note 2: For more information, see https://farmreal.pt/en.
> Source: Smart Rural 21 (n.d.[49]), Penela, https://www.smartrural21.eu/villages/penela_pt/; Farmreal (n.d.[50]), Homepage, https://farmreal.pt/en (accessed on 19 August 2022); Deutscher Bundestag (2018[51]), Reallabore, Living Labs und Citizen Science-Projekte in Europa, https://www.bundestag.de/resource/blob/563290/9d6da7676c82fe6777e6df85c7a7d573/wd-8-020-18-pdf-data.pdf.
> Source: OECD (2021[52]), *Embracing Innovation in Government*, https://trends.oecd-opsi.org/ (accessed on 19 August 2022).

Building more reactiveness and inclusiveness in monitoring and evaluation practices: Improving evidence on support for rural SMEs and entrepreneurs

Monitoring and evaluation systems can be used as a tool to promote institutional dynamism. As well as regularly incorporating monitoring and evaluation outcomes into high-level statements. Quick and small experimentation followed by monitoring and evaluation can help inform scale-up potential for new initiatives.

In terms of network building and facilitating knowledge exchange, RIS are essential because they are fostering cross-cantonal links. Still, the RIS impact across different types of areas within the perimeter can be uneven. Several reports state that SMEs and entrepreneurs in regional centres benefit more from the provided support than the more remote regions and mountainous areas (Egli, 2020[16]; SECO, 2020[12]). The reasoning behind this is that innovation in the peripheral regions functions differently than in the regional centres or the larger agglomerations and that the support currently provided does not sufficiently take geographic specificities into account.

Consequently, better evidence is needed to help RIS evaluate and understand if their activities and programmes match and benefit the different needs existing within the perimeter. Developing a precise understanding of need as well as the current uptake of networking events, coaching opportunities and workspaces usage can help to identify mismatches, define future programming priorities, enhance synergies with other offerings and limit ineffectiveness or cost. Given the important share of expenditure on networking and coaching services, it is important to take steps to collect data to monitor the effectiveness of the programmes offered specifically for rural entrepreneurs. Some guidelines for good practices are available in Box 3.7.

Box 3.7. Guidelines for monitoring and evaluating

Regional innovation policy from SCINNOPOLI

A set of 12 policy recommendations have been formulated as a result of the SCINNOPOLI "Scanning Innovation Policy Impact" project. The nine project partners exchanged numerous experiences in monitoring the impact of regional innovation policy. These policy recommendations are not a story-telling or philosophical approach to monitoring but a set of practical recommendations for the implementation of an effective monitoring system for regional innovation policy.

1. *SMART (Specific, Measurable, Attainable, Relevant and Timebound) policy objectives and SMART indicators*: Policy objectives, as well as monitoring indicators, need to be formulated.

2. *Monitor what you can **influence***: A lot of information is interesting to have but, for monitoring purposes, one should monitor only indicators that can be influenced by the downstream party.

3. *Integrate **feedback-loops** in the monitoring system*: Monitoring results should be used to improve the regional innovation policy. Monitoring is not the end of a process.

4. ***Process orientation***: A key step in the development of an evaluation culture is to recognise the evaluation process as part of a cyclical process of policy design, policy implementation and policy learning.

5. ***Consensus***: The concept of the monitoring system needs to be set up in consensus with all stakeholders (policy makers/practitioners/programme owners/project leaders) and existing monitoring systems need to be considered.

6. *Concise **communication** and promotion of results*: The message and language should be adapted to the targeted public (policy makers, companies, large public and innovation actors). Communication on the innovation policy monitoring process as a whole (objectives, targets, indicators, results) is an indispensable condition of a successful innovation policy.

7. *Monitoring is a **policy tool***: Monitoring innovation policies are only useful when the monitoring results are used by policy makers.

8. ***Embed** monitoring in the regional innovation system*: Monitoring should be embedded in the RIS from the start of its implementation. Adding a monitoring system as an add-on to the RIS will not lead to good results.

9. *Create a **win-win** situation*: All groups involved in the monitoring process should find a benefit in the monitoring system.

10. ***Resources** need to be budgeted*: Resources for the specific support actions defined in the framework of the regional innovation policy as well as resources for the monitoring system itself should be budgeted.

11. ***Long-term** perspective and continuity*: One should search for sustainable indicators, even if the regulatory environment is unstable.

12. ***Coherence***: An innovation policy monitoring system should be based on solid, transparent and clear logic. This logic must be maintained from the lowest level (individual innovation support actions) to the highest (innovation policy design).

Source: OECD (2012[35]), *OECD Reviews of Regional Innovation: Central and Southern Denmark 2012*, https://doi.org/10.1787/9789264178748-en; SCINNOPOLI (n.d.[53]), *Scanning Innovation Policy Impact*, www.scinnopoli.eu (accessed on 19 August, 2022).

At the time of this investigation, the effectiveness of RIS in reaching rural SMEs with their networking and coaching activities is difficult to assess with hard evidence. In 2018, an evaluation of the RIS Framework found that RIS do not hold data on the effectiveness of their interventions on the enterprises in rural regions or on the number of enterprises that were indeed located in rural areas and benefit from their programme (B,S,S Volkswirtschaftliche Beratung AG, 2018[8]). Following evaluations were introduced; now RIS carefully evaluate what they are doing based on an efficiency model and follow up with each SME in which they indicate the degree of satisfaction, as well as the percentage achieved within the NRP perimeter. Still, results are not shared systematically and reduced importance is given to geographical components. Especially, within the NRP perimeter, the goals do not specify different kinds of rural geographies or the level to be achieved at each scale. This also means that there is no analysis done to understand satisfaction differences between rural and non–rural SMEs or whether companies largely come from more regional centres than remote rural places. Consequently, there is also no additional funding to develop specific tools to address specific needs of rurality.

In line with the NRP, which specifically targets rural areas, RIS and SECO could help build more reactiveness and inclusiveness in monitoring and evaluation practices for rural innovation in Switzerland. Each RIS should systematically collect, structure and analyse data about the businesses benefitting from innovation support based on geography. In line with earlier assessments, impact measurements should be improved to assess the value added by the RIS to rural areas and rural SMEs, and to further strengthen geographic data collection. This can be done by setting up a more coherent system for monitoring and evaluation as well as encouraging data sharing on leading practices:

- Consider reinforcing good practices in regular monitoring and evaluation of initiatives within the NRP's mandate. For this, a central strategic unit of RIS in SECO could be set up that works in collaboration with the Federal Statistical Office (FSO) and regional offices based on access to shared data. These need to consider the unique needs of rural regions and underserved populations. Results on good practices should be shared with RIS as part of the regular co-ordination meetings.

- Consider piloting a unified customer relationship management (CRM) system, which would track individuals' access to different services across and between cantons and RIS and could provide the following information:
  - Account for the location (municipality/canton/RIS) of the companies, or the persons, who participate in coaching, information and networking events.
  - Account for the number of companies and location of companies referred by the RIS to other innovation promotion agencies (Innosuisse, etc.).
  - Account for the number and location of companies that are referred to coaches/funding agencies in other cantons of the RIS, as well as the number and location of companies referred to coaches/promotion in other RIS.
  - Account for the number and location of companies that used the individual cantonal antennas (points of entry) and the number of these that have then used: i) a service at the corresponding RIS; and ii) a service at another RIS or innovation promotion agency and the location of these services (B,S,S Volkswirtschaftliche Beratung AG, 2018[8]).

- Advance data sharing and open data practices, between RIS, cantons and the FSO. Include, if necessary, precautionary measures such as aggregation and confidentiality controls that can help provide information while still respecting privacy regulations.

- Consider monitoring trends in non-RIS areas to seek complementarities with RIS programmes.

Increasing and simplifying access to services offered by the RIS through the digitalisation of public services and an online "one-stop-shop" for entrepreneurship support

Despite significant improvements in terms of local contact points and the development of a "no wrong door" policy, SMEs in rural Switzerland face barriers to entry when trying to receive innovation support. In order to address gaps in the accessibility and clarity of services, many RIS have appointed local or regional representation to improve their presence and communication with cantons and sub-regions. Moreover, attempts have been made to reduce the number of service providers and clarify the roles of the different providers within the RIS and outside (Regio Basiliensis, n.d.[25]; 2019[54]; B,S,S Volkswirtschaftliche Beratung AG, 2018[8]). Still, barriers to entering the RIS innovation support seem high for rural SMEs.

Multiple entry barriers can be notified. First, businesses might lack knowledge about the support available and are not targeted with the right communication. Second, points of contact are not locally present or too difficult to access. Especially in rural regions, where the population is less dense, having personal contacts and establishing trust through a continuous exchange is essential. Talking regularly to local people can significantly improve awareness of services and tie them to other networks. Third, if the number of interfaces, offers and actors becomes too great, this can create hesitancy and can make picking the right one a barrier.

As an example of the existing complexity of the RIS system, Figure 3.5. depicts the offers provided within RIS Basel-Jura and the stakeholders involved. Several reports and evaluations observe that there are too many actors involved in innovation support in Switzerland and that roles need to be clarified and presence in rural regions improved (B,S,S Volkswirtschaftliche Beratung AG, 2018[8]; Regio Basiliensis, n.d.[25]; 2019[54]).

From the federal side, Innosuisse and the RIS are the central elements of innovation support and the innovation ecosystem. As a federal agency, the Swiss Innovation Agency, Innosuisse (formerly the Commission for Technology and Innovation), is very proficient at addressing the needs of the science- and technology-based innovators. Successfully linking regional and national innovation support is important to deliver on rural innovation. Companies with lower absorptive capacities, innovating without R&D or being involved in other forms of innovation (e.g. organisational innovation) are not a target of federal policy. In other words, within the "innovation triangle" of knowledge creation-diffusion-absorption, the federal policy addresses the first two elements: knowledge creation and diffusion (OECD, 2011[9]). At the regional level, RIS have successfully taken the role to address more knowledge absorption and diffusion bottlenecks targeting smaller companies innovating in a learning-by-doing and learning-by-interacting mode. It can thus be said that the OECD's recommendation from 2011 on a clearer division of multi-level innovation that delineates innovation promotion based on the innovation triangle has been largely achieved and implemented.

A successive step to further improve the existing innovation ecosystem is to ensure the different federal and regional innovation support systems integrate more smoothly. In particular for rural areas with their economic structures that depend more on exploiting natural resources, such integration needs to widen the scope for further sectoral (innovation) policies, in food and agriculture for example (see also Chapter 4). Regarding the integration of RIS and Innosuisse, co-ordination at the strategic level is ensured through regular meetings and local level integration is lagging. A 2018 evaluation of all RIS mentions that co-ordination still needs to improve with regards to implementation (B,S,S Volkswirtschaftliche Beratung AG, 2018[8]). It becomes especially clear that there is a need to better align the RIS coaching activities and the Innosuisse mentors. Both operate at the regional and local levels offering direct support, yet differentiation can be difficult for companies trying to find the right fit. It is often unclear that RIS offer more general business support while technological innovation is covered by Innosuisse. Furthermore, links to Innosuisse are often facilitated through universities or universities of applied sciences. Regions that do not have these are therefore strategically disadvantaged in providing access to national innovation support.

Figure 3.5. RIS Basel Jura: offers, stakeholders and governance

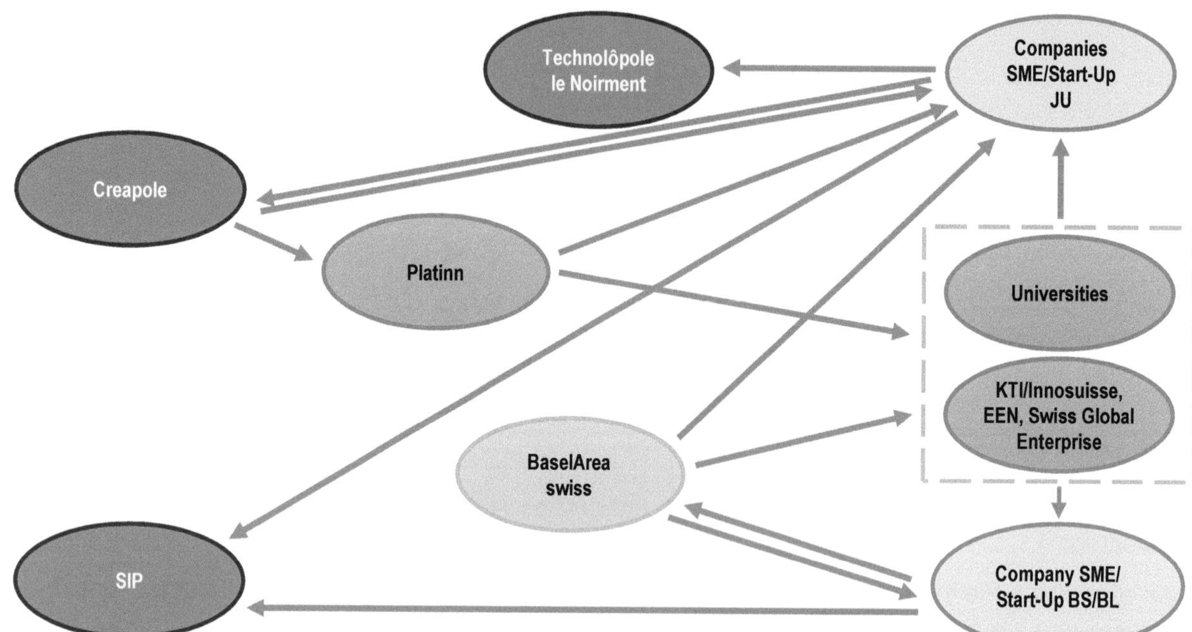

Note: The figure should be read from right to left. Blue arrows indicate to which bodies the SMEs turn to or to whom they are forwarded, orange arrows show the flow of information or the fulfilment of a consulting service of the respective company, light green fields describe the RIS (SMEs and start-ups) target groups, the yellow field BaselAreaswiss represents the RIS management organisations, blue fields show other actors within the RIS and dark green fields describe other important actors outside the RIS. SIP: Switzerland Innovation Park; éCreapole: incubator and accelerator in Delémont, technological Incubator in Noirmont.

Source: regiosuisse (2018[55]), *Regionale Innovationssysteme (RIS) : Evaluation und RIS-Konzept 2020+*, https://regiosuisse.ch/sites/default/fil es/2018-12/RIS%20Evaluation%20und%20RIS-Konzept%202020%2B%20DE.pdf.

Research has shown that co-operation largely works thanks to personal connections and professional links or if RIS coaches and Innosuisse mentors hold both positions at the same time. Further, better integrating processes for companies to flow along the support chains offered by both actors are mentioned. This means that RIS can still improve in putting SMEs and entrepreneurs that have reached a certain level of maturity in touch with Innosuisse support and mentors. Similarly, the other way around, those that are not yet ready for Innosuisse support need to be guided towards the RIS effectively (B,S,S Volkswirtschaftliche Beratung AG, 2018[8]). This is particularly relevant for rural SMEs that are often smaller and less likely to know their way around different innovation support actors and might not have been in touch with either actor yet.

In systems where a multitude of services are provided, the simplification and ease of access for users can be a challenge, in particular for countries in which there is a tailored approach to providing government services. In some countries, simplification of the provision of entrepreneurial services is complemented by physical presence with online services that allow easy navigation of business services according to particular needs. This can reduce complexity and help direct people to the "right" offer in their geographic location without having to actually relocate. In Scotland, UK, for instance, the main regional development agencies, Scottish Enterprise, Highlands and Islands Enterprise and the newest, South of Scotland Enterprise, work with Business Gateway and 32 local authority councils to deliver support to SMEs through a shared national website (https://findbusinesssupport.gov.scot/). The aim of the initiative is to help SMEs find business support wherever they may be in a single location. Behind this website is a business support partnership through which all of the agencies meet and share information to avoid confusion and duplication. In addition, the Enterprise agencies and Business Gateway share a CRM system for all businesses engaging in the public sector, to give an overview of previous and current engagement. Further examples of simplification of the provision of services are available in Box 3.8.

Box 3.8. Encouraging simplification for the delivery of entrepreneurship and innovation support in rural areas

Business Pathfinder Tools, Canada

The Canadian federal government has set up a Business Benefits Finder (see note below), which aims to provide businesses with a list of tailored support. The tool is designed on the basis of questions and answers that help filter through hundreds of federal, provincial and territorial programmes. A key objective of the tool was to develop a site that is fun, interactive and as user-friendly as possible while providing the best results. It also aims to reach people who might not know what they are looking for and equip them with information on what the government can do for them. Importantly, the process does not collect or track individual information. The more questions are answered, the more customised and accurate the results will be. Behind the tool sits a team of four people working on keeping information up to date, summarising programmes and creating the right tags for the programmes. While the page was largely oriented toward business growth in the beginning, due to the COIVD-19 pandemic, it was expanded towards resilience to economic shocks. The tool currently provides information on 16 000 programme streams (some programmes have multiple sub-services) and is advertised through sustained marketing efforts.

Community Futures, Canada

In an effort to address the specific needs of rural entrepreneurs and bring funding for community support and innovation to rural areas, in 1985, the government of Canada established Community Futures. The programme is a community-driven economic development initiative designed to assist communities in Canada's rural areas to develop and implement strategies for dealing with a changing economic environment.

This programme works with 267 Community Futures Development Corporations (non-profits, whose operating funds are provided by federal regional development agencies) to provide services to entrepreneurs in their local communities including standards entrepreneurial and innovation support for example, such as: strategic community planning and socio-economic development; support for community-based projects; business financing, business plan consultation, business planning and business start-up assistance; and access to capital for SMEs and social entreprises.

Rural Partners Network, US

Set up by the Biden-Harris Administration, the Rural Partners Network is an alliance of federal agencies and civic partners working to expand rural prosperity through job creation, infrastructure development and community improvement. The networks bring "boots to the ground" by designating community liaisons to work to simplify access to information for rural communities. They are established as a collaboration of 27 agencies and the White House in an effort to improve access to government resources, staffing and tools, build awareness of rural issues and focus on building rural strategies. It is currently going through the second pilot programme in 14 counties and 10 states.

Business Support Simplification, UK

The Business Support Simplification Programme (BSSP) was initiated by the Department for Business Enterprise and Regulatory Reform (now the Department for Business, Innovation and Skills) for English regions. It aims to make it easier for companies and entrepreneurs to understand and access

---

government-funded grants, subsidies and advice with which to start and grow their businesses. With an estimated 3 000 or more publicly funded business support schemes, existing businesses reported that they were confused by the number of schemes, which discouraged them from applying. Streamlining helps save them time and money when looking for support. Better targeted schemes have more impact on businesses and provide the public sector with a greater value for money from a leaner system. The 3 000 schemes were reduced to 100 or less by 2010 and made available through the nationally sponsored and regionally administered Business Link gateway. With the new UK government in 2010, this process was consolidated into Solutions for Business. The portfolio will contain only 13 products and will no longer be supported by the administrative regions that ceased to exist on 31 March 2011 but rather offered through an Internet portal.

Note: For more information, see http://innovation.canada.ca/.
Source: OECD (2012[35]), *OECD Reviews of Regional Innovation: Central and Southern Denmark 2012*, https://doi.org/10.1787/9789264178748-en; BIS (n.d.[56]), *Solutions for Business: Simplified Business Support*, www.bis.gov.uk/policies/enterprise-andbusiness-support/solutions-for-business-simplified-business-support (accessed 1 September, 2022); Find Business Support (n.d.[57]), *Homepage*, https://findbusinesssupport.gov.scot/ (accessed 1 September, 2022); U.S. Government (n.d.[58]), *Rural Partners Network*, https://www.rural.gov/; CFNC (n.d.[59]), *Supporting Canada's 267 Community Futures Organizations*, https://communityfuturescanada.ca/ (accessed 1 September, 2022).

While the "no door" policy is a first step to simplification, in order to facilitate the provision of business services in rural areas RIS and Innosuisse need to:

- Complement physical entry points with a digital online one-stop-shop to reduce the complexity of the existing system, making support accessible from anywhere and allowing to integrate programmes and measures.

- Designate an outreach person that contacts rural SMEs directly and speaks to them to inform them about offers.

- Develop targeted communication and branding strategies and make sure information is shared in rural areas and through channels in the region, such as entrepreneurs who already live in remote places. This can also include developing specific entry events that inform about the offers of RIS.

- Improve integration of Innosuisse and RIS services by creating shared support roles where the same people take on RIS counselling and Innosuisse mentoring. This way processes for companies to flow along the support chains are offered by both regional and federal actors.

Box 3.9. Simplifying business support ecosystems across rural-urban areas

Entrepreneurial support available wherever you live

Southern Ontario is a cornerstone of the Canadian economy with the region accounting for more than a third of Canada's population, jobs and economic output. The province of Ontario generates nearly half of the country's business R&D spending, almost two-thirds of patent applications and over 40% of Canada's science, technology, engineering and mathematics-related workforce – all critical inputs to drive growth and innovation in the digital economy. The three cities, Ottawa, Toronto and Waterloo, have together been at the heart of Southern Ontario's technology cluster for many years now.

In each city, the sector is supported by a strong business accelerator organisation. These organisations work closely with local universities, researchers, investors, business strategists and mentors, as well as with the government, to provide entrepreneurs and SMEs with the tools, advice and access to finance their need to innovate, commercialise new ideas and technologies, and grow their companies.

Outside of these cities though, the picture is quite different. Rural areas in Southern Ontario have not shared in the recent success of the region's major cities. In the decade following the economic recession of 2008, Ontario saw the creation of 865 000 net jobs. However, 87% of this job growth was concentrated in Ottawa and Toronto, while rural communities experienced the loss of 76 000 jobs over the same period.

Relative to rural areas in other parts of Canada, rural areas in Southern Ontario are relatively close to cities and well connected by roads, rail and broadband services; however, rural entrepreneurs have not had access to the support available to their counterparts in the major cities. Recognising this issue, the Federal Economic Development Agency for Southern Ontario, which provides funding to the three major business accelerators, included a provision in recent funding negotiations to develop rural-urban linkages between the three major business accelerators and innovation centres serving smaller communities and rural areas across the region. The resulting Southern Ontario Scale-Up Platform brings together each major city's business accelerator organisation into a new partnership. A goal of the new platform is to make the programming, advisory services and other support offered by these organisations at their urban locations available to entrepreneurs and SMEs located outside the major cities, by partnering with local innovation centres.

In one example, Invest Ottawa provided funding support to Queen's University in Kingston (196 km from Ottawa) to develop their Launch Lab initiative, including a boot camp for early-stage start-ups, a pre-commercialisation pilot for intellectual property holders and a growth accelerator programme for SMEs. The boot camp has been offered in rural Lanark County and the town of Cornwall (45 723 inhabitants, 103 km from Ottawa) and is being adapted for virtual delivery. Invest Ottawa has also partnered with a local vocational college (St. Lawrence College), with three campuses across Eastern Ontario to develop a business ecosystem pathfinding tool to assist start-ups and scale-ups in connecting with available resources.

The tool called Switchboard (see note below) provides navigation support and visibility to all relevant public support activities in the area of Kingston. Results are clustered and displayed according to which stage of the business circle entrepreneurs are in, based on qualitative analysis. In case entrepreneurs are unsure of their best fit, the tool also provides assessment help and lets people research for support directed at specific needs, including for women and Indigenous people. The page is constantly updated through support providers, making it easily saleable to other regions and allowing for reporting on what kind of support was most searched for. This way it can also be used to assess where needs exist and if the demands are currently met.

By helping rural residents to fulfil business ambitions in their own communities, without having to move into the cities to find the help they need or to commute, the benefits of their efforts may be captured locally, supporting the development of rural communities. Linkages forged via the Scale-Up Platform are also expanding the capacity of the smaller innovation centres outside the major cities, while fostering a stronger network between these centres and the major platform members, creating new opportunities for knowledge sharing and idea development across a wider area.

Note: For more information, see www.myswitchboard.ca.

Promoting innovation through networks: Fostering rural-urban linkages

Rural-urban linkages exist across several dimensions including demographic, environmental and economic aspects (OECD, 2013[60]). Demographic linkages include commuters and migration patterns. This can include young people moving from rural to urban areas for educational or career opportunities, or urban retirees moving to rural areas to enjoy a slower pace of life, a greater sense of community and proximity to nature. Environmental linkages can include shared assets, such as water and amenities for public enjoyment, such as natural beauty spots. Economic linkages include a wide variety of relationships, including trade and supply chain links between firms across the rural-urban continuum, investments and relationships around R&I that support the development and commercialisation of new products and services.

Figure 3.6. Linkages between rural and urban areas within functional regions

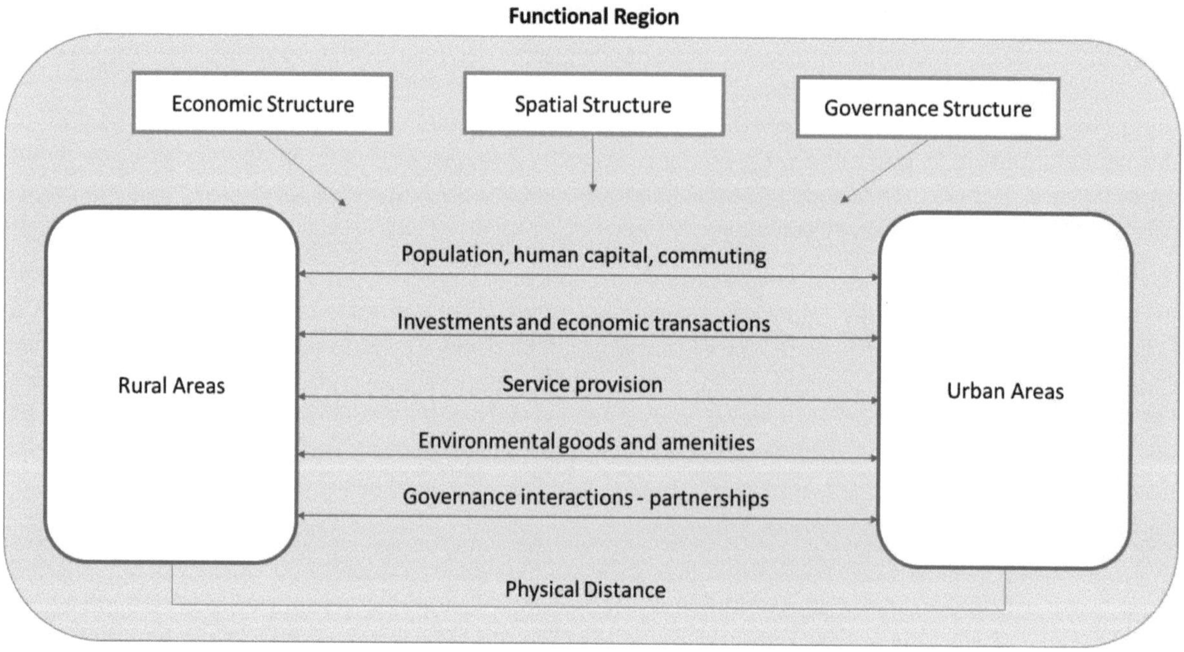

Source: OECD (2013[60]), *Rural-Urban Partnerships: An Integrated Approach to Economic Development*, https://doi.org/10.1787/9789264204812-en.

Linkages tend to be stronger in rural areas that are close to cities. Switzerland has five functional urban areas (FUAs) in which 55% of its population resides, yet only 40% of the population lives in its urban cores, the rest residing in commuting zones. The Swiss commuting zones are characterised by lower-density settlements with respect to the main urban centres. However, firms and workers in these areas benefit from good access to markets, services and agglomeration of talent present in the urban core, benefits often referred to as "borrowed" agglomeration effects. Rural areas close to cities often enjoy environmental amenities and lower land and housing costs than cities, making them both attractive places to live and in which businesses can invest. Overall, the commuting zones in Switzerland grew faster than the cores during the last decade (Veneri, 2018[61]). This also suggests the increased importance of interlinkages.

Entrepreneurs who actively develop rural-urban links and tap into urban clusters are needed to develop vital, competitive rural economies. Geographic proximity matters for innovation and agglomeration or clustering can permit locally concentrated labour markets, specialisation in production and the attraction of specialised buyers and sellers (OECD, 2015[62]). Research on rural innovation has shown that rural entrepreneurs utilise non-local knowledge for more radical innovations and they strategically engage in rural-urban linkages to leverage knowledge outside of their location. This includes urban innovation networks, suppliers or higher education institutions (Mayer, Habersetzer and Meili, 2016[18]). Overall rural-urban links are beneficial to entrepreneurs in three ways:

> *"Rural-urban links help entrepreneurs create a sensibility for the core market demands and trends.*
>
> *Rural-urban linkages help entrepreneurs strategically utilise them to valuate rural assets that have traditionally been perceived as backwards, disadvantages, burdensome, etc.*
>
> *They can be used to combine rural and urban sources of knowledge for innovation, which, in turn, puts a competitive edge on rural businesses." (Mayer, Habersetzer and Meili, 2016[18])*

In light of such learnings, the importance of an open, competitive environment and of innovation systems that are conducive to knowledge flows have increased. This includes cross-border and rural-urban collaboration in innovation, fostering collaborative efforts in which businesses interact and exchange knowledge and information with other partners as part of broader innovation systems. While the shift towards an "open innovation" paradigm, facilitated by the digital transition, has made business innovation more accessible to SMEs, the businesses, especially rural ones, still often find it difficult to identify and connect to appropriate knowledge partners and networks at the local, national and global levels (Cusmano, Koreen and Pissareva, 2018[63]). If countries are already experiencing spatial disparities, there is a danger that rural economies drift further apart if their enterprises are not helped to sufficiently connect and link to agglomeration economies or wider national and global markets.

National co-ordination mechanisms for innovation promotion are built from the bottom up in Switzerland. They are strongly targeted to the sectors determined to be high value-added. Regions (cantons) co-ordinate across themselves in initiatives to support economic development, based on proximity and cultural (language) closeness. While the structure is organic and has merits in how well it adapts to local contexts, it does also mean that cantonal economies have a harder time adapting to change or opportunities outside of their neighbouring regions and less access to the full potential of Swiss resources.

Silos between agencies that perform critical work to develop the framework conditions for rural innovation create gaps in public service provision. Agencies relevant for innovation in rural areas include SECO's RIS, the Federal Office for Agriculture, Innosuisse and the education and labour market agencies. While the entire innovation ecosystem is not under the institutional responsibility of one sole agency, bridging the gaps between agencies and policies is a crucial step toward improving prospects for innovation in rural regions.

Ensuring policy coherence for rural-urban linkages

From a territorial perspective, two policies are dealing with rural-urban links in the broader sense. These are the agglomeration policy (AggloPol) and the policy for rural and mountain areas (P-LRB or PERM). Both policies are cross-cutting policies that work across a range of sectoral policies including aspects such as transport, energy and finance and try to bring a geographical component to them. The two policies are linked and share part of the goals and measures. In that context, the NRP is also considered a sectoral policy and overlaps in geographical terms with both policies (see also Figure 3.7). The agglomeration policy, for instance, covers a heterogeneous spectrum of urban areas ranging from the five main urban centres to other "agglomerations", which include towns in predominantly rural regions covered by NRP (OECD, 2011[9]).

Due to the short geographic distances between Swiss rural and urban areas, policy linkages are crucial. Yet, two different policies exist as tensions have sometimes plagued the relationship between more urban and more rural places and their representatives, as the two often compete for attracting credits and public funding. The split between the agglomeration policy and the policy for rural and mountainous areas, however, does too little to reduce institutional and policy fragmentation, in order to better support existing inter-dependencies among territories. Improved co-ordination between the agglomeration policy and the policy for rural and mountain areas can have a beneficial effect on sectoral policies that function as an enabler to rural innovation. Currently, the Federal Network on Coherent Urban-Rural Spatial Development is facilitating the co-ordination between the policy areas on the federal level. Evaluation reports have stated that existing co-operation mechanisms are insufficiently used and that sectoral policies and topics for rural and mountainous areas are dominating. While, agglomeration programmes provide a large amount of funding to urban areas, there is no equivalent for rural areas. This inhibits making use of synergies between policies and possibly better integrating rural and urban linkages. Research has also stated that there is a need to better define which issues co-operation between the policies could bring added value to and how clarifying roles between the existing bodies can make processes efficient (Schweizerische Eidgenossenschaft, 2019[64]).

Figure 3.7. Regional policy in the plan for coherent spatial development

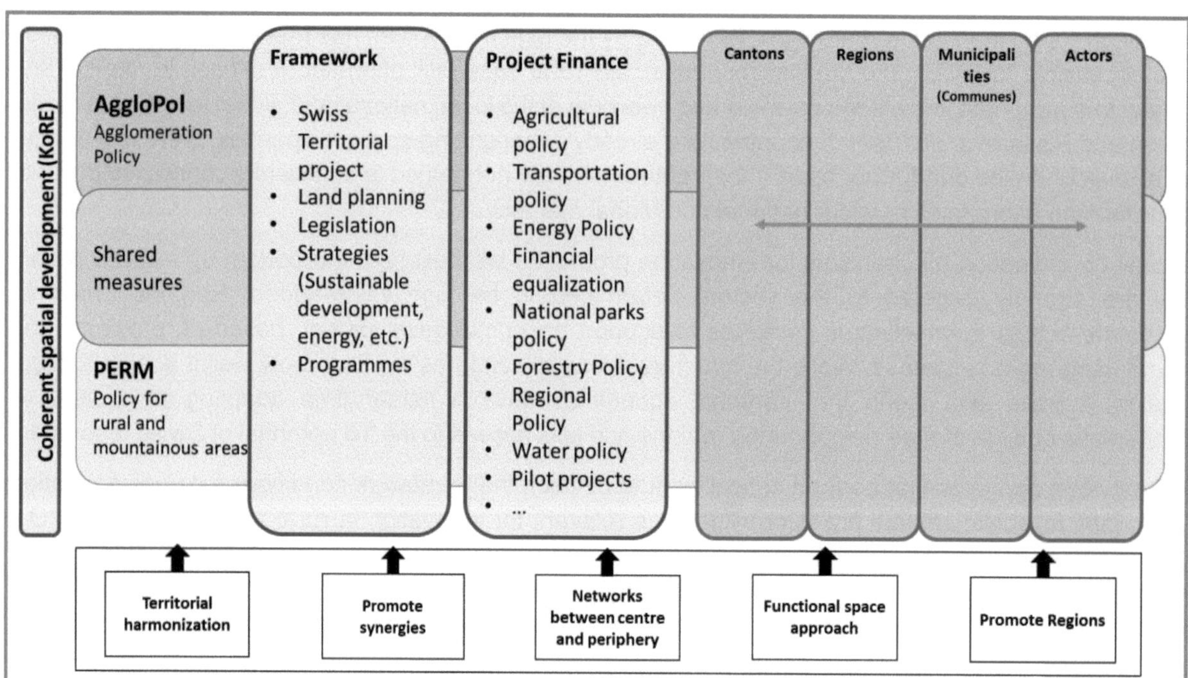

Note: AggloPol: Agglomeration policy; PERM: Policy for rural and mountainous areas; KoRE: Coherent spatial development.
Source: Provided by Federal Department of Economic Affairs, Education and Research EAER, State Secretariat for Economic Affairs SECO, Regional Policy and Spatial Planning DSRE, 2021.

In the context of rural-urban linkages for innovation, the Federal Network on Coherent Urban-Rural Spatial Development could provide added value in further investigating the topic of innovation. For instance, it could investigate and identify which sectoral policies could further strengthen rural-urban linkages and consequently benefit innovation. Furthermore, alignment and more effective co-ordination of the NRP and sectoral policies could also help increase the impact of the NRP, while not necessarily requiring additional funding. Some solutions for this are further explored in Chapter 4, with recommendations for different levels of co-operation between the Agri-Food Knowledge and Innovation System (AKIS) and the RIS.

Regionally, rural-urban coverage of innovation support is ensured through funding and programme conditionality that is agreed upon in ordinances to the NRP. The RIS has the purpose of providing support to regions with less access to resources than those of major urban centres. Their activities also seek to connect entrepreneurs with universities and other knowledge partners in urban centres to benefit innovation in rural areas as well. To address this, regional agencies are allowed to jointly apply for innovation funds for new initiatives through collaborations with metropolitan areas, with the condition that at least 50% of the expenditure on programmes (point of entry and coaching) must be done in non-metropolitan areas. These areas are defined by the NRP perimeter (Figure 3.4). In practical terms, this means that in large cities such as Basel and Geneva, RIS services can only happen because of co-operation with more rural cantons through the RIS. Furthermore, some cantons (Aargau, Solothurn and Zurich) are not part of any NRP-RIS but have their own programmes. Little can be said about how far they contribute to establishing rural-urban links and cater to more rural entrepreneurs.

In 2011, the territorial review of Switzerland (OECD, 2011[9]) stated, that NRP would gain coherence if it covered all regions. It argued that extending the NRP's territorial coverage can reduce economic fragmentation and support polycentric development. Furthermore, it was said that the focus on rural, mountainous and border areas could be broadened to the whole Swiss territory, in order to better take into account existing or potential linkages across regions, especially in terms of urban-rural linkages (OECD, 2011[9]). To this date, the discussion on the enlargement of the perimeter could not be agreed upon, notably because mountainous cantons fear a decrease in assistance for structurally weak regions. Therefore, the above-mentioned 50% funding compromise was created. According to many stakeholders, this compromise does not hinder building linkages between rural and urban areas but continues to ensure financial support primarily targeting less urbanised regions. Yet, some demand a further limitation to the NRP perimeter, to ensure more money is spent on the least urban areas. Formalising this type of compromise further could help ensure stability and provide assurance for all actors involved.

To enhance rural-urban partnerships for rural innovation in Switzerland and reduce institutional and policy fragmentation. The role of the Federal Network on Coherent Urban-Rural Spatial Development as a facilitator could the strengthened. Specifically, the network should assess ongoing co-ordination needs between the agglomeration policy and the policy for rural and mountainous areas. Furthermore, it should also be used to identify synergies for sectoral policies (transport, education, energy, etc.) that have the power to improve innovation in rural areas through much-needed rural-urban links. Therefore, the network should discuss the role of innovation in all sectoral policies and improve alignment and synergies between the NRP and other sectoral policies by focusing on rural-urban links.

Fostering university-industry partnerships in rural regions

Informal co-ordination mechanisms are important to build networks in rural regions. Nevertheless, informal co-ordination mechanisms do not always have the capacity, nor the right information to address the challenges that impact rural regions.

Switzerland has initiatives to build connections between universities and industrial partners. They are established to help generate new innovations, diffuse pre-existing innovations across territories and support the development of SMEs. These successful triple-helix initiatives in Switzerland are mostly university-industry partnerships, which tend to be university-led and focused on high-tech innovation. Rural regions without higher education institutions or high-tech industries are disadvantaged in this setup. Initiatives for innovation co-operation driven by demand from entrepreneurs and the private sector in rural areas can bring more locally driven opportunities to rural regions.

However, often these initiatives occur in denser areas, are driven by the research arm of the partnership and are focused on high-tech innovation. In some cases, antenna campuses of universities have been successful at building projects with local partners, but in areas where no universities are located, there are lower opportunities for innovation through this mechanism. In sparsely populated areas, antennas or university consortia with local research centres have been important for innovation, economic development, education and training in regions without universities (OECD, 2017[65]). Switzerland can benefit from the following action point:

- Promote new initiatives and programmes to better link entrepreneurs to researchers in rural regions.

- Encourage the development of the demand for university linkages among entrepreneurs, such that all research initiatives are not only led by the university teams.

- Establish innovation initiatives that better promote co-operation between entrepreneurs in rural areas and cities. This can be done through regional development strategies, smart specialisation or university-industry linkages that consult with local entrepreneurs to determine the scope, activity and initiative supporting innovation in rural areas. Examples of such initiatives can be found in Boxes 3.10 and 3.11.

- Re-enforce existing initiatives to establish university consortia or research institutions with antennas in rural areas tied to the local economic opportunities.

Box 3.10. Using regional ambassadors and brokers for cluster development strategies

Brainport Development, Eindhoven and South Holland Region, Netherlands

Brainport Development is a cluster collaboration platform that is directly incorporated into a regional development agency. It carries several independent networks that specialise in different activities such as sports, high technology, health technology, automobile industry, food technology, safety programmes, and a designer programme, and currently increasing clusters to include the high-tech software cluster, augmented reality and virtual reality cluster and integrated photonics. Brainport Development focuses on stimulating new projects, investing in start-ups and scale-ups, attracting foreign companies, and helping local companies go abroad. In recent years, the initiative also includes a human capital programme, including a talent programme.

There are a few characteristics that make Brainport stand out among other cluster specialisation initiatives which include:

- Strong attachment to partnership in the public sector, private sector and universities, which includes a board that is composed of the mayor of Eindhoven (location of headquarters), mayors of other participating municipalities, private sector representatives from local businesses, and university members.

- A bottom-up approach and a lack of pre-determination when using existing regional assets, starting from companies that jointly partner up to determine priorities in requesting cluster initiatives, are then accommodated by a project-based approach.

- The use of regional ambassadors as brokers, or "match-makers" to attract activities from national and international resources to the region and to build local buy-in, which contributes to a large part of the annual budget, and annual business investment into start-ups on site.

- The financial participation of all partners (central, regional, local, universities and private sector) in the elaboration of the services offered for the cluster strategy.

A few years after the success of Brainport, a new initiative to bring a similar model to South Holland in the western part of the Netherlands, was initiated. This region is characterised as a region with two big cities, some smaller ones and rural surroundings. The structure of the model in South Holland included several similar characteristics to the original Brainport. It was directed by the Economic Board South Holland, a high-level council that brings together industry, institutions and governments, in combination with the regional development agency, InnnovationQuarter, and therefore had a strong engagement with the private sector, local partners and universities that builds trust and buy-in from local communities. However, it also faced different challenges and opportunities from the original Brainport. They included the following:

- A more diversified mix of chairpersons, industry leaders and local leaders on the board, as a result of a more diversified economic structure and a larger geographical area with more municipalities.
- Difficulties in formulating a joint strategy and common goals due to the diversified economic structure and lack of strong regional cohesion.
- More participation from regional development agencies creates opportunities to mobilise more executive power for regional strategy.
- Many hidden champions with a good market position, and a short and local supply chain that are initially not well connected to regional ecosystems.
- Less informal networks create barriers, with more transparent rules for entry into the market as compared to the Brainport region.

Source: Author interview; Brainport Eindhoven (n.d.[66]), *Brainport Eindhoven*, https://brainporteindhoven.com/int/ (accessed 1 September, 2022).

Box 3.11. University-industry linkages for regional innovation

Encouraging joint projects between universities and firms are one of the strongest drivers of regional innovation across OECD countries. Regions that contain an important share of research universities or laboratories often more easily build connections and generate benefits from spill-overs. Governments tend to support these types of linkages through a variety of tools that include subsidies for joint endeavours, networking events or other kinds of in-kind and programme support.

Evidence from a recent study in Norway found that many successful initiatives are often determined by the characteristics of firms, rather than initiatives from university researchers (Atta-Owusu, Fitjar and Rodríguez-Pose, 2021[67]). When firms are open to collaborations, they are more likely to collaborate with universities that are nearby. However, incentives for universities are not always aligned. Universities may not necessarily gain as much from collaboration and, as they grow in success, they tend to weaken links with local and national firms.

Institute for Systems and Computer Engineering, Technology and Science (INESC TEC), Portugal

As one of the most influential research centres in Portugal, INESC TEC brings academics and companies together to contribute to the competitiveness of the Portuguese economy, while improving local societal impacts. INESC TEC has 13 R&D centres in 5 locations around the northern region in Braga, Porto and Vila Real, and focuses on bringing university and academic knowledge to businesses. Presently, its main sites are in the three cities. The institute has four R&D clusters that include the Power and Energy Cluster; Industry and Innovation Cluster; the Networked Intelligent Systems Cluster; and the Computer Science Cluster. The institute provides management and organisational services, including: legal support and human resource management help; business development services, through industry partnerships, technology licensing, funding opportunities and international outreach; and technical support including communications and business informatics. In 2017, INESC TEC was composed of 725 researchers and received 33% of funding from international sources.

Interface, Scotland, UK

In Scotland, Interface is a regional knowledge connection hub that is the prime tool for businesses to connect with universities looking to participate in partnerships for R&D. The hub has eight associated centres specialising in different sectors. Unlike initiatives that focus on finding businesses for academics who wish to explore areas of R&D, Interface is focused on helping to connect businesses to universities and finding matches that can support the firm's R&D competitively. The request for the linkage to occur comes from the initiative of the firm. Once an inquiry from a firm is received, dedicated staff works to match the firm with a university and find funding opportunities for their endeavours.

Academy for Smart Specialisation, Karlstad University and Region Värmland, Sweden

The regional government of Värmland, Sweden, leverages university-industry ties through its regional development and smart specialisation strategies, which now place the initiative within a local university (OECD, 2020[68]).

As part of a regional smart specialisation strategy, the regional government integrated the Academy for Smart Specialisation, an applied research facility with tailored training programmes and an interdisciplinary platform, into its region's Research and Innovation Strategy for Smart Specialisation 2015-2020. The initiative promotes new specialisation and skills in forest-based bioeconomy, ICT, healthcare, industry 4.0 and tourism with an approach reflecting the sustainability, inclusive growth and well-being goals of the regional development strategy.

While the success of smart specialisation in Värmland is attributed to the institutional "mobilisation" of regional actors, political agencies and place-based leadership, it also faced several challenges due to changes in regional governance, and a lack of funding and business engagement. To address some of these issues, the region of Värmland is now working on mainstreaming the academy within the local higher education institution at Karlstad University.

Source: Interface (n.d.[69]), *Interface: Homepage*, https://interface-online.org.uk/ (accessed on 1 September, 2022); INESC TEC (n.d.[70]), *INESC TEC: Homepage*, https://www.inesctec.pt/en (accessed on 1 September, 2022).

Co-ordination for addressing shortages in labour skill supply

One of the key challenges for rural regions is shortages in skills, and in particular digital skills. In a 2021 survey of regional government officials in OECD countries, skills shortages were one of the top barriers to innovation in rural regions (OECD, 2020[71]). Often this is an outcome of demographic change due to an ageing population and inter-regional migration patterns that often result in a "brain drain" (OECD, 2021[72]; 2020[13]). Often rural areas suffer from a loss of new talent that may either migrate because of work or training opportunities elsewhere. Yet, a relatively high-skilled population is important for innovation and start-ups need a skilled workforce to bring innovations to the market. While R&D investments are often thought of as critical for innovation for some regions, investments in human capital, education and training can encourage innovation focused on the well-being of rural regions to the forefront (OECD, forthcoming[31]). In Switzerland, this issue goes outside of the scope of the RIS mandate but is nevertheless a critical barrier for cantonal and regional authorities.

Among active labour market policy expenditures, the Swiss federal and cantonal governments primarily spend public funds to support reskilling across territories. According to a report from 2010, the largest spending on skilling for the labour force is on supported employment and rehabilitation, training, temporary employment in the public sector and intermittent pay (Duell et al., 2010[73]). Recent statistics on expenditure on initiatives for training and entrepreneurship through the public employment services indicate that training initiatives are the major source of government expenditure in 2018 targeted at reskilling and encouraging more start-up activities (Figure 3.8). In Switzerland, active labour market policies delivered through the public employment services are focused only on training, at 0.16% of GDP.[4] Cantonal and regional governments also deliver programmes to support regional development based on local needs and, as such, the offer for programmes to support labour market skilling is larger than just those provided by the public employment services.

Figure 3.8. Active labour market policies for skills and start-up support

Expenditure on programmes to support skills upgrading and new entrepreneurship, 2018

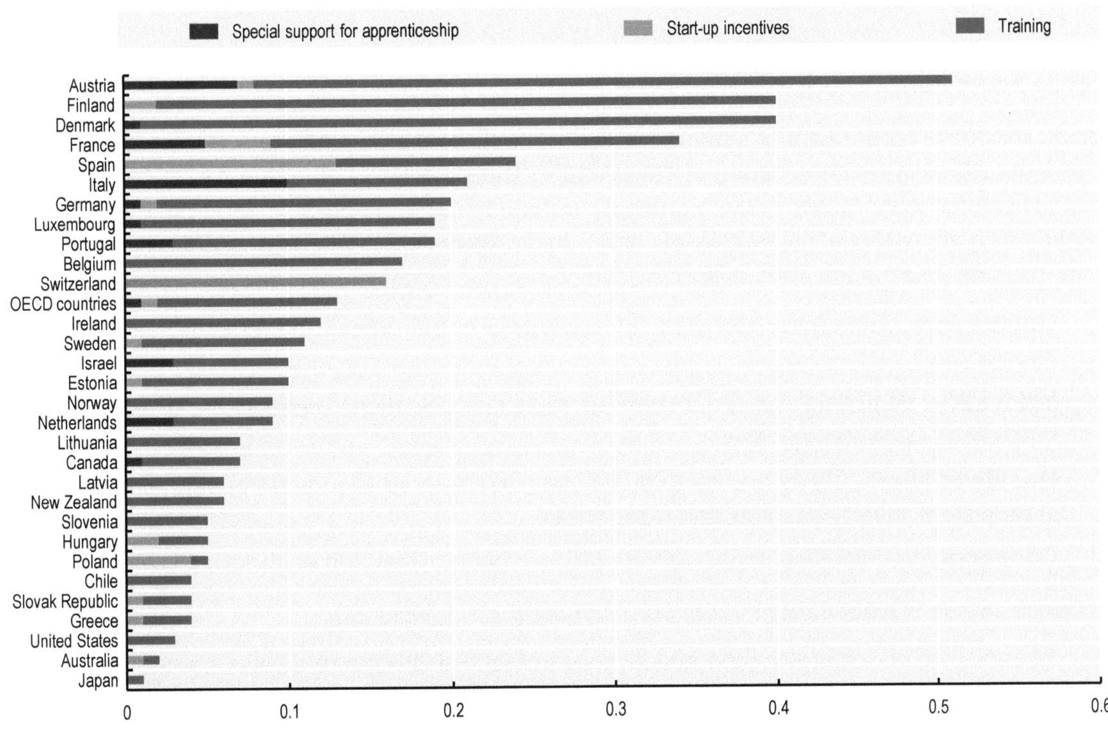

Note: All values are reported as expenditures as a share of GDP. Training expenditures include institutional training, integrated training and workplace training. The category for job rotation was excluded as only Finland and Spain included expenditures for such initiatives at 0.01% of GDP. The figure above excludes the Czech Republic and Mexico, which have no reported expenditure for such initiatives.
Source: OECD (2021[74]), *Active Labour Market Policies: Connecting People with Jobs*, https://www.oecd.org/employment/activation.htm (accessed on 15 June 2021).

Currently, Switzerland has regional and cantonal employment councils but it is unclear whether they are able to meet the needs of rural regions. More bold actions such as setting up an inter-agency co-ordination body at the centre of government that addresses skills and other cross-cutting issues, such as the one in the US described in Box 3.12, may be worth considering. For the most part, individuals are responsible for seeking retraining courses. Upskilling is often an initiative by the employee or contingent on the willingness of the employer. In other OECD countries, such as France, support for continuous training and upskilling is individualised and is provided as a benefit to workers rather than an offer through employers (Perez and Vourc'h, 2020[75]). Such an arrangement removes requirements to be employed or to direct skills towards current employment needs for gaining access to skills training. In its most recent version, the individual training accounts also allow for training certification across all fields. While some local employers provide ample opportunities for upskilling, it is not clear that individuals would always have the same preferences as employers for training needs. Furthermore, services focusing on upskilling workers through cantonal initiatives or the public employment system could further benefit from a regional perspective. This includes initiatives that target providing support for new entrants in the labour market (such as apprentices), start-up entrepreneurship training, continuous training and lifelong learning (Fazekas and Field, 2013[76]) as well as programmes that target regional integration of migrants into the labour market (Liebig, Kohls and Krause,

2012[77]; OECD, forthcoming[78]). In particular, training in formal management practices is important for innovation, in particular in small businesses. Similarly, the effective adoption of automation and digitalisation requires strong managerial skills in SMEs. In this regard, evidence suggests that targeted programmes that combine ICT solutions with management training and advisory services can be especially effective for innovation (Cusmano, Koreen and Pissareva, 2018[63]).

Box 3.12. High-level co-ordination on rural affairs in the US

The White House Rural Council, US

Under an executive order of the Obama-Biden Administration, the US undertook a mission to bring the concerns of rural areas into the centre of government. The initiative, in an attempt to improve the voice of rural constitutes in the policy-making process, worked to reinforce co-ordination on a wide range of issues across government at different levels and within different agencies. The objectives of the council were to focus on job creation and economic development by focusing on:

1. **Opportunity**: Increasing the flow of capital to rural areas, job creation and workforce development.
2. **Innovation**: Including the expansion of telecommunications, renewable energy and new markets for rural communities.
3. **Quality of life**: Including access to quality healthcare, education and housing, and particularly in persistent poverty counties and tribal areas.
4. **Conservation**: Including expansion of outdoor opportunities and economic growth.

The council carried this out through three core functions which included:

1. Streamlining and improving the effectiveness of federal programmes serving rural America.
2. Engaging stakeholders, including farmers, ranchers and local citizens, on issues and solutions in rural communities.
3. Promoting and co-ordinating private sector partnerships.

The Rural Council Members were chaired by the Secretary of Agriculture and included 30 government bodies including the Department of Commerce, the Department of Labor, the Department of Education, the Department of the Treasury, the Office of Science and Technology Policy, the Small Business Administration, the Council of Economic Advisers and regional authorities such as the Delta Regional Authority and the Appalachian Regional Commission.

Source: U.S. White House (2022[79]), *White House Rural Council*, https://obamawhitehouse.archives.gov/administration/eop/rural-council, (accessed on 1 September, 2022).

Key messages

- Co-ordination with agencies that target upskilling, lifelong learning and educational programmes that enable students to discover their creative and entrepreneurial potential are particularly important for these regions.
- Co-ordination with cantonal and public employment partners on regional skills development and digital skills strategies is an avenue for integration of concerns over the perceived limited level of skills in different regions.

References

ARE (n.d.), *Projets-modèles pour un développement territorial durable 2020-2024*, Office fédéral du dévelopment regional, https://www.are.admin.ch/are/fr/home/developpement-et-amenagement-du-territoire/programmes-et-projets/projets-modeles-pour-un-developpement-territorial-durable/2020-2024.html. [46]

Atta-Owusu, K., R. Fitjar and A. Rodríguez-Pose (2021), "What drives university-industry collaboration? Research excellence or firm collaboration strategy?", *Technological Forecasting and Social Change*, Vol. 173, p. 121084, https://doi.org/10.1016/j.techfore.2021.121084. [67]

B,S,S Volkswirtschaftliche Beratung AG (2018), *Regionale Innovationssysteme (RIS) Evaluation und RIS-Konzept 2020+*, https://regiosuisse.ch/sites/default/files/2018-12/RIS%20Evaluation%20und%20RIS-Konzept%202020%2B%20DE.pdf. [8]

BIS (n.d.), *Solutions for Business: Simplified Business Support*, Department for Business Innovation and Skills, London, http://www.bis.gov.uk/policies/enterprise-andbusiness-support/solutions-for-business-simplified-business-support (accessed on 1 September 2022). [56]

BMWi (2018), *Reallabore als Testräume für Innovation und Regulierung*, Bundesministerium für Wirtschaft und Energie, https://www.bmwi.de/Redaktion/DE/Downloads/S-T/strategiepapier-reallabore.pdf?__blob=publicationFile&v=16. [44]

Brainport Eindhoven (n.d.), *Brainport Eindhoven: Homepage*, https://brainporteindhoven.com/int/ (accessed on 1 September 2022). [66]

CFNC (n.d.), *Supporting Canada's 267 Community Futures Organizations*, Community Futures Network of Canada, https://communityfuturescanada.ca/ (accessed on 1 September 2022). [59]

Council for Spatial Planning (2019), *Megatrends und Raumentwicklung Schweiz*, https://regiosuisse.ch/sites/default/files/2019-07/megatrends_de.pdf. [27]

Cusmano, L., M. Koreen and L. Pissareva (2018), "2018 OECD Ministerial Conference on SMEs: Key Issues Paper", *OECD SME and Entrepreneurship Papers*, No. 7, OECD Publishing, Paris, https://doi.org/10.1787/90c8823c-en. [63]

Deutscher Bundestag (2018), *Reallabore, Living Labs und Citizen Science-Projekte in Europa*, https://www.bundestag.de/resource/blob/563290/9d6da7676c82fe6777e6df85c7a7d573/wd-8-020-18-pdf-data.pdf.   [51]

Duell, N. et al. (2010), "Activation Policies in Switzerland", *OECD Social, Employment and Migration Working Papers*, No. 112, OECD Publishing, Paris, https://doi.org/10.1787/5km4hd7r28f6-en.   [73]

e2 Entrepreneurial Ecosystems (n.d.), *Homepage*, http://www.energizingentrepreneurs.org.   [36]

EC (2021), "Long-term vision for rural areas: For stronger, connected, resilient, prosperous EU rural areas", European Commission, https://ec.europa.eu/regional_policy/en/newsroom/news/2021/06/30-06-2021-long-term-vision-for-rural-areas-for-stronger-connected-resilient-prosperous-eu-rural-areas.   [29]

Egli, R. (2020), "Regionale Innovationssysteme (RIS) der Regionalpolitik (NRP) aus der Perspektive peripherer Regionen", https://regiosuisse.ch/sites/default/files/2020-04/Fachartikel%20regiosuisse%20Regionale%20Innovationssysteme%20%28RIS%29%20der%20Regionalpolitik%20%28NRP%29%20aus%20der%20Perspektive%20peripherer%20Regionen.pdf.   [16]

Farmreal (n.d.), *Homepage*, https://farmreal.pt/en (accessed on 19 August 2022).   [50]

Fazekas, M. and S. Field (2013), *A Skills beyond School Review of Switzerland*, OECD Reviews of Vocational Education and Training, OECD Publishing, Paris, https://doi.org/10.1787/9789264062665-en.   [76]

Fedlex (2012), *Federal Act on the Promotion of Research and Innovation*, https://www.fedlex.admin.ch/eli/cc/2013/786/en.   [3]

Find Business Support (n.d.), *Homepage*, https://findbusinesssupport.gov.scot/ (accessed on 1 September 2022).   [57]

Freshwater, D. et al. (2019), "Business development and the growth of rural SMEs", *OECD Regional Development Working Papers*, No. 2019/07, OECD Publishing, Paris, https://doi.org/10.1787/74256611-en.   [19]

Government of Canada (2022), *Women Entrepreneurship Strategy*, https://ised-isde.canada.ca/site/women-entrepreneurship-strategy/en.   [38]

Government of Canada (2021), *Women's Enterprise Initiative in British Columbia*, https://www.canada.ca/en/pacific-economic-development/services/support/womens-enterprise.html (accessed on 19 August 2022).   [32]

Government of Canada (2021), *Women's Enterprise Initiative in the Prairie Provinces*, https://www.canada.ca/en/prairies-economic-development/services/support/womens-enterprise.html (accessed on 19 August 2022).   [33]

IEA (2021), *Net Zero by 2050*, International Energy Agency, https://www.iea.org/reports/net-zero-by-2050.   [40]

INESC TEC (n.d.), *INESC TEC: Homepage*, https://www.inesctec.pt/en (accessed on 1 September 2022).   [70]

Innosuisse (2022), "Innovation boosters", Swiss Innovation Agency. [5]

Innosuisse (2022), *Mission*, Swiss Innovation Agency, https://www.innosuisse.ch/inno/en/home/about-us/mission.html. [4]

Interface (n.d.), *Interface: Homepage*, https://interface-online.org.uk/ (accessed on 1 September 2022). [69]

Jungsberg, L. et al. (2020), "Key actors in community-driven social innovation in rural areas in the Nordic countries", *Journal of Rural Studies*, Vol. 79, pp. 276-285, https://doi.org/10.1016/j.jrurstud.2020.08.004. [21]

Lee, N. and A. Rodriguez-Pose (2012), "Innovation and spatial inequality in Europe and USA", *Journal of Economic Geography*, Vol. 13/1, pp. 1-22, https://doi.org/10.1093/jeg/lbs022. [20]

Liebig, T., S. Kohls and K. Krause (2012), "The labour market integration of immigrants and their children in Switzerland". [77]

Mahroum, S. et al. (2007), *Rural innovation*. [22]

Mayer, H. (2020), "Slow innovation in Europe's peripheral regions: Innovation beyond acceleration", in Döringer, S. and J. Eder (eds.), *Schlüsselakteure der Regionalentwicklung - welche Perspektiven bietet Entrepreneurship für ländliche Räume?*, Verlag der Österreichischen Akademie der Wissenschaften. [14]

Mayer, H., A. Habersetzer and R. Meili (2016), "Rural-urban linkages and sustainable regional development: The role of entrepreneurs in linking peripheries and centers", *Sustainability*, Vol. 8/745, https://doi.org/10.3390/su8080745. [18]

McKenzie, D. and C. Woodruff (2021), "What works in training entrepreneurs?", https://voxdev.org/topic/firms-trade/what-works-training-entrepreneurs. [47]

OECD (2021), *Active Labour Market Policies: Connecting People with Jobs*, OECD, Paris, https://www.oecd.org/employment/activation.htm (accessed on 15 June 2021). [74]

OECD (2021), *Delivering Quality Education and Health Care to All: Preparing Regions for Demographic Change*, OECD Rural Studies, OECD Publishing, Paris, https://doi.org/10.1787/83025c02-en. [72]

OECD (2021), *Embracing Innovation in Government*, https://trends.oecd-opsi.org/. [52]

OECD (2021), *OECD Regional Outlook 2021: Addressing COVID-19 and Moving to Net Zero Greenhouse Gas Emissions*, OECD Publishing, Paris, https://doi.org/10.1787/17017efe-en. [39]

OECD (2020), *Questionnaire on Enhancing Innovation in Rural Regions*, OECD, Paris. [71]

OECD (2020), *Rural Well-being: Geography of Opportunities*, OECD Rural Studies, OECD Publishing, Paris, https://doi.org/10.1787/d25cef80-en. [13]

OECD (2020), *The Circular Economy in Cities and Regions: Synthesis Report*, OECD Urban Studies, OECD Publishing, Paris, https://doi.org/10.1787/10ac6ae4-en. [41]

OECD (2020), *The Geography of Higher Education: Evaluation of the Academy for Smart Specialisation*, OECD, Paris, https://www.oecd.org/cfe/smes/Evaluation_Academy_Smart_Specialisation.pdf. [68]

OECD (2019), *OECD Regional Outlook 2019: Leveraging Megatrends for Cities and Rural Areas*, OECD Publishing, Paris, https://doi.org/10.1787/9789264312838-en. [10]

OECD (2017), *OECD Territorial Reviews: Northern Sparsely Populated Areas*, OECD Territorial Reviews, OECD Publishing, Paris, https://doi.org/10.1787/9789264268234-en. [65]

OECD (2015), *The Innovation Imperative: Contributing to Productivity, Growth and Well-Being*, OECD Publishing, Paris, https://doi.org/10.1787/9789264239814-en. [62]

OECD (2013), *Rural-Urban Partnerships: An Integrated Approach to Economic Development*, OECD Rural Policy Reviews, OECD Publishing, Paris, https://doi.org/10.1787/9789264204812-en. [60]

OECD (2012), *OECD Reviews of Regional Innovation: Central and Southern Denmark 2012*, OECD Reviews of Regional Innovation, OECD Publishing, Paris, https://doi.org/10.1787/9789264178748-en. [35]

OECD (2012), *OECD Territorial Reviews: Småland-Blekinge, Sweden 2012*, OECD Territorial Reviews, OECD Publishing, Paris, https://doi.org/10.1787/9789264169517-en. [34]

OECD (2011), *OECD Territorial Reviews: Switzerland 2011*, OECD Publishing Paris, https://doi.org/10.1787/9789264092723-en. [9]

OECD (forthcoming), *Multi-level Governance Arrangements for Migrant Integration: A Policy Perspective*, OECD Publishing, Paris. [78]

OECD (forthcoming), *Understanding Innovation in Rural Regions*, OECD Publishing, Paris. [31]

OECD/EC (2020), "Policy brief on recent developments in youth entrepreneurship", *OECD SME and Entrepreneurship Papers*, No. 19, OECD Publishing, Paris, https://doi.org/10.1787/5f5c9b4e-en. [30]

Perez, C. and A. Vourc'h (2020), "Individualising training access schemes: France – the Compte Personnel de Formation (Personal Training Account – CPF)", *OECD Social, Employment and Migration Working Papers*, No. 245, OECD Publishing, Paris, https://doi.org/10.1787/301041f1-en. [75]

Regio Basiliensis (2019), *Audit RIS Region Basel-Jura*, https://www.regbas.ch/de/assets/File/downloads/Audit_RIS_Basel-Jura_Schlussbericht_def_DE.pdf. [54]

Regio Basiliensis (n.d.), *Interkantonales Umsetzungsprogramm zur Regionalpolitik 2020-2023 der Region Basel-Jura*, https://www.regbas.ch/de/assets/File/UP-Basel-Jura_NRP_2020-2023_24_6_2020.pdf. [25]

regiosuisse (2018), *Regionale Innovationssysteme (RIS) : Evaluation und RIS-Konzept 2020+*, https://regiosuisse.ch/sites/default/files/2018-12/RIS%20Evaluation%20und%20RIS-Konzept%202020%2B%20DE.pdf. [55]

regiosuisse (n.d.), *Eine Praxis-Toolbox zur Förderung der Kreislaufwirtschaft in Regionen, Gemeinden und Städten*, https://regiosuisse.ch/kreislaufwirtschaft. [43]

regiosuisse (n.d.), *Financial Instruments and Measures within the Framework of the NRP*, https://regiosuisse.ch/index.php/en/financial-instruments-and-measures-within-framework-nrp. [11]

regiosuisse (n.d.), *Wissensgemeinschaft «Kreislaufwirtschaft und Regionalentwicklung»*, https://regiosuisse.ch/wissensgemeinschaft-kreislaufwirtschaft-und-regionalentwicklung. [42]

Schweizerische Eidgenossenschaft (2019), *Agglomerationspolitik des Bundes 2016+*, https://www.are.admin.ch/are/de/home/staedte-und-agglomerationen/strategie-und-planung/agglomerationspolitik-des-bundes-2016-.html. [64]

SCINNOPOLI (n.d.), *Scanning Innovation Policy Impact*, http://www.scinnopoli.eu. [53]

SECO (2020), *Botschaft über die Standortförderung des Bundes 2020-2023*, Staatssekretariat für Wirtschaft, https://www.seco.admin.ch/seco/de/home/Standortfoerderung/botschaft_standortfoerderung/Botschaft_zur_Standortfoerderung2020-2023.html. [6]

SECO (2020), "NRP-Pilotmassnahmen für die Berggebiete 2020-2023", Staatssekretariat für Wirtschaft, https://regiosuisse.ch/sites/default/files/2020-07/NRP_Pilotmassnahmen_DasWichtigsteInK%C3%BCrze_Juli2020_DE.pdf. [12]

SECO (2020), *Weissbuch Regionalpolitik*, Staatssekretariat für Wirtschaft, https://regiosuisse.ch/sites/default/files/2020-07/SECO%20%282020%29%20%C2%ABWeissbuch%20Regionalpolitik%C2%BB.pdf. [17]

SECO (2018), *Concept RIS 2020+*, Staatssekretariat für Wirtschaft, https://regiosuisse.ch/sites/default/files/2018-12/RIS%20Concept%20RIS%202020%2B%20FR.pdf. [15]

SECO (2017), *The New Regional Policy of the Federal Government (brochure)*, State Secretariat for Economic Affairs. [7]

SERI (2016), *Research and Innovation in Switzerland 2016*, State Secretariat for Education, Research and Innovation, https://www.sbfi.admin.ch/sbfi/en/home/services/publications/data-base-publications/research-and-innovation.html. [2]

Shearmur, R., C. Carrincazeaux and D. Doloreux (2016), *The geographies of innovations: beyond one-size-fits-all*, Edward Elgar Publishing, https://doi.org/10.4337/9781784710774.00006. [23]

SIPBB (n.d.), *Swiss Smart Factory*, Switzerland Innovation Park Biel/Bienne AG, https://www.sipbb.ch/en/forschung/swiss-smart-factory/. [45]

Smart Rural 21 (n.d.), *Penela*, Smart Rural Areas in the 21 Century, https://www.smartrural21.eu/villages/penela_pt/. [49]

Swiss Federal Council (2018), *Overview of Innovation Policy*, https://www.sbfi.admin.ch/sbfi/en/home/services/publications/data-base-publications/innovation-policy.html. [1]

U.S. Department of Commerce (2022), "Women-owned and Indigenous small businesses thrive with EDA and MBDA support", https://www.commerce.gov/news/blog/2022/03/women-owned-and-indigenous-small-businesses-thrive-eda-and-mbda-support. [37]

U.S. Government (n.d.), *Rural Partners Network*, https://www.rural.gov/. [58]

Veneri, P. (2018), "Urban spatial structure in OECD cities: Is urban population decentralising or clustering?", *Regional Science*, Vol. 97/4, pp. 1355-1374, https://doi.org/10.1111/pirs.12300. [61]

White House (2022), *White House Rural Council*, https://obamawhitehouse.archives.gov/administration/eop/rural-council. [79]

Wilkinson, A. (2017), *Strategic Foresight Primer*, European Political Strategy Centre. [28]

Wojan, T. and T. Parker (2017), *Innovation in the rural nonfarm economy: its effect on job and earnings growth, 2010-2014*. [24]

World Bank (2020), "Global experiences from regulatory sandboxes", World Bank, Washington, DC, https://openknowledge.worldbank.org/handle/10986/34789. [48]

Zentralschweiz innovativ (2020), *Zinno-Ideencheck für Berggebiete*, https://www.zentralschweiz-innovativ.ch/innovationangebot/ideenscheck_berggebiete/. [26]

Notes

[1] For more information, see https://www.oecd.org/regional/regional-policy/thenewruralparadigmpoliciesandgovernance.htm

[2] Anecdotally, this has been associated to a rise in exchange rates that crowded out R&D jobs in 2017. Early analysis with the 2019 updates in the R&D survey seems to suggest that R&D jobs increased from 2017 to 2019, but no knowledge of the distribution of jobs over territories or sectors is currently known.

[3] See Pa.Iv 20.433, https://www.parlament.ch/en/ratsbetrieb/suche-curia-vista/geschaeft?AffairId=20200433.

[4] Additional expenditure on active labour market policies and related programmes are administered by cantonal agencies, rather than specifically through public employment services.

4 The agricultural innovation system in Switzerland

This chapter describes the Swiss agricultural innovation system (AIS). It identifies the actors in agricultural innovation and their roles, describes the main trends in public investments in agricultural research and development (R&D), discusses the impact of agricultural policies on AIS, and describes initiatives to foster agri-food innovation. It also depicts institutional co-ordination between regional innovation systems (RIS) and the Federal Office for Agriculture's (FOAG) advisory services at the canton level.

Switzerland is a small open economy with a high gross domestic product (GDP) per capita and relatively low inflation and unemployment. Framework conditions for research and innovation (R&I) in Switzerland are remarkably good, including a strong and stable macroeconomy and institutional framework, high quality of life, significant equality, reliable legal framework, sophisticated financial system and generally favourable taxation, among others. Innovation also benefits from a strong human resource base with a well-educated labour force, high investment in R&D, a strong science base, outstanding innovation performance of the economy and good positioning in international networks. Switzerland is a federal country with a federal innovation policy. There are national programmes and initiatives but no centralised innovation policy (OECD, 2021[1]).

The following sections of this chapter outline the actors and funding in the Swiss agricultural innovation system (AIS), agricultural policies in Switzerland, and specific Swiss initiatives that foster agri-food innovation and institutional co-ordination between the RIS, FOAG and cantonal offices.

Scene-setting for the Swiss AIS

Agriculture plays a relatively minor and declining role in the Swiss economy. In 2017, it contributed to only 0.7% of GDP and 2.6% of total employment (World Bank, 2021[2]). However, the sector is perceived as an important element in maintaining food security, an economic pillar in decentralised settlement and mountainous regions, and as a provider of environmental benefits and maintenance of cultural landscapes, all of which are highly valued by Swiss society.

Agricultural policies in Switzerland seek to find a balanced solution for addressing a variety of commercial, social and environmental objectives. The result is a system of market protection in combination with a set of payments to farmers that provides income support as well as incentives for certain types of farming practices.

Farmers are highly supported by agricultural policies such as broad market price support measures and direct payments. This protection allows maintaining land and agricultural activities for non-productive uses. It also slows structural adjustment and can negatively affect innovation and sustainable productivity. As farmers receive large subsidies, these can create disincentives for innovation and sustainable productivity growth. As these subsidies decrease, there is more room for innovation services that support farmers, the agri-food chain and related services industries.

Business development, innovation, and competitiveness of the farm sector and the food industry are hindered by trade policies that raise the prices for imported inputs and shield producers from competition. Although the level of agricultural support in Switzerland, as measured by the Producer Support Estimate (PSE), has declined gradually, it is still one of the highest among OECD countries. Support to farmers (as a percentage of gross farm receipts) declined from close to 80% of gross farm receipts in the late 1980s to slightly less than 50% in 2020 (OECD, 2021[3]).

The Swiss AIS is sophisticated and advanced. It is comprised of national institutions (FOAG, Secretariat for Education, Research and Innovation [SERI], the Swiss Innovation Agency Innosuisse, the Swiss National Science Foundation [SNSF], the Swiss Confederation's centre of excellence for agricultural research Agroscope, etc.) that provide the general (agricultural) innovation framework and fund and/or carry out agricultural R&D. The Swiss AIS is also composed of cantonal agricultural offices that implement agricultural policy (direct payments and support for structural improvements) and execute advisory services and other agricultural matters. The role of the private sector and the public-private initiatives (e.g. AGRIDEA, Star'Terre) has been crucial for the sector.

General investment in research is relevant and high in the Swiss innovation system (OECD, 2014[4]). Both the public and the private sector invest heavily in research, and research intensity is above the OECD median. Public expenditure on R&D makes up a significant share of the government budget, accounting for 3.37% of GDP in 2017 (World Bank, 2021[5]). As a share of GDP, public expenditure on R&D is higher than the OECD median, placing Switzerland in the top half of OECD performers (3.5% of GDP in 2019). Higher education expenditure on R&D is among the highest in the OECD area (Figure 4.1).

An important part of the public expenditure on R&D goes to research at Swiss universities and research centres such as the Swiss Federal Institutes of Technology (ETH Zurich and EPFL), which include research institutes like the Paul Scherrer Institute (PSI), the Swiss Institute for Materials Science and Technology (EMPA) and the Universities of Basel, Bern, Geneva, Svizzera Italiana (USI) and Zurich, among others. These universities and research institutes are well placed in global rankings of world-class universities and publications. They received, in 2019, about a 61% of total R&D funding from the public sector (Table 4.1).

Figure 4.1. Science and innovation in Switzerland

Comparative performance of national science and innovation system, 2014

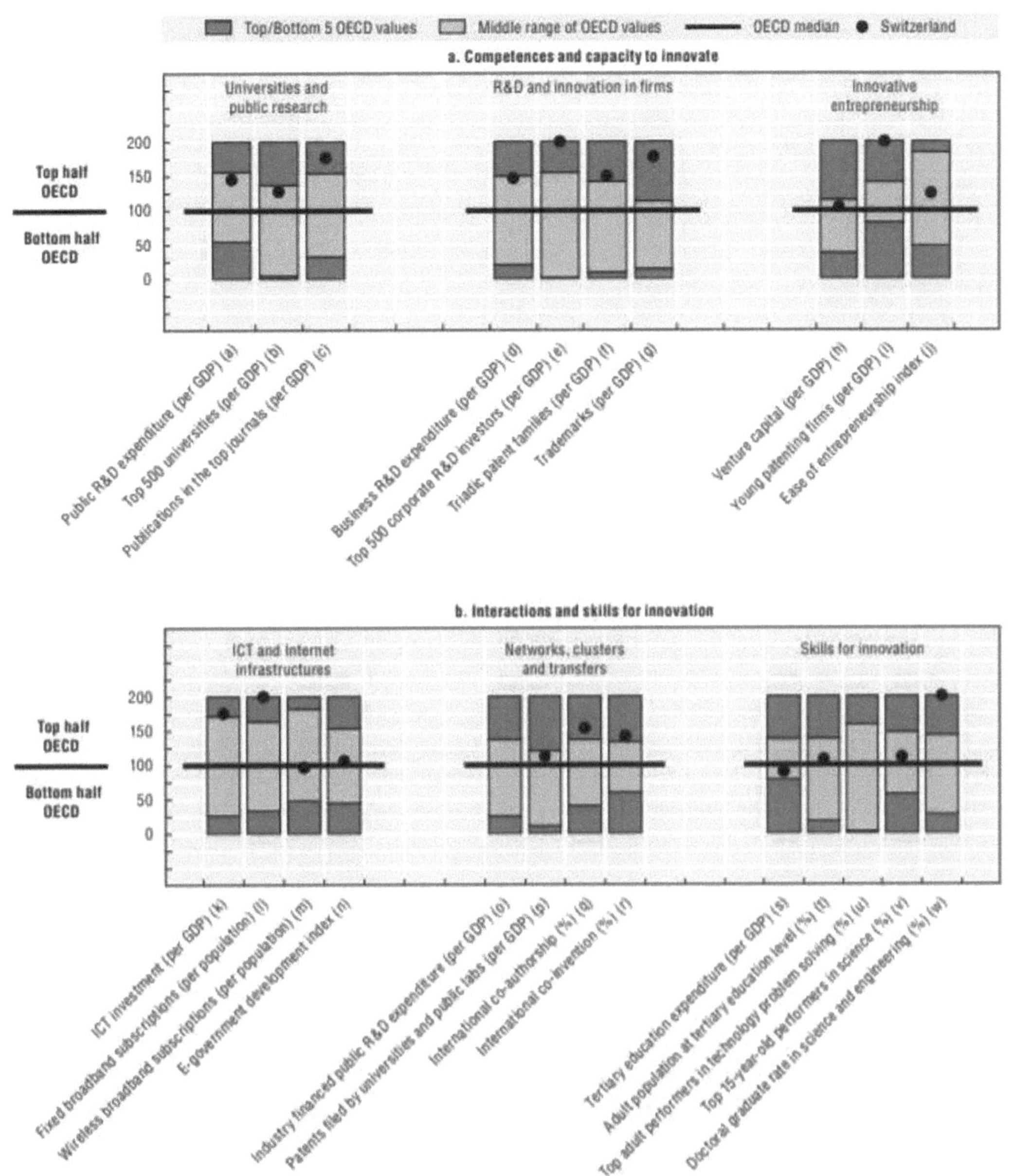

Source: OECD (2016[6]), *OECD Science, Technology and Innovation Outlook 2016*, https://dx.doi.org/10.1787/sti_in_outlook-2016-en.

Table 4.1. Public Budget Outlays on Research and Development by purpose, 2019

Item	Current Million CHF	Percentage
Research financed by the General University Funds (FGU)	4 319.8	61.43
Other civil research[1]	1 862.6	26.49
Political and social systems, organisation and processes	198.4	2.82
Exploration and exploitation of space	183.5	2.61
Industrial production and technology	169.8	2.41
Agriculture	155.4	2.21
Energy	42.9	0.61
Defence	25.8	0.37
Environment	23.1	0.33
Health	16.9	0.24
Education	12.6	0.18
Transport, telecommunications and other infrastructure	9.5	0.14
Exploration and exploitation of the terrestrial environment	8.9	0.13
Culture, leisure activities, ideology and media	2.7	0.04
Total public budgetary allocations in R&D	**7 032.0**	**100.00**

Note:
1. Non-distributable research.
Source: FSO (2021[7]), *Federal Statistics Office*, https://www.bfs.admin.ch/bfs/en/home.html.

Nevertheless, some limitations faced by the innovation framework include the lack of competition in some sectors of the economy that sometimes reduces the incentives to innovate. Barriers to entrepreneurship are still high: these include difficulties in financing new innovative businesses. Moreover, there is no well-defined national innovation policy framework (see Chapter 3 for more details).

Actors and funding of the Swiss AIS

Agricultural innovation is the process whereby individuals or organisations bring new or existing products, processes or ways of the organisation into use for the first time in a specific context in order to increase effectiveness, competitiveness, resilience to shocks or environmental sustainability. They thereby contribute to food security and nutrition, economic development and sustainable natural resource management (OECD, 2019[8]). The Swiss AIS is fully integrated into the general innovation policy and institutional framework. The economy-wide framework for science, technology and innovation provides the underlying incentive structure in all sectors of the economy (see Chapter 3 for more details).

AIS involve a wide range of actors who enable, guide, fund, perform and facilitate innovation. The key players include policy makers, researchers, teachers, advisors, farmers, private companies and consumers. AIS around the world are increasingly driven by economy-wide process and organisational innovations, developments in information and communication technology (ICT) and the bioeconomy.

The Swiss AIS is highly sophisticated and advanced and is comprised of national institutions that provide the general agricultural innovation framework and fund and/or carry out agricultural R&D. The Swiss AIS is also comprised of cantonal agricultural offices that provide advisory services and also implement agricultural policy. Table 4.1 shows a diagram depicting its main institutions.

Figure 4.2. The Swiss AIS

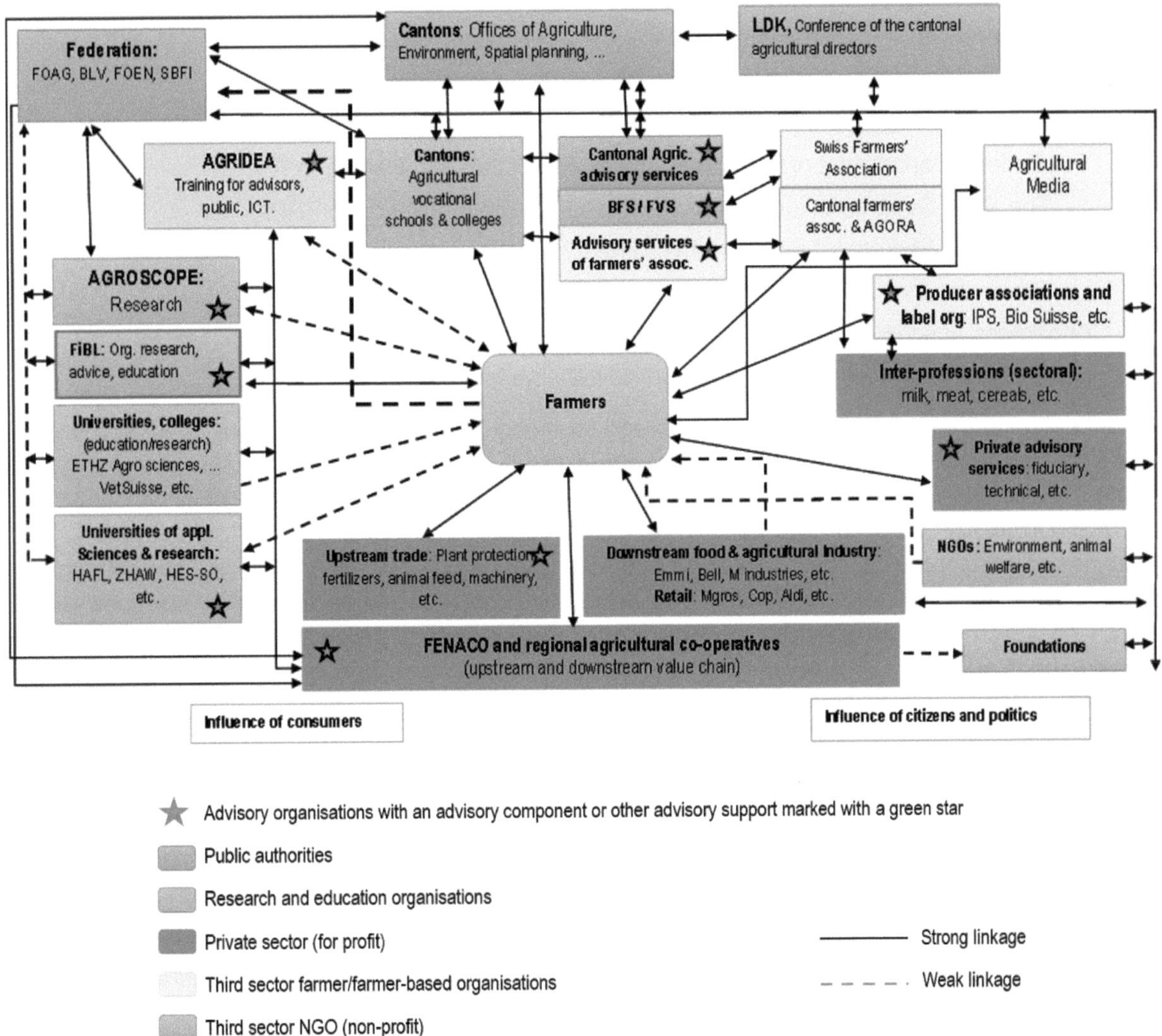

Note: This figure is attributed to AGRIDEA (2021[9]). Abbreviations used in this graphic are original and refer to German names. They include BLV, which is FSVO (Federal Food Safety and Veterinary Office) and SBFI which is SERI.

Source: AGRIDEA (2021[9])), *AKIS and Advisory Services in Switzerland*, Swiss Association for the Development of Agriculture and Rural Areas.

Actors in the AIS

R&D institutes

The government plays a role in the governance and funding of the AIS, by setting, implementing and monitoring policy, as well as evaluating programmes, policies, knowledge and R&D organisations.

Knowledge generators include universities, research institutes, government bodies and companies. Most public research takes place in universities and they are the main actors in public research. There are more than 50 accredited university colleges, universities or other organisers of higher education, with at least 1 university and/or university college in every canton (Swiss Universities, 2021[10]). Apart from universities, some research institutes and private and public actors offer knowledge to the food and agriculture sectors.

Research is carried out by universities, applied science universities and vocational schools and colleges, while knowledge transfer and advisory services are carried out by cantons and certain private institutions.

Key public institutions involved in innovation in agriculture and the food and nutrition sector at the national level are:

- The Federal Office for Agriculture (FOAG).
- The Federal Food Safety and Veterinary Office (FSVO).
- The Federal Office for the Environment (FOEN).
- The Federal Department of Economic Affairs, Education and Research (EAER):
  - The State Secretariat for Education, Research and Innovation (SERI).
  - The State Secretariat for Economic Affairs (SECO).
  - The Swiss Innovation Agency (Innosuisse).
- 26 cantons agricultural offices.
- The Swiss National Science Foundation (SNSF), an independent agency.

Main education and research institutions in the agri-food sector are the Swiss Federal Research Institute for the Agri-food Sector (Agroscope), the Swiss Federal Institute of Technology (ETH Zurich), the Research Institute of Organic Agriculture (FiBL), the School of Agricultural, Forest, and Food Science (HAFL), the Vetsuisse (University of Zurich) and Zurich University of Applied Sciences (ZHAW), among many other universities. Agroscope is directly under the auspices of FOAG (AGRIDEA, 2021[9]). The cantons are responsible for the universities (including VetSuisse) and the universities of applied sciences (HAFL, ZHAW, University of Applied Sciences and Arts of Western Switzerland [HES-SO], etc.). These universities undertake both education and research in the areas of agriculture, forestry, food and environmental science (AGRIDEA, 2021[9]).

Agricultural research and education are funded by the federal government and by the cantons. The federal government finances the agricultural research institute Agroscope, a major research centre, and in part the FiBL. However, the FiBL is privately operated and receives private funding as well. The ETH Zurich agro sciences faculty is funded by the federal government. The cantons finance the agricultural schools as well as agricultural education and extension centres and higher agricultural training courses (AGRIDEA, 2021[9]). Box 4.1 describes the main public institutions of the AIS.

Public AIS institutions are located and spread out across the country (Figure 4.3). For instance, there are 5 agricultural universities, 11 Agroscope centres, 1 organic agricultural research centre (FiBL), 3 AGRIDEA centres and more than 30 agricultural colleges and advisory/extension services that provide agricultural technical assistance.

Figure 4.3. Public AIS institutions in Switzerland

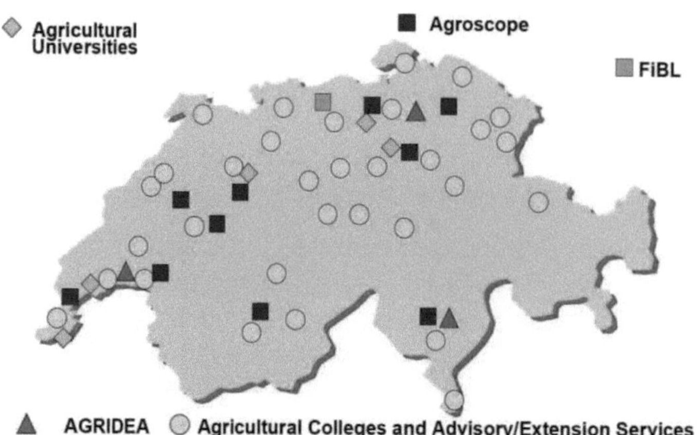

Source: FOAG (2021[11]), *ERI-Project OECD Information Request*, Federal Office for Agriculture.

Box 4.1. Brief description of main AIS institutions

The **Federal Office for Agriculture (FOAG)** is the Swiss Confederation's competency centre for all things relating to the agricultural sector. The FOAG is a part of the Federal Department of Economic Affairs, Education and Research (EAER) and has under its authority Agroscope, which is the Swiss centre of excellence for agricultural research. The department, on the basis of the Agricultural Act, promotes and designs agricultural policy instruments and implements them together with cantonal authorities and farmers' associations (FOAG, 2021[12]).

The **Federal Food Safety and Veterinary Office (FSVO)** promotes the health and well-being of humans and animals through enforcing measures of food safety and healthy eating for humans, and animal health and welfare for animals. The department is supported by the Federal Food Chain Unit in implementing legislation in the areas related to plant health, food and feed, and animal diseases and welfare. The FSVO is organised into specialist divisions that work closely with other parties in their respective disciplines. This includes, for example, the Swiss Veterinary Service in addition to a number of committees to incorporate expert knowledge into policy design and development (FSVO, 2021[13]).

The **Federal Office for the Environment (FOEN)** is responsible for the sustainable use of natural resources such as land and water domestically, as well as for international environmental policy. It is also responsible for the protection against natural disasters, safeguarding the environment and human health, and preserving biodiversity and landscape quality. This is meant to tackle the main changes facing the environment through designing policies related to climate protection, biodiversity conservation and sustainable resource management. The FOEN also creates a space for dialogue between the different cantons as well as other types of stakeholders and actors on a variety of topics related to the environment (FOEN, 2021[14]).

The **State Secretariat for Economic Affairs (SECO)** is the Swiss federal government's centre of expertise in key matters related to economic policy. The centre aims to ensure sustainable economic growth, improve employment and fair working conditions, and provide a stable environment for regulatory, economic and foreign trade policy. SECO is responsible for a number of directorates such as the Labour Directorate, Economic Policy Directorate, Foreign Economic Affairs Directorate, Promotion Activities Directorate and the Organisation, Law and Accreditation Directorate. Through its directorates' operations, the agency helps design legislations related to export and location promotion. The secretariat also addresses issues related to economic policy, foreign trade and economic co-operation, involvement in international organisations and tourism promotion (SECO, 2021[15]).

Agroscope, under the auspices of the FOAG, is the Swiss centre of excellence for agricultural research. The centre works to promote sustainable agriculture and growth of the food sector, while preserving the environment and its resources, thereby contributing to an improved overall quality of life. As such, **Agroscope** is responsible for R&D along the entire value chain of the agro-food sector including agriculture, nutrition and the environment. It also provides guidance for policy-making authorities and encourages knowledge exchange and technology transfer with different actors in the field (Agroscope, 2021[16]).

The **Swiss Federal Institutes of Technology (ETH Zurich)** is a university of science and technology that is dedicated to the study of a varied range of disciplines, which allows knowledge to be shared and combined in original and future-oriented ways. It consists of 16 departments covering a broad academic spectrum with various strategic initiatives, competency centres and networks that encourage interdisciplinary co-operation. The university is built upon Swiss values of freedom, individual responsibility, entrepreneurial spirit and open-mindedness, which has granted it a leading rank amongst scientific educational institutions globally (ETH Zurich, 2021[17]).

The **Research Institute of Organic Agriculture (FiBL)** involves non-governmental public institutions or non-profit organisations functioning as foundations or associations in various European countries. They are legal independent entities that group themselves under the partnership of the FiBL Group. The common goal of these entities is the continuous development of organic agriculture and the creation of added value along the chain of the food system through research, knowledge transfer, advisory services, hands-on projects and public relations expertise. The group works in partnership with the actors and stakeholders in the field on projects related to food security and nutrition, preserving natural resources and promoting organic farming and a sustainable agro-food system. The FiBL Group currently comprises FiBL Switzerland (founded in 1973), FiBL Germany (2001), FiBL Austria (2004), ÖMKi (Hungarian Research Institute of Organic Agriculture) (2011), FiBL France (2017) and FiBL Europe (2017) (FIBL, 2021[18]).

The **School of Agricultural, Forest, and Food Science (HAFL)** is an institution that teaches and researches in disciplines related to agricultural, forestry and food sciences. It uses a holistic, multifaceted and innovative scientific research approach to develop solutions to address current and future challenges in a number of areas pertaining to its five divisions (agriculture, forest science, food science and management, MSc programmes, and transdisciplinary subjects) and it does so through two main areas of operations teaching as well as research, consulting and continuing education (BFH, 2021[19]).

AGRIDEA is the Swiss agricultural extension centre, mainly providing support for cantonal extension services and any organisation working in agriculture. It acts as a competency centre for the production, exchange and distribution of research knowledge and expertise. AGRIDEA provides a network for various kinds of small or big actors in the agricultural sector and rural areas. The centre has three locations in Cadenazzo, Lausanne and Lindau that are committed to delivering cutting-edge solutions and research publications related to efficient and sustainable agriculture and vigorous rural development. As such, AGRIDEA plays a central role in the Swiss agricultural knowledge system (AKIS), which connects science and farming and creates new synergies that open a number of opportunities in the agro-food industry (AGRIDEA, 2021[20]).

Established in 2013, the **State Secretariat for Education, Research and Innovation (SERI)** is part of the federal department of EAER. It is responsible for building bridges between these different sub-disciplines knowing that they are interdependent and all connected to the overall well-being and prosperity of Swiss society. The department is leading collaboration on national and international matters related to education, research and innovation (ERI), and is responsible for co-ordination efforts of the canton authorities, private sector actors, academic institutions as well as other types of organisations. SERI has an annual total budget of CHF 4.5 billion for the year 2021, which is distributed amongst its 8 divisions that specialise in different areas of ERI design and implementation. This means that SERI is responsible for the design and implementation of innovation policy at the federal level, through its application of the Research and Innovation Promotion Act. It also provides funding for projects that are put forward by the SNSF (see below), while overseeing the conduct of Innosuisse. Between 2017 and 2020, SERI allocated CHF 2.5 billion towards projects put forward by the European Framework Programmes for Research and Innovation and CHF 625 million towards projects put forward by Innosuisse (SERI, 2021[21]).

The **Swiss National Science Foundation (SNSF)** is the leading Swiss institution for promoting science and research and was established in 1952 to provide financial aid to research projects and initiatives and to support upcoming scientists in a variety of academic disciplines. In 2020, the SNSF had a budget of CHF 937 million, which was awarded entirely to new proposals adding to over 6 000 projects employing 20 000 researchers (SNSF, 2021[22]). The foundation is at the forefront of research collaboration and is leading many initiatives in conjunction with higher education institutions, all while conducting an evaluation of third-party-led research projects. The SNSF is committed to maintaining the reputable level of quality of Swiss research by operating under high standards of excellence and accountability. To continue to do so, the foundation is proud to be operating autonomously as a private entity that values fairness, impartiality and equal access to opportunity (SNSF, 2021[22]).

Innosuisse is the Swiss Innovation Agency responsible for promoting R&I in areas of science that would benefit the Swiss economy and society at large. The agency employs a special outlook on the importance of combining knowledge and R&D and promotes collaboration between private market entities and academic institutions to maintain a sustainable innovative state of the economy that nurtures start-ups. However, Innosuisse provides support for projects in accordance with the subsidiarity principle, that is it only supports projects if there is a possible risk of lost market potential and implementation of innovation without funding. Therefore, the yearly budget varies considerably depending on the number of project proposals approved by the agency. For example, during the first 6 months of 2020, 208 out of 359 projects received were approved, thus amounting to a total budget of CHF 63 million, for the first half of 2020. In addition to its regular funding activities, the agency also launched 2 new funding initiatives in 2021 and, during the first 6 months of the year, 72 projects under the impulse innovation programme were approved, totalling CHF 33.1 million (Innosuise, 2021[23]). Innosuisse also benefits from close collaboration with both SNSF and SERI at the national level, in addition to international exchanges through its membership of the European network of leading national innovation agencies (TAFTIE) (Innosuise, 2021[23]).

Vocational training

Vocational training is a common responsibility of the Swiss Confederation that sets the legal framework and the cantons that offer the training courses, e.g. in agricultural colleges. These colleges provide vocational education and training to people aged between 16 and 20 years old, professional education and training to people aged 20 and older and to farmers with an advanced federal diploma. Moreover, the professional organisations define the content of the vocational training, for example its objectives, requirements and topics, among others. The professional organisations responsible for vocational training in the field of agriculture have recently started a reform process. This process will consider and take into account emerging concerns and issues such as the role of digitisation, entrepreneurial issues and innovation skills, resource management, biodiversity, etc.

Advisory services

Knowledge intermediaries are those sharing and spreading knowledge between actors. Cantons (the public sector) have traditionally provided advisory services in the Swiss AIS. Agricultural offices of the 26 cantons are responsible for agricultural advisory services, as well as for the cantonal veterinarians and food control authorities. The offices provide extension services such as information and documentation for farmers, training courses, advice/extension in public and private interest, and project support. Since 2008, the cantons' public agricultural advisory services have been financed exclusively by the cantons. Some cantons like Bern, Geneva, Jura, Neuchâtel, Vaud and Zurich, grant (full or partial) advisory mandates to the cantonal farmers' associations, which then operate the cantonal advisory services. Moreover, the cantonal agricultural advisory services are independent. They do not depend on the FOAG (AGRIDEA, 2021[9]).

Private sector and non-profit organisations also provide extension services. AGRIDEA, for example, is a non-profit association. The services of the three AGRIDEA advisory centres are financed by a mandate from the FOAG, membership fees and private funds from the sale of products. AGRIDEA provides services to cantons (training courses, publications, information technology [IT] solutions and other services), while for farmers it mainly provides publications and IT solutions (AGRIDEA, 2021[9]).

Private sector actors include several firms and consultants with varying competencies and knowledge areas. Some companies provide advice to farmers, e.g. on plant production and risk management. Companies selling stable equipment provide the main advice on silos and provide service and advice on robot milking equipment. A number of research centres at universities aim to have close relationships with businesses to diffuse knowledge and innovation. Some of these are directly related to the agricultural and food sectors. Private or farmer-based advisory services such as agricultural fiduciary services play an important role in the areas of accounting, business and tax advice. The Swiss Farmers' Association runs a private consultancy centre (Agriexpert) on topics such as fiduciary services, legal issues, farm transfers, etc.

As mentioned above, advisory services are provided at the canton level by the agricultural offices and are generally well perceived. Nevertheless, in general, AIS actors may need to improve their co-ordination and collaboration mechanisms, particularly to improve the link between basic research, applied research, advisory services and technology adoption by the farmer. Knowledge exchange and transfer between research and agricultural sector in advisory services need to remain up to date. There are many factors that influence this exchange and transfer of practical experience toward advisors and researchers in the field of agriculture. In recent times, there is increased ease of exchange and access to knowledge and information sharing due to the effects of digitalisation and the central role played by the Internet. This facilitates the emergence of new opportunities, which fit the changing information needs and expectations regarding access to AIS topics. At the same time, the novelty of some aspects of digitalisation in application poses a challenge for agricultural research (AGRIDEA, 2021[20]).

AGRIDEA mainly provides services to cantons but also has direct contacts with farmers. The areas of consultancy that are most in demand are business and farm management, diversification and risk mitigation, agro-environmental measures and financing concerns. These advisory services are financed through national and cantonal public government funds and private contributions such as membership fees and cost-recovery from farmers.

Agricultural extension lies within the individual jurisdiction of the 26 cantons. As such, it is in many cases small in structure; therefore, cantons that have exceptionally small agricultural sectors seek co-operation with their neighbouring cantons. However, on the national level, cantons participate in a common forum for the exchange and protection of interests (AGRIDEA, 2021[20]).

Some of the most used forms of communication concerning advisory services include telephone, face-to-face meetings on or off the farm, virtual communication channels and group assistance outside the farm. Advisory services are dominated by individual advice followed by group advice. These services are provided by a group of highly qualified individuals – 80% of whom have over 3 years of professional experience in the field. Additionally, there is a relatively high level of collaboration in the sector between public authorities, farmer-based or professional groups, and academic or research institutions. Agricultural extension services continue to thrive under public support in areas of nutrient production and pesticide use, conservation of biodiversity, and value creation within the sector (AGRIDEA, 2021[20]).

Farmers and farmer organisations

Farms structure in Switzerland continues to consolidate. The number of farm holdings has decreased by around 30% from 2000 to 2020 (Table 4.2). In 2020, there were 49 363 agricultural holdings, which is a decline of 1.3% compared to 2019 (FSO, 2021[7]). Size holdings greater than 10 hectares represent 72% of total holdings. In 2020, around 15% of total farms are using organic production systems. The average farm size in Switzerland was 21 hectares in 2020 and the country has witnessed a structural change as farm size has increased constantly since 1990, when the average was around 11 hectares. There are around 150 000 employees in the agri-food subsector in the country (FSO, 2021[7]).

Table 4.2. Farm holdings by size, 2000 and 2020

Farm size	2000	Percentage	2020	Percentage
Less than 1 hectare	3 609	5.1	2 064	4.2
From 1 to 3 hectares	4 762	6.8	3 139	6.4
From 3 to 5 hectares	5 393	7.6	2 408	4.9
From 5 to 10 hectares	13 149	18.6	6 284	12.7
From 10 to 20 hectares	24 984	35.4	14 005	28.4
From 20 to 30 hectares	11 674	16.6	10 287	20.8
From 30 to 50 hectares	5 759	8.2	8 114	16.4
50 hectares and more	1 207	1.7	3 062	6.2
Total	**70 537**	**100.0**	**49 363**	**100.0**

Source: FSO (2021[7]), *Federal Statistics Office*, https://www.bfs.admin.ch/bfs/en/home.html.

Farmers are organised in different chambers by sub-sector. The Swiss Farmers' Union is the umbrella organisation of Swiss agriculture. It is made up of representatives from 25 cantonal professional organisations and various trade associations.

Farmers are the main users of knowledge and innovation generated in the AIS. The agricultural structure is characterised by small- and medium-sized enterprises (SMEs), which can affect their innovative capacity. Traditionally, farmers participate in field experimentation but, even when farmers' involvement in innovation generation projects is highly regarded, adoption of innovation in some agricultural sub-sectors is relatively lower than the national average (AGRIDEA, 2021[9]).

The farmers' organisations under the Swiss Farmers' Union play a key role in the AIS. Among other things, they are also responsible for designing vocational training for farmers. The Vocational Training Organisation (OdA AgriAliForm) groups ten organisations from the agricultural and equestrian sectors which are involved in vocational education and training (AGRIDEA, 2021[9]).

Agroindustry

Upstream and downstream value-added partners play a key role for agricultural enterprises. Upstream are the suppliers of plant protection products, fertilisers, animal feed, machinery, equipment and services that provide the inputs necessary for agriculture. Upstream suppliers are important intermediaries of innovation on farms. Downstream is the whole agri-food industry as a consumer of agricultural products. Domestically, a significant market position in the upstream and downstream value chains is held by the FENACO agricultural co-operative association and its affiliated regional agricultural co-operatives. The agricultural co-operatives are run by farmers. FENACO is an important supplier to the farms and the food industry with high market shares (AGRIDEA, 2021[9]).

National label certification associations such as Bio Suisse or IP-Suisse also are farmer-based and have cantonal sections. Also important are the sectoral associations (Interprofession milk, Proviande, Swissgranum, Swisspatat, etc.), which involve the players along the entire value chain, from production to processing and marketing, and play a major role in industry standards, market issues, representation of interests and sales promotion, among other things.

Business development, innovation and competitiveness of the farm sector and the food industry are hindered by trade policies that raise the prices for imported inputs and may shield producers from the competition (OECD, 2014[4]). Successful participation in such value chains requires unencumbered access to the best inputs at the lowest prices as well as regulations and technical standards that facilitate the exchange of semi-processed and finished products with partner countries.

The Swiss food and beverage industry overall has a relatively strong position in comparison to the main competitors. However, this situation is mainly driven by particular sub-sectors such as cocoa and chocolate manufacturing or beverages (e.g. mineral water): these subsectors count for more than 70% of total agri-food exports. Over recent years, as is evident in 2019 (Figure 4.4), Switzerland's leading export category under the agro-food sector has been headed by beverages at USD 4.03 billion, cocoa and cocoa-related products at USD 1.8 billion and dairy products at USD 1.47 billion (UN-COMTRADE, 2021[24]).

Figure 4.4. Swiss main agri-food exports, 2019

Export values

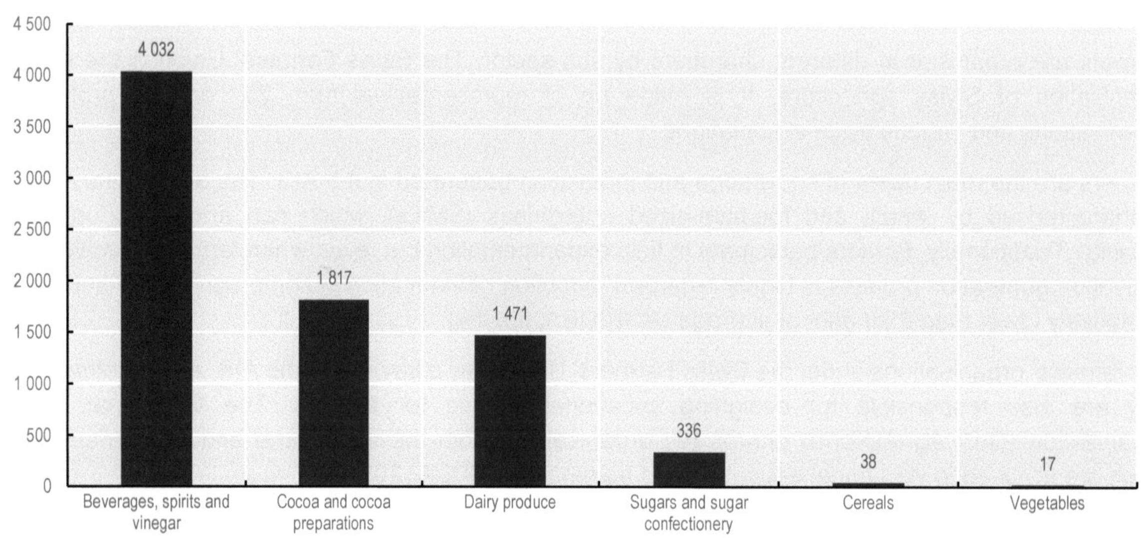

Source: UN-COMTRADE (UN-COMTRADE, 2021[24])

On the other hand, some of the less competitive sub-sectors in Switzerland are meat and dairy, which rely mainly on domestic primary agriculture for their inputs, although some dairy producers successfully serve high-value niche markets. These industries as well as the weak animal feed sector have to pay relatively high prices for their material inputs. Additionally, these less competitive sectors have experienced relatively low labour productivity growth and are relatively labour intensive.

Lastly, according to the Eurostat innovation survey (2017[25]), food processing firms in Switzerland tend to be more innovative than all-manufacturing firms. Around 87.5% of food processing firms reported having introduced some innovation in 2012-14 compared to 80.6% of all-manufacturing firms (Figure 4.5). The share of innovative firms among food processing firms is higher in Switzerland than in other countries in the EU. In international comparison, the gap between food processing and all-manufacturing firms in Switzerland is significant without being too wide.

Figure 4.5. Share of innovative firms in selected countries, 2014

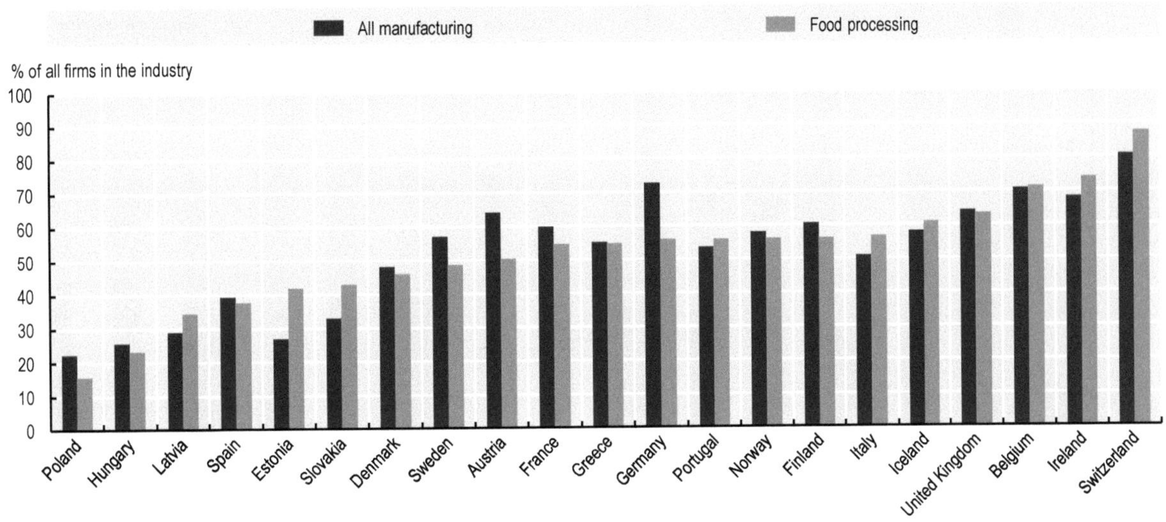

Source: Eurostat (2017[25]), *Community Innovation Survey*, http://ec.europa.eu/eurostat/data/database.

Networks

The AIS has several thematic networks at the national and cantonal levels, which play a major role in the exchange of knowledge, experience, networking and solving current problems. The networks mainly bring together experts, researchers, decision-makers, multipliers and also farmers. AGRIDEA alone, for example, is involved in over 150 thematic networks every year.

Agricultural media play an important role in the transfer of knowledge between the AIS actors and farmers. This media report on new products, practical application of innovations, examples, key research results and important technical or agricultural policy topics. The most important ones are BauernZeitung (farmer-owned), Schweizer Bauer (private), and Agri (farmer-owned, French-speaking Switzerland). Other publications include agricultural research (Agroscope), cantonal farmers' association newspapers, newsletters, etc. (AGRIDEA, 2021[9]).

Funding of the AIS

The public sector continues to be the main source of funding in the AIS of Switzerland, with the SNSF as the leading contributor (CHF 938 million total budget in 2020 for all subsectors of the economy) to research performed in public or private organisations (SNSF, 2021[22]). Based on observed allocations, government budget expenditures on R&D for agriculture are typically more variable than total R&D expenditure over time, reflecting changes in government priorities from year to year. However, private funding in agriculture is also relevant, with total business expenditures on R&D (BERD) in Switzerland amounting to around 2.5% of GDP in 2016 (OECD, 2019[8]). Nonetheless, agriculture R&D represents only 2.2% of total R&D public outlays (FSO, 2021[7]).

Since 2006, there has been a gradual increase in spending on the development of AIS, with agricultural knowledge generation receiving most of the funding, from close to CHF 250 million in 2006 to around CHF 375 million in 2020. These changes also depict the difference in the distribution of the funds. While agricultural knowledge generation still receives the highest percentage, funding for agricultural education has also grown compared to previous years (Figure 4.6).

Figure 4.6. Evolution and composition of the AIS public budget, 2006-20

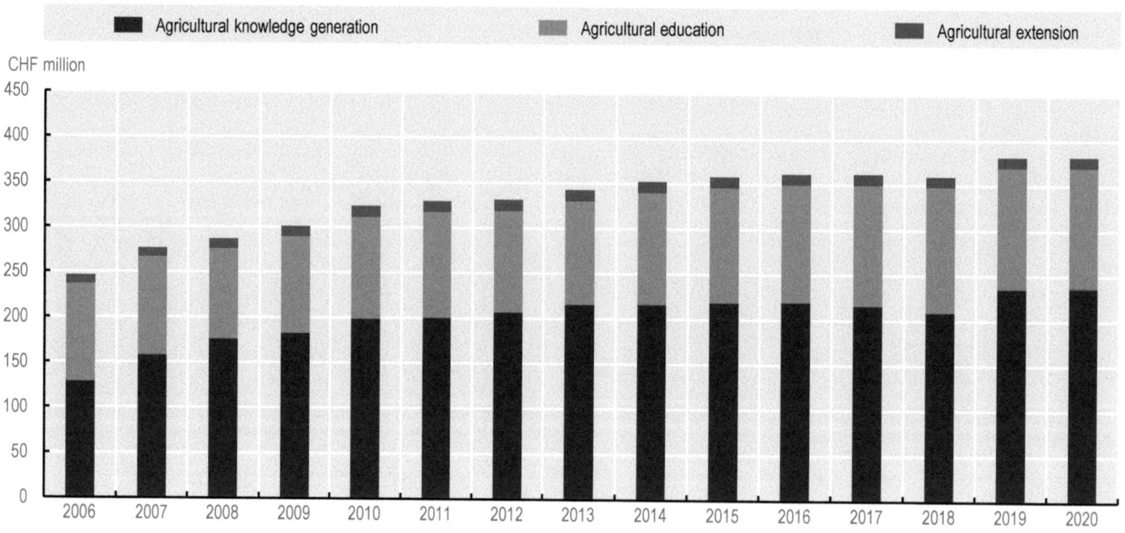

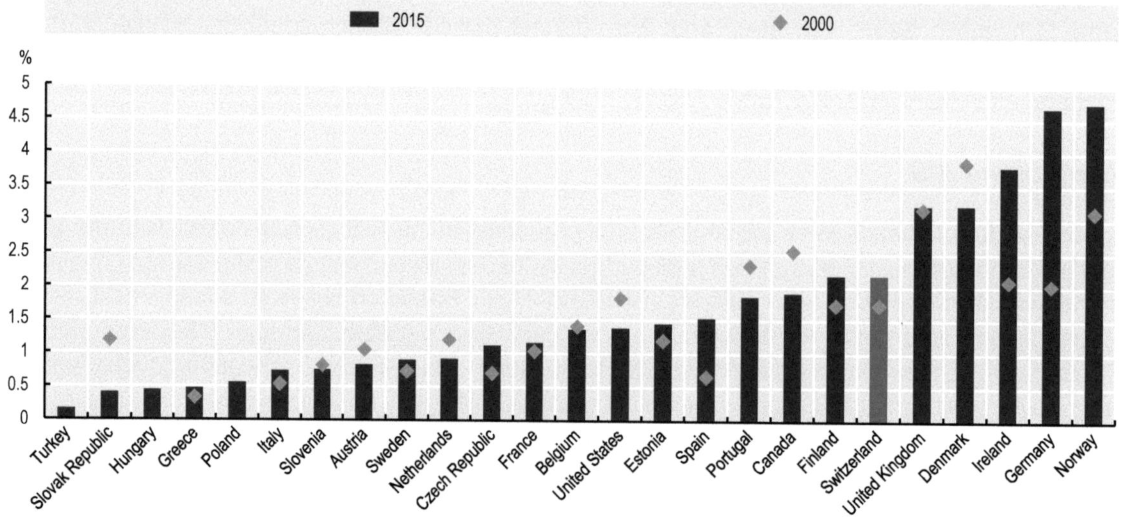

Source: OECD (n.d.[26]), "Producer and Consumer Support Estimates", http://dx.doi.org/10.1787/agr-pcse-data-en.

When looking at trends in research intensity within R&D in the agricultural sector, it is evident that Switzerland ranks amongst the mid- to high-performing countries of the OECD (Figure 4.7). Swiss government expenditure on agricultural R&D grew from 1.7% to around 2.2% share of total expenditure on R&D between 2000 and 2015 respectively.

Figure 4.7. Agricultural R&D intensity in selected countries, 2000 and 2015

Government budget appropriations or outlays for R&D (GBAORD) as a percentage of agricultural value-added

Note: 2002 instead of 2000 for Estonia. Public expenditure on R&D is government budget appropriations or outlays for R&D comes from OECD R&D statistics, and value-added from OECD GDP statistics.
Source: OECD (2017[27]), *OECD Research and Development Statistics*, https://stats.oecd.org/ (Accessed 1 September, 2022).

Almost half of the General Services Support Estimate (GSSE) expenditure finances the AIS. AIS, infrastructure expenditure, and inspection and control, among other support services, have one of the highest shares in agricultural value-added and composition in Switzerland (Figure 4.8). While Japan and Korea have a higher share of infrastructure support services, Switzerland ranks the highest in AIS support services provided. Between 2018 and 2020, the country had a 16% share of the support services in agricultural value-added.

Figure 4.8. General Services Support Estimate, share in agricultural value-added and composition, 2018-20

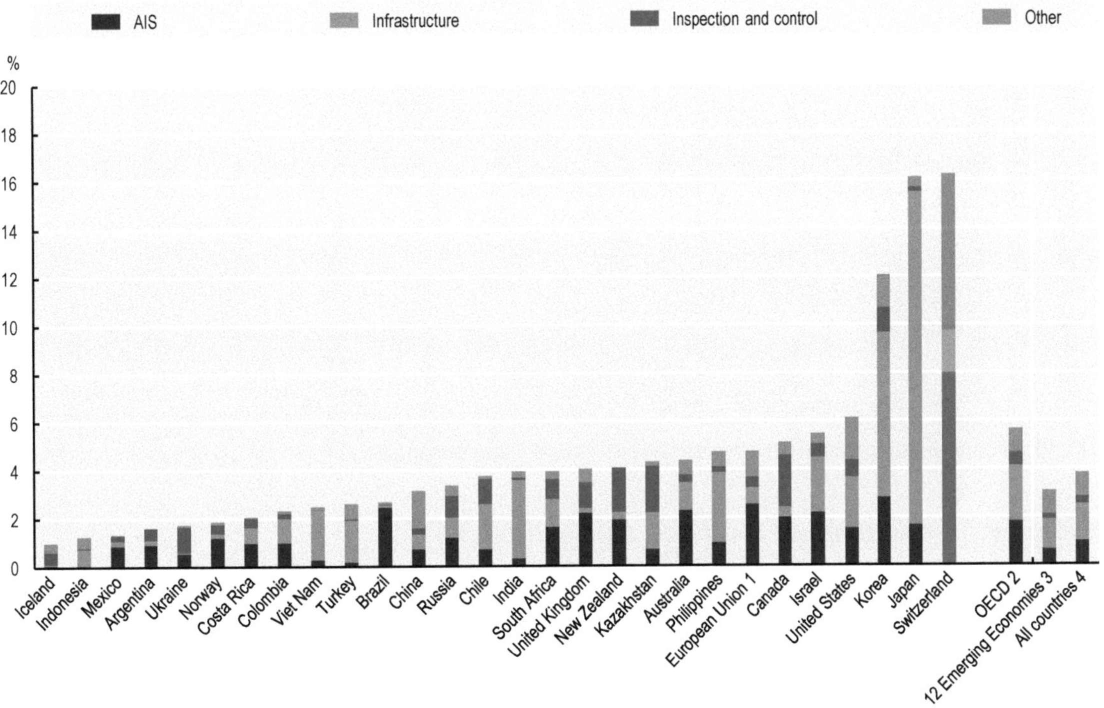

Note: "AIS" refers to the agricultural knowledge and innovation system. "Other" includes the marketing and promotion, cost of public stockholding and miscellaneous categories of the GSSE. Countries are ranked according to the share of total GSSE in agricultural value-added.

Due to missing value-added data, the 2018-20 average GSSE is related to agricultural value-added data for 2017-19 except for Japan and the United States (2016-18) and for Canada and New Zealand (2015-17).

1. EU28 for 2018-19, EU27 plus UK for 2020.

2. The OECD total does not include the non-OECD EU member states. Latvia and Lithuania are included only for 2018-20. Costa Rica became the 38th member of the OECD in May 2021. In the data aggregates used in this report, however, it is included as one of the 12 emerging economies.

3. The 12 emerging economies include Argentina, Brazil, China, Costa Rica, India, Indonesia, Kazakhstan, the Philippines, the Russian Federation, South Africa, Ukraine and Viet Nam.

4. The "All countries" total includes all OECD countries, non-OECD EU member states and emerging economies.

Source: OECD (2021[3]), *Agricultural Policy Monitoring and Evaluation 2021: Addressing the Challenges Facing Food Systems*, https://dx.doi.org/10.1787/2d810e01-en; OECD (n.d.[26]), "Producer and Consumer Support Estimates", http://dx.doi.org/10.1787/agr-pcse-data-en.

The main public institutions that provide funding to the AIS are the Federal Council through Innosuisse, the SNSF and FOAG, while the main beneficiaries are the universities and institutional research centres like Agroscope (Figure 4.9).

Figure 4.9. Main public institutions and funding of the AIS for 2019, in CHF Million

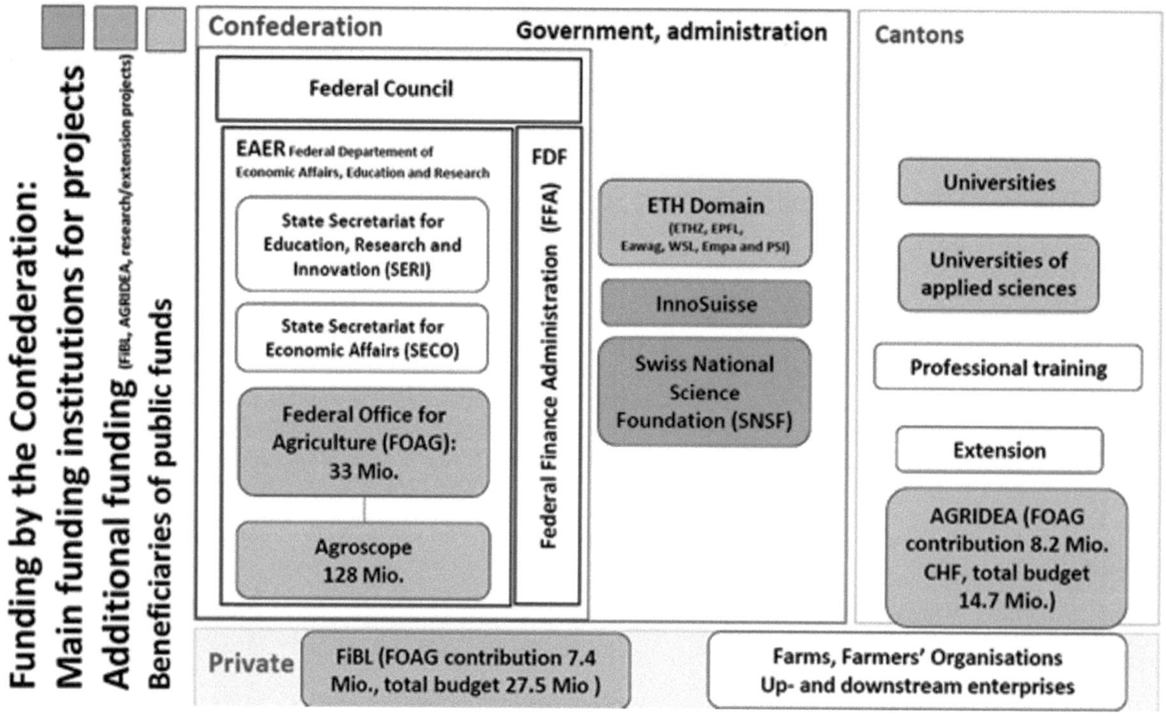

Source: FOAG (2021[11]), *ERI-Project OECD Information Request*, Federal Office for Agriculture.

International co-operation in food and agricultural R&D

International co-operation in agricultural R&D offers universal benefits. While this is generally true given the public good nature of many innovations in agriculture, it is particularly the case where global challenges are being confronted (e.g. climate change) and when initial investments are exceptionally high. The benefits of international co-operation for national systems stem from the specialisation it allows and from international spill-overs. In countries with limited research capacity, scarce resources could then be used to better take into account local specificities.

Switzerland has a long tradition of international co-operation in agricultural R&D. A number of forms of international co-operation are specifically prevalent in the Swiss AIS and are often financed or operated through the main current research funding organisations.

For example, the European Union (EU) Framework Programme for Research and Innovation was first established to encourage cross-border collaboration on research amongst countries in the EU in addition to within them, individually. It currently acts as a tool to create opportunities for R&I in a number of areas. Switzerland has been an active participant in this framework, though it is considered a non-associated third country for the submission of project proposals in programmes and initiatives. As such, project participants based in Switzerland can apply to participate in collaborative projects, which will not be funded by the European Commission but by the Swiss SERI. This means that there are a number of limitations that apply to Swiss participants as they cannot be responsible for co-ordination of projects despite taking a lead in it, for example. However, with a total budget of EUR 95.5 billion, the framework is sure to attract a lot of promising project proposals from participants in member countries and Switzerland can learn by association from collaborating on such projects with them (SERI, 2021[21]).

Agricultural policies in Switzerland

Although agriculture plays a relatively minor and declining role in the Swiss economy, the sector is perceived as an important element in maintaining food security and increasingly as a provider of positive externalities such as environmental benefits and animal welfare, which are highly valued by Swiss society. Hence, agricultural policies and related support to agriculture are an important part of the Swiss political landscape (OECD, 2015[28]). Agricultural policies in Switzerland seek to find a balanced solution for addressing a variety of commercial, social and environmental objectives. The result is a system of market protection in combination with an elaborate set of payments to farmers that provides income support as well as incentives for certain types of farming practices (OECD, 2015[28]).

The level of agricultural support in Switzerland, as measured by the Producer Support Estimate (PSE) as a share of gross farm receipts, has declined gradually but is still one of the highest amongst OECD countries. Figure 4.10 shows that Switzerland is one of the top three countries that support the most its agriculture, just after Iceland and Norway, but way above the OECD average. Support to producers remains high: around 50% on average in 2018-20, almost 3 times the OECD average (OECD, 2021[3])

Figure 4.10. Producer Support Estimate by country, 2000-02 and 2018-20

Percentage of gross farm receipts

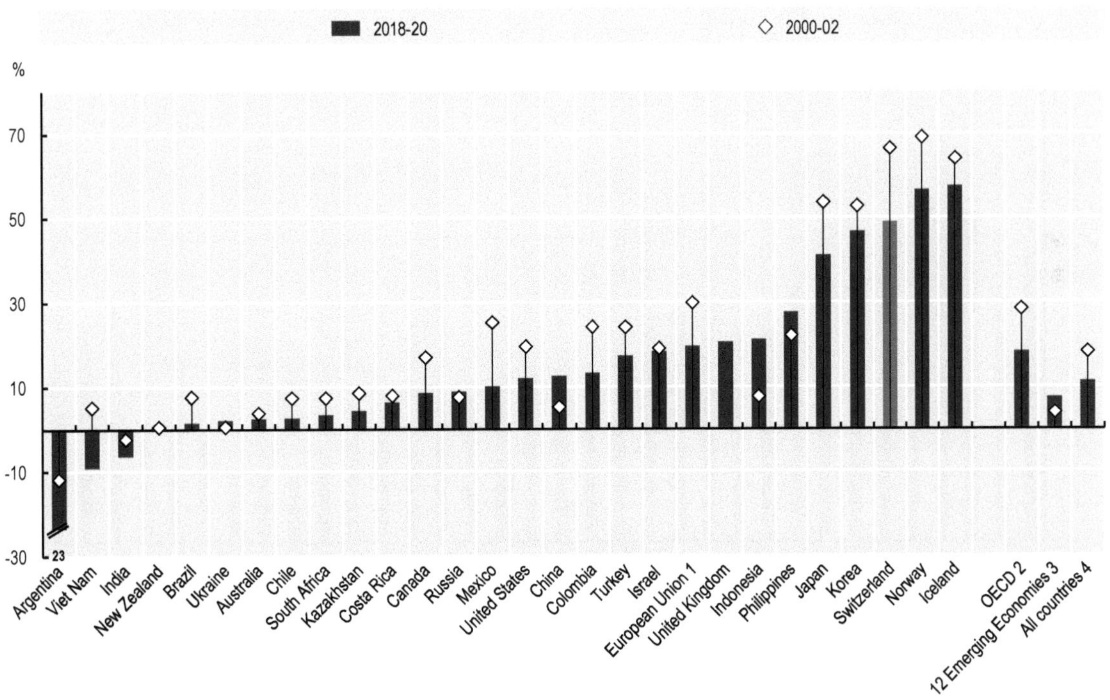

Note: Countries are ranked according to the 2018-20 levels.
1. EU15 for 2000-02, EU28 for 2018-19 and EU27 plus UK for 2020.
2. The OECD total does not include the non-OECD EU member states. Latvia and Lithuania are included only for 2018-20. Costa Rica became the 38th member of the OECD in May 2021. In the data aggregates used in this report, however, it is included as one of the 12 emerging economies.
3. The 12 emerging economies include Argentina, Brazil, China, Costa Rica, India, Indonesia, Kazakhstan, the Philippines, the Russian Federation, South Africa, Ukraine and Viet Nam.
4. The "All countries" total includes all OECD countries, non-OECD EU member states and emerging economies.
Source: OECD (2021[3]), *Agricultural Policy Monitoring and Evaluation 2021: Addressing the Challenges Facing Food Systems*, https://dx.doi.org/10.1787/2d810e01-en; OECD (n.d.[26]), "Producer and Consumer Support Estimates", http://dx.doi.org/10.1787/agr-pcse-data-en.

There have been some important changes in the structure of support, as direct payments partly replaced market price support (MPS). MPS, mainly due to tariff rate quotas (TRQs) with high out-of-quota tariffs, remains the main component of support. Over the past 30 years, MPS fell from 80% to around 50% of total producer support. Nonetheless, average domestic prices were on average 46% above world prices in 2018-20 (OECD, 2021[3]). Potentially most production- and trade-distorting support (mainly MPS) also declined from around 80% to less than 50% of producer support between 1986 and 2020, while payments considered less distorting grew (Figure 4.11).

The country provides direct payments to farms (almost all subject to environmental cross-compliance). These increased over time: while they represented around 20% of support to farmers in the 1980s, their share rose to almost 50% in recent years. Most are general area payments to all agricultural land, payments to maintain farming in less favoured conditions and payments to farmers who voluntarily apply stricter farming practices related to environmental and animal welfare. Expenditures for general services (GSSE) are high in Switzerland. GSSE relative to agricultural value-added rose from 11% in 2000-02 to 16% in 2018-20 and is among the highest of countries covered by this report. Total support for agriculture as a share of GDP fell from 2% in 2000-02 to 1% in 2018-20 (OECD, 2021[3]).

Figure 4.11. Switzerland: Level and Total Support Estimate (TSE) composition by support categories, 1986-2020

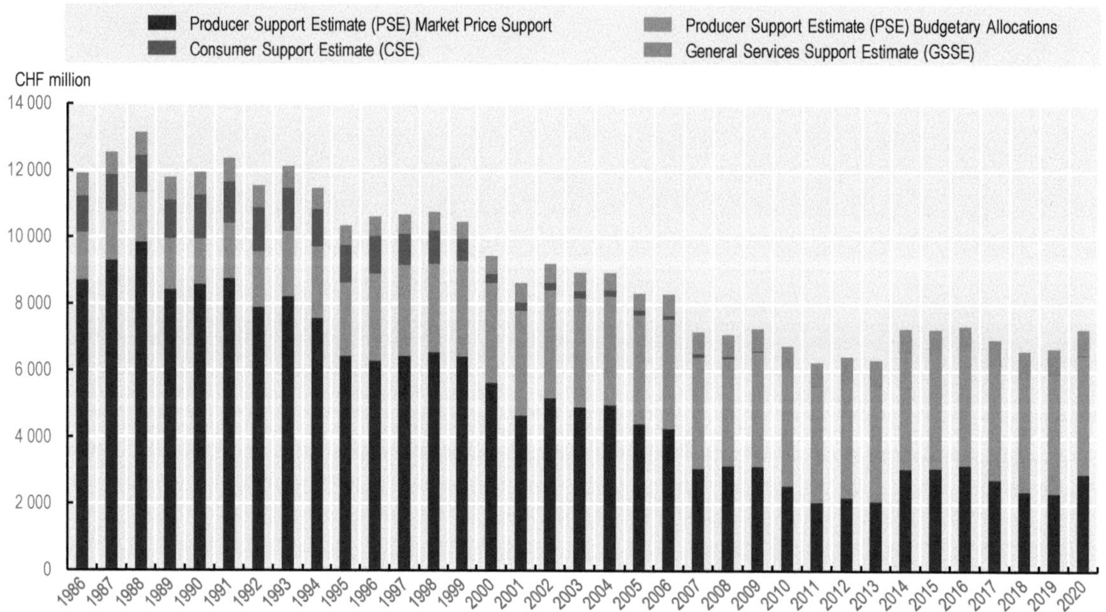

Source: OECD (2021[3]), *Agricultural Policy Monitoring and Evaluation 2021: Addressing the Challenges Facing Food Systems*, https://dx.doi.org/10.1787/2d810e01-en; OECD (n.d.[26]), "Producer and Consumer Support Estimates", http://dx.doi.org/10.1787/agr-pcse-data-en.

Agricultural policies' performance can be improved by making the distinction between policies that address market failures (the provision of positive externalities and public goods as well as the avoidance of negative externalities) and those that address income problems. Current policies combine both aspects and seek to address market failures by a combination of cross-compliance conditionalities and differential payment rates to stimulate certain farming practices. Direct payments have reached such a high level relative to what farmers earn by selling their products on the market that price and market signals appear to play only a secondary role in guiding their decisions. This hampers structural adjustment in the farm sector and, more generally, limits the development of an innovative and competitive food-producing sector that contributes to food security objectives and continues to produce high-quality products (OECD, 2015[28]).

The competitiveness of the Swiss food and beverage industry is almost entirely driven by sub-branches that source most of their raw material inputs abroad or where inputs are non-agricultural (chocolate, coffee and beverages like mineral water). As previously seen, chocolate together with beverages accounts for 70% of the exports of the Swiss agro-food industry. While meat and dairy processing continue to be less competitive and rely on agricultural public support (OECD, 2015[28]; UN-COMTRADE, 2021[24]).

Specific Swiss initiatives that foster agri-food innovation

Knowledge diffusion and adoption are some of the most difficult challenges in R&D and the knowledge and innovation system. Policy incentives for the adoption of innovation include a wide range of regulatory and financial approaches, including business investment support and support for public-private co-operation arrangements and participation in networks. In primary agriculture, training, extension and advisory services can facilitate the transfer and successful adoption of innovation (OECD, 2014[4]).

In the case of Switzerland, given the relatively large number of small-scale farmers, extension and advisory services become essential. Advisory services are crucial in facilitating farmers' access to technology and knowledge, in farmers' effective participation in innovation networks and in the ability to formulate their specific demands – in particular, to support the diffusion of innovation in small-scale farms and agro-firms.

R&D projects

Switzerland has an important number of initiatives on R&D, for instance, the platform *Projets de recherche, évaluations et études externes* provides access to research and evaluation projects and external studies which are supported by the FOAG. Projects range from the field of plant protection initiatives to sustainability, water, healthcare, etc. The platform provides both shorter summaries of the projects as well as longer detailed versions. This is meant to share knowledge and provide ideas for future projects that can build upon the blueprints of the existing projects on this database. Users can search for projects by category (field), type, project status and period. The projects listed here represent only a small fraction of all R&D projects; moreover, most projects carried out by Agroscope, FiBL etc. do not receive direct funding from the FOAG.

Steady investment in R&D projects is required to improve agriculture's sustainability. At the canton level, there are many initiatives like the one in the canton of Vaud, for example (which accounts for 10% of the Swiss agricultural surface), which offers a supportive environment for innovation in the agro-food sector and encourages collaboration between researchers, entrepreneurs, and cantonal and federal entities (Vaud, 2020[29]).

Furthermore, for example, in the area of Swiss agricultural R&D, certain players are leading the way for the future of innovation in this field. One of them is the Communauté d'Études pour l'Aménagement du Territoire (CEAT), which is a pioneering research institution that works on projects dealing with territorial planning. Another player is Agroscope, which is making incredible headway in identifying future challenges in the Swiss agricultural and food processing sector and their respective smart farming solutions. Lastly, the Geodetic Engineering Laboratory (Topo) is producing research findings that revolve around geodesy, monitoring and cartography, sensors and satellite positioning for agricultural growth purposes (Vaud, 2020[29]). These are only a few examples of the innovation projects and initiatives carried out in the agro-food sector.

Agri-food Innovation hubs

For agricultural innovation, it is important to have a holistic approach to achieve sustainable agriculture. The country has many important hub initiatives. For instance, Swiss Food Research is a network that helps the generation and cultivation of ideas that promote the growth of innovation in the agro-food ecosystem. The Innosuisse innovation network is made up of over 160 businesses, start-ups, universities and research institutions all contributing to the growth of the Swiss agro-food industry. The network and its members operate under the guidance of the 17 goals for sustainable development proposed by the United Nations (UN). The canton of Zurich is home to many thriving projects that experiment with drones and imaging, agricultural robots, soilless agriculture and other forms of smart agriculture (Swiss Food Research, 2021[30]).

Another effort is the NTN IB Swiss Food Ecosystems – Funding Next Generation's Food Ecosystem. The NTN Innovation Boosters are 12 initiatives supported by Innosuisse that intend to cultivate innovation through developing ideas and testing their implementation. The initiatives are built upon principles of knowledge exchange and transfer between all actors and stakeholders that are involved in the value chain of a sector. This includes educational and research institutions, private actors and public government entities that collaborate on 600 projects that have a collective allocation of CHF 21.3 million (Swiss Agro Food, 2021[31]).

Of the 12 NTN initiatives, the Swiss Food Ecosystem aims to provide cutting-edge solutions to current and future food and agricultural issues that require collaboration and a holistic approach to innovation. The initiative provides financial and administrative support to the promising ideas proposed and the support is provided through Suisse Agro Food Leading house. Many of the projects undertaken by the initiative focus on smart nutrition solutions, bioeconomy efficiency solutions and sustainable packaging solutions (Swiss Agro Food, 2021[31]).

The Swiss Food & Nutrition Valley is an innovation ecosystem that involves institutions based mostly in the canton of Vaud as well as the canton itself, but there are other cantons involved. It is a national initiative that is reinforcing and promoting innovation in food and agriculture both within Switzerland and internationally. It tackles challenges stemming from food security concerns, agricultural support and nutritional value by providing sustainable solutions for the future of food through the utilisation of advancements in science and technology. Switzerland has a high density of scientific research institutions and start-ups working in agro-food and robotics innovation, making it a cultivating environment for research in this sector to thrive and continue to benefit the world's food concerns. This initiative brings together different actors and stakeholders with the aim of contributing to advances in five areas: precision nutrition, sustainable proteins, food systems 4.0, the future of farming and sustainable packaging (Swiss Food & Nutrition Valley, 2021[32]).

Precision nutrition is a scientific approach to explaining the relationship between the body's genetic makeup and the food it consumes to explain trends in health and nutrition. Sustainable proteins refer to the process of producing proteins from alternative plant-based sources, but also to making meat production more sustainable. Food systems 4.0 is the process of digitalisation of food production that is implemented along the entirety of the food supply chain. This is also tied to the future of farming, which focuses on new ways of growing food using all sorts of sophisticated technologies to grow food sustainably and efficiently. Lastly, sustainable packaging is the process by which packaging is made to be more eco-friendly, having a minimal impact and a low carbon footprint to contribute to sustainable waste management (Swiss Food & Nutrition Valley, 2021[32]).

Agropole involves mostly the canton of Vaud and is a physical space (campus) that acts as an ecosystem for different types of innovators in the agro-food sector to work and collaborate. This stimulates innovation through knowledge exchanges between academics, farmers, manufacturers, retailers, investors and so on. Furthermore, this bridges the gaps in communication between actors on the food value and supply chain and thus, accelerate the rate at which sustainable innovative solutions are implemented in agriculture. As an accelerator, Agropole has helped bring many new sustainable solutions to the market in order to benefit the environment, economy and society to the point where it is now expanding its campus by constructing additional buildings to continue to grow its collaborative space (Agropole, 2021[33]).

The canton of Fribourg's Agri & Co Challenge is an initiative that aims to attract promising project proposals – of which it currently funds 16 prize winners for 2018 collectively amounting to CHF 500 000 in total funding. This initiative has been a great propelling force towards increased collaboration on innovative projects, value chain creation and overall sustainable economic development. During its last period of selection in 2018, the initiative received 154 project proposals from 53 countries through its Relocation Program or Remote Collaboration Program. The Relocation Program allows the winners to operate at the St.-Aubin Innovation Space for 2 years under a CHF 30 000 grant in addition to administrative support. The Remote Collaboration Program, on the other hand, allows winners who are not interested in relocating their operation to still have access to Swiss markets and develop long-term partnerships with local actors (Agri&Co Challenge, 2021[34]).

Star'Terre is an inter-canton (Fribourg, Geneva and Vaud) platform that supports local projects aiming to solve food consumption issues in the Geneva region through agro-food innovative solutions. The platform supports farmers, entrepreneurs and other stakeholders in their efforts to innovate, share knowledge and create sustainable food production. It offers a base of knowledge systems that are meant to provide ease of access to information, a vast network of actors with diversified skillsets and resources, a hub that solves problems and answers questions, complementary dedicated administrative support and guidance, in addition to visibility to interested outside parties through a distinct platform (Star'Terre, 2021[35]).

Star'Terre is working to increase synergies between agriculture and innovation entrepreneurship, given that both are dependent on total commitment to daily business conduct while being subjected to changes in the market environment. The industries must constantly reinvent themselves to remain adapted to success factors while making sure that every stage of the value chain is operating as efficiently and as sustainably as possible. Many of these agro-entrepreneurial initiatives rely on funding from federal and regional entities, such as *L'ordonnance sur la promotion de la qualité et de la durabilité dans le secteur agroalimentaire* (OQuaDu), *Projets de développement régional* (PDR), AgrIQnet, and *regiosuisse* (Star'Terre, 2021[35]).

Innovativi Puure, in the canton of Zurich, works on making the agricultural sector adaptable to the types of changes that affect it by increasing its viability. It aims to motivate different actors in this sector to keep reinvesting in development and sustainability through employing process and specialisation expertise. This co-operative and goal-oriented initiative views innovation as a logical business process of renewal and remaining up to date. It offers services such as Puure info, Puure plan, Puure coaching, Puure project and Puure price to support farmers in operating sustainably and implementing change and innovative solutions. These services are meant to provide educational platforms and resources, guide through the process of a business plan creation, coach through the stages of project conception, help realise a project through financing and consulting, and ensure its sustainable success over the long run once it is up and running (Innovativi Puure, 2021[36]).

Another agricultural innovation initiative is the *Konzept zur Förderung von Innovationen in der Landwirtschaft* in the canton of Lucerne. This is a project lasting about 9 months and aims to promote innovation use in agricultural development. The project perpetuates a culture of evaluation of the business, agricultural and political factors that strengthen innovation within agriculture. It employs intensive research and subject experts to assess whether a proposed initiative fits the standards of the New Regional Policy (NRP) and is thus eligible for funding (regiosuisse, 2021[37]). Agricultural hubs are key for technology adoption and technology transfer, an example of these hubs is depicted in Box 4.2.

Box 4.2. Agri-Food innovation hubs: Incubators and accelerators

H-Farm: Linking innovation, entrepreneurship and education from a young age, Italy

Established in 2005, H-Farm is located in Sile River Natural Park in an area known as Ca' Tron, one of the largest single agricultural estates in Italy, bordering Venice, in Italy's northeast region. The multi-purpose facility operates as an incubator, business consultancy and education service provider for entrepreneurs looking to start new businesses and accelerate pre-existing ones. The philosophy of the founders of the hub is to place education at the heart of operations. It offers entrepreneurs a physical location in a rural region, housing, entertainment and educational services to support entrepreneurship and consists of a boarding school focused on the farming industry, a boarding school in Treviso with virtual classes (in virtual reality) for students 3 to 16 years old, various other programmes for young students and courses for entrepreneurs in a variety of industries.

Cultivator, Regina, Saskatchewan, Canada

Cultivator is a credit union lead accelerator focused on supporting companies working in the agri-tech space. While the location of the accelerator is technically within the metropolitan area of Regina, the hub is built for bringing talent to work on issues related to the agricultural sector and self-identifies as a hub for rural development in the Canadian Prairies. The programme started in 2019. The accelerator was built to create an innovation hub that provided the programming, resources, mentorship, funding and space founders to accelerate the growth of local tech start-ups. The initiative was founded by Conexus Credit Union (Conexus) and supports founders by providing coaching, mentorship, product development, customer discovery, investor readiness, space, perks and hiring support.

Source: H-Farm (2021[38]), *About Us*, https://www.h-farm.com/en/corporate/about; Cultivator (2022[39]), *Homepage*, https://www.cultivator.ca/ (accessed on 1 September, 2022).

Intellectual property rights (IPRs) for biological innovations

IPRs, knowledge networks and knowledge markets are of growing importance in fostering innovation. Reinforcing linkages across participants in the AIS (researchers, educators, extension services, farmers, industry, non-governmental organisations, consumers and others) can help match the supply of research to demand, facilitate technology transfer and increase the impact of public and private investments. Partnerships can also facilitate multi-disciplinary approaches that can generate innovative solutions to some problems.

The characteristics of different types of IPRs used to protect biological innovations are shown in Table 4.3. Following EU regulations, patents cannot be issued for new plant varieties or new breeds in relation to conventional biological processes. However, they can be granted if the invention is not specific to a specific sort of plant or specific breed. The Swiss Federal Institute of Intellectual Property issues patents in their modern forms in line with the patent regulation. It works alongside governmental agencies, trade groups and businesses to administer Swiss indications of source (tells consumers the geographic origin of a product, where it was produced or processed) both within Switzerland and internationally.

Plant variety protection is similar to an issued patent. These rights declare that the party that has created a new plant variety has reserved all rights to it. The FOAG issues these rights under Article 7 of the Agriculture Act and there is a requirement that the plant should be new, distinguishable, uniform and stable. The protection means that no other actor-exempt breeders can use the specific plant or identical plant variations in any form.

Figure 4.12 showcases the intellectual property (IP) protection metrics of Switzerland compared to other OECD members. Panel A indicates that Switzerland stands at 85.8% on the international IP index in 2021 and is lower in terms of percentage compared to some other countries that are leading in the level of IP submissions. These indices examine the environment that IP is governed within different countries. Panel B looks specifically at plant variety protection within Switzerland in five-year intervals between 1965 and 2015, which indicates a significant increase in the last decade. Lastly, Panel C portrays that Switzerland, alongside Finland, is a leading country in the World Economic Forum (WEF) Intellectual Property Protection Index measures.

Figure 4.12. Intellectual property protection

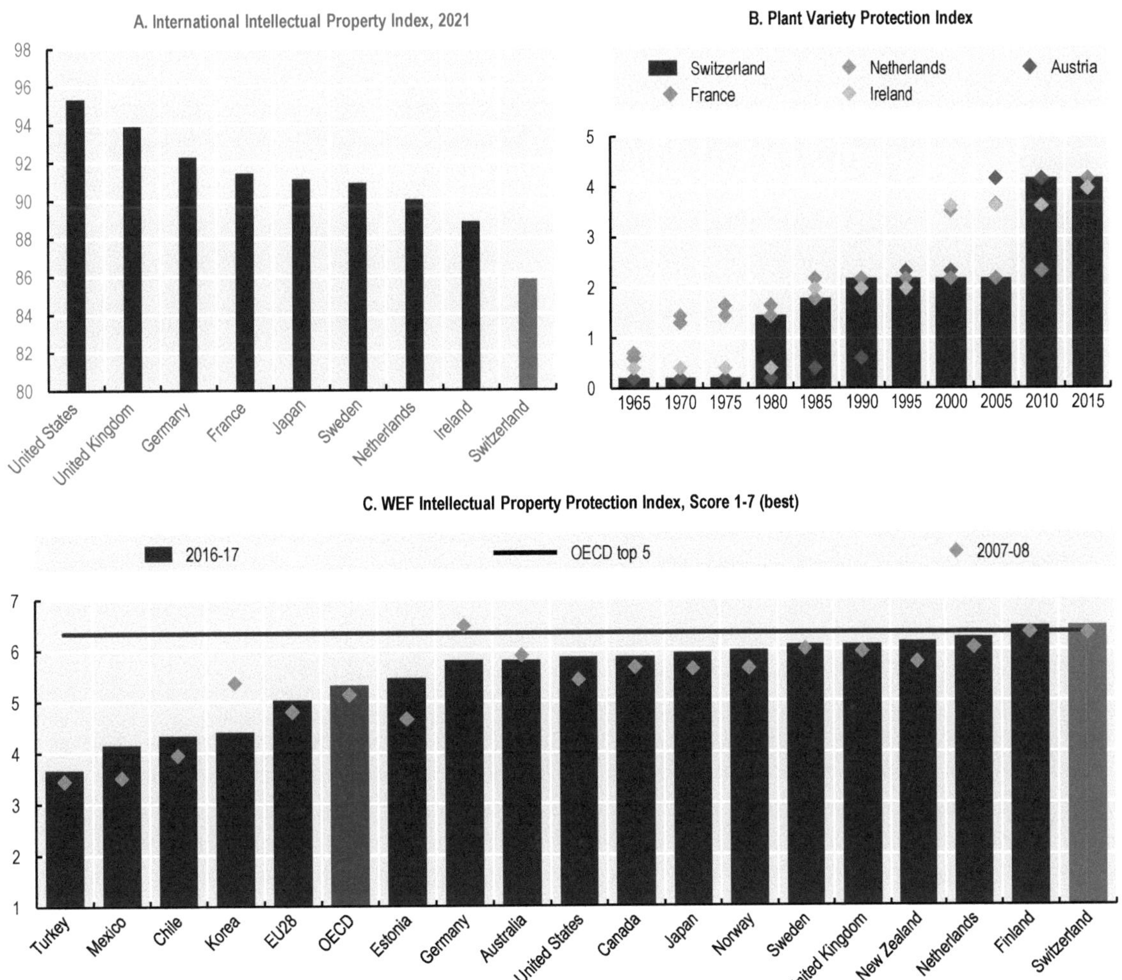

Note: OECD top 5 refers to the average of the scores for the top 5 performers among OECD countries (Finland, Luxembourg, the Netherlands, New Zealand and Switzerland). Indices for EU28 and OECD are the simple average of member-country indices.
Source: Statista (Statista, 2021[40]); Campi, M. and A. Nuvolari (2020[41]), "Intellectual property rights and agricultural development: Evidence from a worldwide index of IPRs in agriculture (1961-2018)", https://www.econstor.eu/handle/10419/228145/; World Economic Forum (2017[42]), *The Global Competitiveness Report 2016-2017: Full Data Edition*, https://www3.weforum.org/docs/GCR2016-2017/05FullReport/TheGlobalCompetitivenessReport2016-2017_FINAL.pdf.

Publications outcomes

Publications and citations are indicative of the progress that research on innovation has reached. Overall progress to create and adopt relevant innovations can be usefully monitored, including using proxy measures, such as the number of patents or bibliographic citations (OECD, 2014[4]). It should be noted, however, that although the number of patents is an informative proxy, it is not a comprehensive indicator of the outcomes of the innovation system, as not all innovations are patented and not all patents are used. Other IPR systems exist for plant varieties rather than patents and are frequently used for food processing innovations. In addition, numbers must be complemented with indicators of patent quality (Table 4.3).

Table 4.3. Agriculture and food publications or R&D outcomes (accumulated 1996-2020)

Country	Agro publications % of the country's total	Agro citations % of the country's total	Agro publications % of the world total	Agro citations % of the world total
United States	6.0	6.6	17.9	24.5
United Kingdom	5.7	7.8	5.0	7.7
Germany	5.9	7.2	4.5	5.7
Japan	5.5	6.2	3.7	3.3
Canada	8.0	9.1	3.5	4.6
France	6.5	8.5	3.4	4.6
Italy	6.2	6.2	2.8	2.6
Netherlands	6.4	7.4	1.6	2.5
Spain	9.3	11.7	3.3	3.7
Sweden	7.3	8.3	1.2	1.7
Switzerland	**6.2**	**7.0**	**1.1**	**1.8**

Source: SJR (2021[43]), *International Science Ranking*, http://www.scimagojr.com (accessed on 1 September, 2022).

Institutional co-ordination: RIS, the FOAG and cantonal offices

Improved co-ordination between the local level and regional and national governments and across sectors and institutions within the government enable a stronger, opportune response, better utilisation of resources and more accurate targeting of resources to address the greatest need. Promoting collaboration in areas of innovation and policy making related to agricultural and rural development is key to the successful and sustainable role they play in economic well-being (Cervantes-Godoy, forthcoming[44]). Policy integration not only reduces redundancy and conflict but also maximises efficiency and creates collective synergies. However, establishing effective integration is quite tricky (OECD, 2012[45]).

The New Regional Policy (NRP) was created in 2008 as the answer to the development needs of cantons with mountainous regions, rural regions and the border regions of Switzerland. The NRP also aims to support the creation and maintenance of workplaces in these regions by reducing the disparities between the different regions (HES-SO Valais Wallis, 2021[46]). The introduction of RIS within the framework of the NRP established the RIS organisations as a central link between the federal government and the cantons in the operational implementation of an innovation-based regional policy. By 2021, Switzerland had six RIS covering significant parts of the country. The RIS are inter-cantonal economic areas and focus on demand and need-driven innovation services, specifically targeting SMEs (see Chapter 2 for more details).

In summary, the RIS is an intricate, multi-dimensional innovation system that promotes networking and facilitates access to the various skills available on regional, cantonal and national levels. This includes skills and knowledge of academic institutions, private companies, trade associations and other stakeholders. The Swiss Confederation co-finances six RIS initiatives: RIS Basel-Jura (BL, BS, JU), RIS Mittelland (BE), RIS Eastern Switzerland (AI, AR, GL, GR, SH, SG, TG, Zurich mountain area), RIS Southern Switzerland (TI, GR), RIS Western Switzerland (BE, FR, VD, VS, NE, GE, JU) and RIS Central Switzerland (LU, NW, OW, SZ, UR, ZG). Every RIS has a different governance mechanism unique to the characteristics of cantons and regions.

In the field of agricultural policy, the agricultural offices of the cantons are in charge of implementing the federal agricultural policy, particularly the programmes related to direct payments to farmers. However, these offices also are in charge of co-financing rural infrastructure projects and providing extension services. Additionally, many cantons have set up their own agricultural innovation programmes or initiatives.

In the field of regional policy, the RIS works collaboratively with different partners to design and implement a wide array of programmes and solutions related to training and research, sharing information and raising awareness, conducting comprehensive preliminary analysis, building networks, transferring technology, protecting IP, supporting incubators, coaching, in addition to financing innovative project proposals. However, when it comes to agriculture and food, the RIS and FOAG, together with the agricultural offices at the cantonal level, have limited interaction. Most farmers do not know of the RIS programmes. The New Regional Policy (NRP) RIS operates under a budget of CHF 40 million non-repayable funds per year and 50 million grants.

Fostering co-ordination amongst different ministries results in the arrival of effective policy solutions. Consequently, this will lead to ease of conduct between different levels of government (municipal, cantonal and federal). Policy co-ordination apparatuses that involve all government levels are fundamental to resolving discrepancies between sectoral priorities and the objectives of policies. Additionally, they must assess foreign and domestic policies, and how actors from different sectors and institutions can apply them (OECD, 2021[3]).

Some best practices of institutional inter-governmental co-ordination suggest that high-level political backing is important to enhance co-ordination. This suggestion has been raised previously in Chapter 3 of this report where an example from the United States is provided. Hereby, simple mechanisms often work best while overlapping functions and blurred accountability make co-ordination difficult (OECD, 2017[27]). Flexible and adaptive co-ordination mechanisms, which sometimes are informal, may work better than rigid and prescriptive ones, as they have a better chance to be sustained and become self-reinforcing even as leaders change. In the case of Switzerland, for example, the supreme responsibility for the co-ordination of Switzerland's policy making generally lies with the Federal Council. This applies to different policy areas but the example found is related to sustainable development strategy, where the Federal Office for Spatial Development (ARE) heads the Interdepartmental Sustainable Development Committee (ISDC). This committee serves as a platform for knowledge sharing and a forum to cultivate interdepartmental co-operation, thereby working to align objectives and address policy conflicts at the national level (OECD, 2022[46]). Routine reporting procedures, combined with a careful assessment and monitoring of obstacles and measures to resolve them, are essential links in the accountability chain.

A platform for knowledge exchange and access to information would best be established as a website. This website can have two main tabs, one outlining institutional offers and services that farmers can access, the other geared towards knowledge sharing and peer learning for researchers, academics and the like. This online platform can be incorporated as a part of a new structure of supply chain known as "net chains" (a combination of networks and chains). Net chains serve as a web or network of connections that focus on consumers (in this case farmers) as well as other stakeholders who are interested in different forms of information exchange. Such a platform would also help outline the knowledge base and analytical tools that are made available to farmers, policy makers and other stakeholders to monitor progress, evaluate agricultural and innovation policies, and guide decisions making processes. The government plays a critical role in data collection, which permits the creation and implementation of efficient, evidence-based policy. This would be taking into consideration the results of monitoring and evaluation of said policies and making relevant information readily accessible to any concerned party (farmers, investors, etc.) on a shared network (online platform).

Generally, excellence in agro-food research and innovation attracts investment from investors looking to promote and benefit from this type of research collaboration. Government efforts to promote investment at different stages of innovation typically require the provision of data and information necessary to incentivise investors in their decision to invest. This can be made easily available on an online platform for knowledge sharing. Well-educated farmers using this platform will also become more aware of the types of resources, training and advisory services available to them. Given the variety of stakeholders that will stand to benefit from the platform, funding for it can be raised through government contribution and/or private investment. In the Netherlands, for example, the government promotes private investment through the provision of tax incentives, which further strengthens public-private partnerships.

References

Agri&Co Challenge (2021), *Homepage*, http://agricochallenge.org/?lang=fr (accessed on 1 September 2022). [34]

AGRIDEA (2021), *AGRIDEA - Swiss Association for the Development of Agriculture and Rural Areas*. [20]

AGRIDEA (2021), *AKIS and Advisory Services in Switzerland*, Swiss Association for the Development of Agriculture and Rural Areas. [9]

Agropole (2021), *Homepage*, https://www.agropole.com/ (accessed on 1 September 2022). [33]

Agroscope (2021), *Homepage*, https://www.agroscope.admin.ch/agroscope/en/home.html (accessed on 1 September 2022). [16]

BFH (2021), *School of Agricultural, Forest, and Food Science (HAFL)*, Bern University of Applied Sciences. [19]

Campi, M. and A. Nuvolari (2020), "Intellectual property rights and agricultural development: Evidence from a worldwide index of IPRs in agriculture (1961-2018)", *LEM Working Paper Series*, No. 2020/06, https://www.econstor.eu/handle/10419/228145/. [41]

Cervantes-Godoy, D. (forthcoming), "Aligning agricultural and rural development policies in the context of structural change". [44]

Cultivator (2022), *Homepage*, https://www.cultivator.ca/ (accessed on 1 September 2022). [39]

ETH Zurich (2021), *Homepage*, Eidgenössische Technische Hochschule Zürich (Swiss Federal Institutes of Technology), https://ethz.ch/en.html. [17]

Eurostat (2017), *Community Innovation Survey*, http://ec.europa.eu/eurostat/data/database. [25]

FIBL (2021), *Research Institute of Organic Agriculture FiBL*, https://www.fibl.org/en/ (accessed on 1 September 2022). [18]

FOAG (2021), *ERI-Project OECD Information Request*, Federal Office for Agriculture. [11]

FOAG (2021), *Federal Office for Agriculture*. [12]

FOEN (2021), *Federal Office for the Environment*. [14]

FSO (2021), *Federal Statistics Office*, https://www.bfs.admin.ch/bfs/en/home.html. [7]

FSVO (2021), *Federal Food Safety and Veterinary Office*. [13]

H-Farm (2021), *About Us*, https://www.h-farm.com/en/corporate/about. [38]

Innosuise (2021), *Innosuise - Swiss Innovation Agency*, https://www.innosuisse.ch/inno/en/home.html (accessed on 2021 September 1). [23]

Innovativi Puure (2021), *Was match Innovativi Puure?*. [36]

OECD (2022), *Policy Coherence for Sustainable Development Toolkit*, Policy Coordination, OECD, Paris, https://www.oecd.org/governance/pcsd/toolkit/goodpractices/Policy%20Coordination.pdf. [46]

OECD (2021), *Agricultural Policy Monitoring and Evaluation 2021: Addressing the Challenges Facing Food Systems*, OECD Publishing, Paris, https://doi.org/10.1787/2d810e01-en. [3]

OECD (2021), *OECD Science, Technology and Innovation Outlook 2021: Times of Crisis and Opportunity*, OECD Publishing, Paris, https://doi.org/10.1787/75f79015-en. [1]

OECD (2019), *Innovation, Productivity and Sustainability in Food and Agriculture: Main Findings from Country Reviews and Policy Lessons*, OECD Food and Agricultural Reviews, OECD Publishing, Paris, https://doi.org/10.1787/c9c4ec1d-en. [8]

OECD (2017), *OECD Research and Development Statistics*, https://stats.oecd.org/ (accessed on 1 September 2022). [27]

OECD (2016), *OECD Science, Technology and Innovation Outlook 2016*, OECD Publishing, Paris, https://doi.org/10.1787/sti_in_outlook-2016-en. [6]

OECD (2015), *OECD Review of Agricultural Policies: Switzerland 2015*, OECD Review of Agricultural Policies, OECD Publishing, Paris, https://doi.org/10.1787/9789264168039-en. [28]

OECD (2014), *Analysing Policies to Improve Agricultural Productivity Growth, Sustainably: Revised Framework*, OECD, Paris, http://www.oecd.org/tad/agricultural-policies/Analysing-policies-improve-agricultural-productivity-growth-sustainably-december-2014.pdf. [4]

OECD (2012), *OECD Science, Technology and Industry Outlook 2012*, OECD Publishing, Paris, https://doi.org/10.1787/sti_outlook-2012-en. [45]

OECD (n.d.), "OECD, "Producer and Consumer Support Estimates", *OECD Agriculture statistics (database)*, https://doi.org/10.1787/agr-pcse-data-en. [26]

regiosuisse (2021), *La plateforme du développement régional en Suisse*. [37]

SECO (2021), *State Secretariat for Economic Affairs*. [15]

SERI (2021), *State Secretariat for Education, Research, and Innovation*. [21]

SJR (2021), *International Science Ranking*, SCImago Journal Rank, http://www.scimagojr.com. [43]

SNSF (2021), *Key Figures of the Swiss National Science Foundation*, Swiss National Science Foundation, https://data.snf.ch/key-figures. [22]

Star'Terre (2021), *Homepage*, https://www.starterre.ch/ (accessed on 1 September 2022). [35]

Statista (2021), *https://www.statista.com/*. [40]

Swiss Agro Food (2021), *NTN Innovation Booster -Swiss Food Ecosystems*. [31]

Swiss Food & Nutrition Valley (2021), *Enabling Innovation for a Better Food System*, [32]
https://swissfoodnutritionvalley.com/ (accessed on 1 September 2022).

Swiss Food Research (2021), "Innovations for a future-oriented food system". [30]

Swiss Universities (2021), *Accredited Swiss Higher Education Institutions*, [10]
https://www.swissuniversities.ch/en/topics/studying/accredited-swiss-higher-education-
institutions.

UN-COMTRADE (2021), *UN-COMTRADE*, https://comtrade.un.org/ (accessed on [24]
1 September 2022).

Vaud (2020), *AGRITECH: An innovation domain of the canton of Vaud*, https://www.invest- [29]
vaud.ch/Portals/4/Files/Factsheets/EN_2020/%5BEN%5D_FS_DI_Agritech.pdf.

World Bank (2021), *Research and Development Expenditure (% of GDP) - Switzerland*, World [5]
Bank, Washington, DC,
https://data.worldbank.org/indicator/GB.XPD.RSDV.GD.ZS?locations=CH.

World Bank (2021), *World Development Indicators*, World Bank, Washington, DC, [2]
https://databank.worldbank.org/source/world-development-indicators.

World Economic Forum (2017), *The Global Competitiveness Report 2016-2017: Full Data* [42]
Edition, https://www3.weforum.org/docs/GCR2016-
2017/05FullReport/TheGlobalCompetitivenessReport2016-2017_FINAL.pdf.

Annex A. OECD recommendations to improve agricultural innovation systems

Improving governance of agricultural innovation systems is key

- Establish a longer-term strategy for agricultural innovation to guide operational objectives and associated expenditures, taking into account long-term challenges such as climate change, as well as societal demand.
  - Ensure coherence between innovation and growth strategies.
  - Improve the integration of agricultural innovation objectives in government-wide innovation strategy.
  - Improve involvement of stakeholders in the definition of objectives, starting at an early stage of the process.
  - Include measurable targets in the definition of objectives; and monitor progress towards objectives.
- Improve co-ordination between research organisations, public and private and at the national and subnational levels:
  - If missing, create a specific national institution (e.g. a national council) to co-ordinate objectives and monitor policy, and ensure continuity in programming.
  - Clarify mandates of organisations to avoid duplication or undersupply in one area (for example between research and knowledge transfer).
- Develop coherent evaluation procedures at different levels (researchers, projects, institutions, system) that include some independent evaluation and cover a wide range of indicators of efforts, outputs and impacts to allow for future improvements. Ensure evaluation criteria are consistent between levels and with objectives.

Strengthen linkages within the national innovation system to increase efficiency and responsiveness to needs

- Facilitate linkages within the agricultural innovation system (between research, advisory services, education, government, farmers and agri-food companies) and with other experts and stakeholders.
- Promote and enable research co-operation across sectors, so that food and agriculture benefit from advances in other sectors and generic research, such as genetics and digital technologies.
- Remove institutional constraints to public research organisations to engage in co-operation activities with the private sector.
- Facilitate the organisation of producers and industry to enable them to contribute more effectively to the agricultural innovation system.

- Facilitate the emergence of public-private partnerships (PPPs) for research and innovation, when they bring additional benefits. Provide guidelines for successful PPPs and, in particular, ensure objectives are shared and institutional arrangements are clear, including the sharing of costs and benefits between partners, which should be commensurate.
- Create and support poles of competitiveness, or poles of excellence to facilitate co-operation.
- Explore further opportunities to share public infrastructure with the private sector.
- Identify areas where local companies and researchers could collaborate to develop local or niche products and innovations.
- Support the functioning of local, national and international networks for innovation and the participation of researchers and stakeholders in these networks.
- Strengthen the links between research and development (R&D) and technical assistance, for example by adding technology transfer components to research projects or by encouraging networking between researchers, advisors and producers. Simplify research programming to improve effectiveness and transparency.
- Simplify the programming of R&D and innovation funding, and provide clear information to improve access. For example, streamline funding programmes and build a single platform that informs on all of the sources of available government funding. When relevant, include information on subnational sources.
- Review the efficiency of research funding mechanisms to ensure higher impact. Consider greater use of incentives that incentivise transdisciplinary and system-based approaches and wider stakeholder involvement that increases relevance.
- Explore ways to generate new (breaking through) ideas to overcome current constraints, for example through demand-driven funding mechanisms.
- In cantons where research is organised by commodity sector, create cross-sector thematic areas and projects, or broaden the scope and membership of existing commodity research systems.
- Explore ways to generate new, breakthrough solutions to current and future challenges.

Strengthen private contribution to R&D and innovation for food and agriculture to increase the impact

- Enhance the involvement of processing industries and retailers in innovation, by making them an integral part of the system, from the priority setting stage to the financing and commercialisation of innovation stages.
- Evaluate programmes that support innovation in private companies to ensure they are efficient and reach intended beneficiaries. In particular, monitor whether they reach agri-food companies. If private companies have access to tax incentives for R&D, evaluate the system to ensure it stimulates additional research activities.
- Strengthen and harness the capacity of private companies to participate in research partnerships via project funding, support to networking, training activities and effective intellectual property rights (IPR) protection.
  - Ensure appropriate protection of IPR and improve enforcement when needed, to attract private funding while allowing for further use for research purposes, as with plant breeders' rights.
- Explore alternative sources of funding for research and innovation:
  - This could include farmers' contributions and revenues from royalties or intellectual property.
  - Investigate the demand and supply for venture capital for agri-food companies and identify a possible role for the government to ease constraints.

    o   Lower barriers to foreign direct investment (FDI) in agricultural R&D if they exist.

Facilitate international R&D co-operation

- Explore opportunities for public research to engage in bilateral, regional and multilateral co-operation in R&D and technology transfer.
- Remove institutional constraints on public research organisations to hire foreign researchers or trainees.
- Provide positive incentives such as support to student and staff exchange, and sharing of equipment and laboratories.

Strengthen farm advisory systems to facilitate adoption

- There is no one-size-fits-all or preferred model for farm advisory systems.
- Encourage a diverse supply of relevant advice from diverse public and private suppliers.
- Ensure needs are met:
  - Review current systems and identify needs and gaps.
  - Ensure advisory services cover technical, financial and organisational aspects and sustainability improvements.
  - Ensure advice is accessible to all types of farmers, using new (digital) technologies.
- Focus public role on services that the private sector may underprovide:
  - Target the needs of small, semi-subsistence farmers to broaden their opportunities.
  - Strengthen environmental performance by providing targeted advice on sustainable technologies and practices, and use experience to better understand issues and needs.
- Explore the scope for including support to technical assistance and research projects within agri-environmental policies, in case of under-provision.
- Facilitate the sharing of experiences through networking and the development of databases.
- Ensure advisors have up-to-date knowledge, possibly through certification and facilitate continuous training.

Facilitate knowledge sharing and information dissemination

- Continue developing information systems to guide policies, research and innovation, and facilitate knowledge sharing.
  - Include market intelligence (big data) and research results.
  - Monitor innovation adoption in form and farm surveys, surveys to generate data on innovation and better understand motivations and barriers to adoption.
  - Monitor environmental performance in surveys.
  - Use innovative methods to reduce collection costs and improve farm and firm participation, drawing on experience from other countries.
  - Develop indicators and tools to evaluate the performance of the agricultural innovation systems in general, and innovation policy regularly, taking longer-term effects into account.
- Promote the integration of research data and sharing of experience at the international level.

- Improve public understanding of the importance of innovation in food and agriculture, in the sector and society, and build trust in science through increased transparency and education.

Reference

OECD (2019), *Innovation, Productivity and Sustainability in Food and Agriculture: Main Findings from Country Reviews and Policy Lessons*, OECD Food and Agricultural Reviews, OECD Publishing, Paris, https://doi.org/10.1787/c9c4ec1d-en. [1]

Annex B. Additional figures

Figure A B.1. R&D spending by destination, shares of R&D spending by Swiss typology, 2012-19

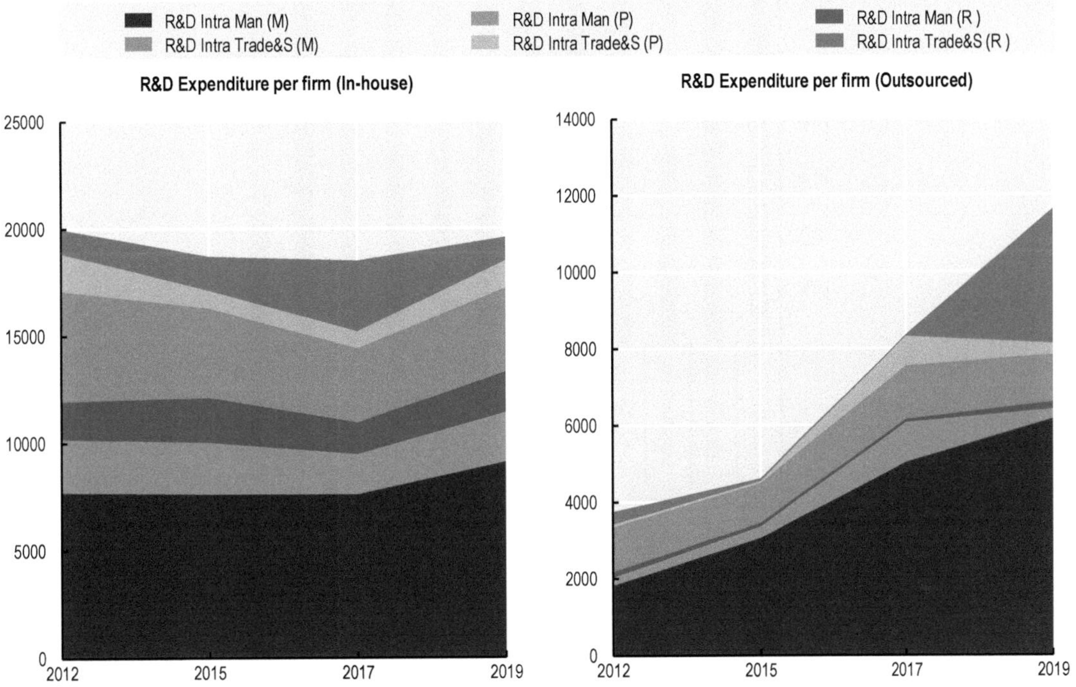

Note: The mining sector has been removed for visualisation purposes but accounted for at most 0.1% of firms in rural regions in 2017. All currency is in Swiss Francs (2015). The figure refers to the destination of any expenditure of the firm. In some cases, the final destination of expenditure may both be inward and outward for each expenditure. The figure is only indicative of general trends.
Source: Swiss Research and Development Survey.

Figure A B.2. R&D expenditure by destination

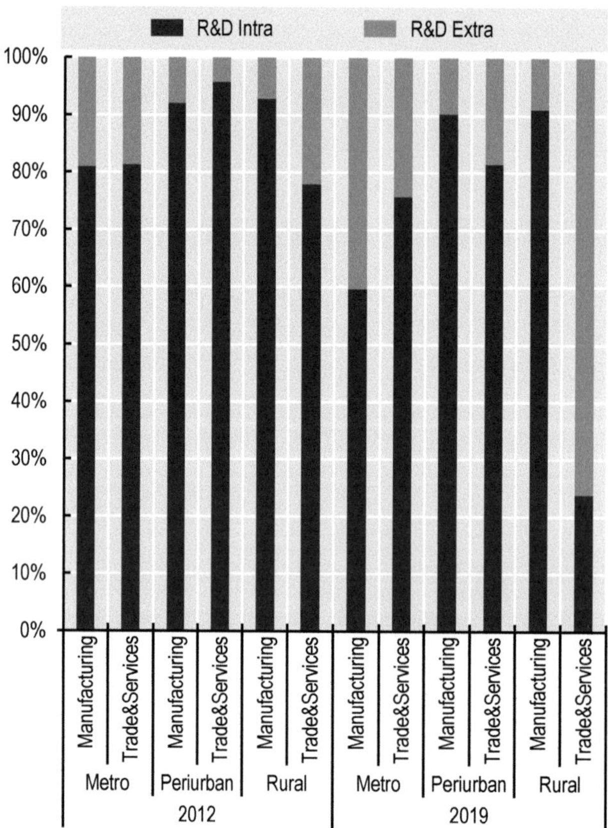

Note: The mining sector has been removed for visualisation purposes but accounted for at most 0.1% of firms in rural regions in 2017. Currency is in Swiss Francs (2015). All currency is in Swiss Francs (2015). The figure refers to the destination of any expenditure of the firm. In some cases, the final destination of expenditure may both be inward and outward for each expenditure. The figure is only indicative of general trends.
Source: Swiss Research and Development Survey.

Printed by Libri Plureos GmbH in Hamburg,
Germany